D0648295

BROADCASTING AND BARGAINING

Broadcasting and Bargaining

Labor Relations in Radio and Television

edited by
ALLEN E. KOENIG

The University of Wisconsin Press
Madison, Milwaukee, and London
1970

Published by
THE UNIVERSITY OF WISCONSIN PRESS
Box 1379, Madison, Wisconsin 53701
The University of Wisconsin Press, Ltd.
27–29 Whitfield Street, London, W. 1

Printed in the United States of America by
North Central Publishing Co., St. Paul, Minnesota

SBN 299–05521–3
LC 76–98123

The Authors

CHARLES G. BAKALY, JR., is a partner in the Los Angeles law firm of O'Melveny and Myers and a specialist in labor relations. He has handled broadcasting cases for the American Broadcasting Company, the Columbia Broadcasting System, and the Radio Corporation of America, and is co-chairman of the American Bar Association's Committee on Practice and Procedure under the National Labor Relations Act. Mr. Bakaly is a graduate of Stanford University and received the J.D. degree from the University of Southern California. His articles have appeared in the *Labor Law Journal* and the *Los Angeles Bar Bulletin*.

EVELYN F. BURKEY is executive director of the Writers Guild of America, East, Inc., in New York City, and has served as the assistant executive secretary of the Authors League of America, Inc., and the acting director of evening studies, Washington Square College of Arts and Sciences at New York University. Miss Burkey is a graduate of New York University and pursued graduate studies there. She is second vice-president of the New York chapter of the National Academy of Television Arts and Sciences, and a member of that organization's editorial board for *Television Quarterly*.

ROBERT L. COE, who is lecturer and special assistant to the School of Radio-Television at Ohio University in Athens, has worked in broadcast engineering and management for forty-five years. Before his appointment to Ohio University he was for twelve years vice-president of the American Broadcasting Company's television network, and had previously served as director of station relations for the DuMont Television Network. Mr. Coe planned, organized, and built television stations KSD-TV (St. Louis, 1947) and WPIX (New York, 1948). In 1938 he constructed the world's first radio facsimile newspaper in St. Louis.

BARRY G. COLE is an associate professor in the departments of radio and television and mass communications at Indiana University. He received the B.S. degree from the University of Pennsylvania and the A.M. and Ph.D. degrees from Northwestern University. He is editor of *Commercial Television: An Overview*, to be published in the spring of 1970, and is writing a book on public policy and broadcasting. His articles have appeared in *Educational Broadcasting Review*, the *Journal of Broadcasting*, and *Australian Quarterly*.

ROBERT COULSON is executive vice-president of the American Arbitration Association in New York City. He is also chairman of the arbitration committees of the Section on Corporation, Banking, and Business Law and of the Section on International and Comparative Law of the American Bar Association. Mr. Coulson received an A.B. degree from Yale University and an LL.B. degree from Harvard University. He is the author of *How to Stay Out of Court*, and his articles have appeared in the *American Bar Association Journal, Labor Law Journal, The Business Lawyer, Insurance Law Journal, Arbitration Journal*, and the *New York Law Journal*.

A. EDWARD FOOTE is managing editor of *Educational Broadcasting Review* at the Ohio State University, where he is a Ph.D. candidate in communications. He is a graduate in mathematics from Florence State College, studied broadcasting at New York University, and holds a Master's degree from the University of Southern Mississippi. He has worked in commercial and educational television, as well as advertising.

RICHARD N. GOLDSTEIN is vice-president, labor relations, for the National Broadcasting Company. He received the B.S. degree from the Cornell School of Industrial and Labor Relations and the LL.B. degree from Yale Law School. Before joining NBC in 1957, he practiced labor law in New York City.

GARY GUMPERT is an associate professor of communication arts and sciences at Queens College of the City University of New York. He was formerly director of instructional television development and utilization and assistant professor in the division of radio-television-education at the University of Wisconsin. Mr. Gumpert received the B.S. degree from Temple University, the A.M. from Michigan State University, and the Ph.D. from Wayne State University. He has contributed chapters to several books on communications media, and articles to the *NAEB Journal* and *Social Work Education Reporter*.

DARREL W. HOLT is associate professor of radio and television at Ohio University in Athens. He was formerly assistant professor of radio-television-film at the University of Kansas, and before teaching had been co-owner of a radio station. He received the A.B. degree from Washington State University, and the A.M. and Ph.D. from Northwestern University. His articles have appeared in *Educational Broadcasting Review.*

CHARLES F. HUNTER is professor of education and radio-television-film and chairman of the latter department at Northwestern University in Evanston, Illinois. He was formerly director of broadcasting at the University of Missouri at Kansas and assistant professor of radio at the University of Missouri at Columbia, and has been an educational producer for NBC television in Chicago. Mr. Hunter received the B.S. and A.B. degrees from Southeast Missouri State College, the Ph.M. from the University of Wisconsin, and the Ph.D. from Cornell University. He has contributed to a number of professional publications.

ALLEN E. KOENIG is director of publications and communications for the American Association of University Professors in Washington, D.C., and editor of the *AAUP Bulletin.* He has served on the faculties of the Ohio State University, the University of Wisconsin-Milwaukee, and Eastern Michigan University. In July, 1967, he became the first editor of *Educational Broadcasting Review,* successor to the *NAEB Journal.* Mr. Koenig received the A.B. degree from the University of Southern California, the A.M. degree from Stanford University, and the Ph.D. degree from Northwestern University. He is co-editor of *The Farther Vision: Educational Television Today* (Madison: University of Wisconsin Press, 1967), and has written on the subject of broadcasting-labor relations and other media topics for the *Journal of Broadcasting, Journal of the University Film Association, NAEB Journal, Educational Broadcasting Review,* and *Preaching: A Journal of Homiletics.* Mr. Koenig has worked in commercial radio and television in Los Angeles and San Francisco.

ROBERT A. LENIHAN is regional director for the National Association of Broadcast Employees and Technicians, assigned to the eleven western states, and has served the union since 1953 as organizer, contract negotiator, general representative, arbitration representative, and special assistant to the president. Mr. Lenihan served two years on the California Governor's Advisory Committee on Educational Television, under Governor Edmund Brown.

JAMES L. LOPER is vice-president and general manager of Community Television of Southern California (Channel 28 in Los Angeles), and the former director of broadcasting at the California State College at Los Angeles. He is the president of the Western Radio and Television Association, chairman of the Labor Committee, Educational Television Stations, of the National Association of Educational Broadcasters, and an editorial board member of *Educational Broadcasting Review*. Mr. Loper is a graduate of Arizona State University and holds an A.M. degree from the University of Denver and the Ph.D. from the University of Southern California. His articles have appeared in *Western Speech, Journal of Broadcasting, Educational Broadcasting Review*, and the *Journal of the University Film Producers Association*.

JAMES E. LYNCH is professor of speech and chairman of mass communications in the Department of Speech of the University of Massachusetts. He has taught at Indiana University, the University of Michigan, the University of Iowa, and the Ohio State University, and has been a frequent contributor to *Speech Teacher, NAEB Journal, Educational Broadcasting Review, Speech Monographs*, and *Television Quarterly*. He is the author of two chapters of *Communicative Arts and Sciences of Speech* (Charles Merrill, 1967), and the editor of *Radio and Television in the Secondary Schools*. Mr. Lynch received the A.B., A.M., and Ph.D. degrees from the University of Michigan.

MARTIN J. MALONEY is professor of radio-television-film at Northwestern University in Evanston, Illinois. He has taught at Stanford University and the University of Chicago, and has produced some five hundred scripts for radio, television, and film and contributed a number of professional articles to journals and textbooks. Mr. Maloney received the A.B. and A.M. degrees from the University of Kansas, and the Ph.D. degree from Northwestern University.

CLAUDE L. McCUE is the executive secretary of the Los Angeles local, and western regional director, of the American Federation of Television and Radio Artists, and the chairman of the Hollywood, California, Committee of Broadcast Unions. He has studied at Stanford University and at the University of San Francisco, and received the J.D. degree from Hastings College of Law of the University of California.

THOMAS J. McDERMOTT, JR., is a partner in the law firm of Kadison, Pfaelzer, Woodard and Quinn, Los Angeles. He is a specialist in labor law, and the attorney for Southern California Educational Television. He received both the A.B. and J.D. degrees from the University of California at Los Angeles and is a past president of the UCLA Law Alumni Association.

RICHARD J. MEYER is director of the School Television Service of WNDT (Channel 13) in New York City, and in addition to serving as a communications consultant to a number of organizations, is developing minority group policies for the National Association of Educational Broadcasters as chairman of its Committee on Programming Practices. He is a graduate of Stanford University, from which he also holds a Master's degree, and was awarded the Ph.D. from New York University, and a post-doctoral Russell Sage Fellowship in Journalism and the Behavioral Sciences at Columbia University. His articles have appeared in the *Journal of Broadcasting, Educational Broadcasting Review, AV Communication Review, Film Comment, Public Opinion Quarterly,* and other periodicals.

ROBERT R. MONAGHAN is associate professor of speech at the Ohio State University in Columbus. He was formerly assistant professor of journalism at the University of Oregon, general manager of the Oregon Association of Broadcasters, and a producer for the National Broadcasting Company in San Francisco. He is a graduate of Olivet College, holds a Master's degree from Stanford University, and a Ph.D. from Michigan State University. Mr. Monaghan's articles have appeared in *Educational Broadcasting Review, Journal of Communication, Quarterly Journal of Speech,* and *Behavioral Science.*

TIMOTHY J. O'SULLIVAN is the international president of the National Association of Broadcast Employees and Technicians, AFL-CIO, CLC. Before his election to that office by the 1968 convention, he served as the union's international representative in the midwestern United States, as its director in Canada, and as the director in the western United States. He attended Ball State Teachers' College, Muncie, Indiana, and served during World War II as an aerial navigator in the United States Eighth Air Force. From 1946 to 1950 he was news editor of radio station WGL, Fort Wayne, Indiana.

GREGORY SCHUBERT is station manager of WBGU-TV and assistant professor of speech at Bowling Green University, Bowling Green, Ohio. He received the A.B. and A.M. degrees from Miami University (Oxford), and is a Ph.D. candidate at the Ohio State University. Mr. Schubert has also been employed as a producer and director of WBGU-TV, where he has written and directed several films.

THOMAS C. WARNOCK is assistant general manager and program director of WOSU radio at the Ohio State University in Columbus. He is also associate director of the Institute for Education by Radio and Television. He received the A.B. degree from Denison University and the A.M. degree from the Ohio State University, where he is now working toward the Ph.D. degree.

Preface

While studying as an undergraduate in Los Angeles I took a part-time job as a radio news editor for KFAC. There I worked under news director Dick Joy, who was also a freelance announcer for the Columbia Broadcasting System's "Playhouse 90." At least once a week Dick and I would have coffee or breakfast together. The topic of our conversation would inevitably turn to the business of broadcasting. What fascinated me most about Dick's conversation was his knowledge about one particular broadcasting union. Several years later I entered graduate school and eventually wrote both my master's and doctoral theses on Dick's union — the American Federation of Television and Radio Artists. While working on these projects and during subsequent research I was amazed by the paucity of studies on broadcasting unions. Since management and labor are sensitive about revealing what happens behind closed doors, it is not too surprising to find that little systematic research has been conducted.

The authors represented here, however, open the subject to examination. The chapters are original and cover four major areas: An historical overview of the broadcasting industry and its unions; legal decisions rendered by the National Labor Relations Board and courts, and arbitration awards concerning labor and management; specific problem areas confronting the industry and unions, such as black employment; and a look at what the future may hold for labor and broadcasting. For those who have no knowledge of existing labor unions in broadcasting, it would be helpful to first read chapter 3, "Broadcasting Unions: Structure and Impact."

I wish to thank all of the contributing authors for their courage and honesty.

A. E. K.

January 1970

Contents

Part I

RADIO AND TELEVISION
UNIONISM IN FOCUS

1 The Collision of Radio, Unions, and Free Enterprise

by MARTIN J. MALONEY

Marshall McLuhan has remarked that the content of a new medium of communication is an old medium. In other words, when a new communication device appears, it does so because it has become technically possible and therefore inevitable, rather than because it answers any special need in society. Being thus without clearly defined purpose, the new medium begins to operate by taking over some of the functions of older media and translating them into its own special language. Thus, radio in the twenties absorbed some of the functions of the newspaper and the vaudeville stage; thus, television in the forties and fifties absorbed much of radio, film, and theater.

All this is observably true of the newer communication media in the United States, but the process by which the absorption takes place has never been adequately described. What is the nature of this process? Let us offer some hypotheses. First, we suggest that any new discovery is characterized by means of metaphor. The discoverers and their colleagues, or the individuals who first encounter the new phenomenon, at once seek to put it in the perspective of the familiar. When motion pictures first appeared, for example, they were sometimes seen in the perspectives of fantasy, deception, and trickery; the great George Méliès, a pupil of the magician Robert-Houdin, regarded cinematography as a new kind of prestidigitation.[1] Radio, to Marconi and the inventors who followed him, was literally "wireless telegraphy" or "wireless telephony." Television was sometimes seen, by journalists of the twenties, as radio with pictures: "'Television' is, or will be, for the eye, what radio already is for the ear — we shall be able to see as well as hear what is going on in remote and near places"; and again, as motion pictures in the home: "It would be possible to transmit to a whole continent a film play in which Charlie Chaplin is the hero. In fact, the film could be dispensed with entirely. Chaplin might as well cavort before a modified, filmless moving picture camera, for successive images of him on a ground glass could be transmitted directly into millions of homes."[2] The uses to which these new devices were at first put developed to some extent from such metaphors.

Second, we argue that these early metaphoric identifications of new media determine what social organizations will be thought appropriate to use and control them. Radio is a case in point. To link the new invention with the existing telegraph was to indicate that it be used for point-to-point communications and to identify it generally with transportation and the military. To add the distinguishing label "wireless," of course, suggested a maritime use. Naturally, then, we should expect government agencies, and especially those concerned with maritime affairs, to have most to do with radio in its early stages of employment.

Finally, we point to the fact that these "appropriate" social organizations come to the new medium with certain biases and predispositions derived from their own past experience, and that these predispositions tend to affect the developing styles and content of the new medium. And here, at last, we may refer to the unions which have become part of the organizational structure of broadcasting. As we shall see, the first unions were organized in radio at a time when trade unionism was the acceptable, and almost the only, formula for resolving employees' economic and other work problems. The unionizing of broadcasting probably did nearly as much to place radio firmly within the field of business enterprise as did the invention of the commercial. More than this, specific unions brought to the new media (especially to television) the biases derived from experience in other, meta-phorically related, areas; is it really so surprising that television took on the realistic, dramatic style of theater and screen, in view of the fact that the early set-designers, costumers, and lighting technicians in TV were committed to that style?

The discussion which follows is not meant to document this complex process in full, but to suggest some of its ingredients: the development of trade unionism in the United States into a widely accepted formula for dealing with certain economic problems; the early, preunion history of radio, and the attempts to charac-terize and categorize the new medium; and the origins and devel-opment of some of the principal unions in broadcasting.

Trends and Patterns in the American Labor Movement

The general pattern of American trade union development has been a fairly simple one. The organizations have tended, over a fairly long period of time, to increase steadily in numbers and power, and to take into the union fold a broader and broader range of occupations as they did so. In an America which has been shifting, as David Riesman has remarked, from a cultural and economic stress on production to a stress on consumption, this has meant, inevitably, that service trades must be unionized — among them, the various activities associated with broadcasting.

Unions have existed in the United States since the end of the eighteenth century; once the Revolution had resulted in the crea-tion of a new state, they appeared. The first of them is said to have been a short-lived association of Philadelphia shoemakers, organ-ized in 1792.[3] It was followed by the Federal Society of Journey-man Cordwainers of Philadelphia and the Franklin Typographical Society of Journeyman Printers of New York, among others. These unions, like their present-day descendants, were concerned primarily with improving the lot of the workman on the job; they sought higher pay, shorter hours, union control of apprentices, and a closed shop. To enforce one or another of these demands, several strikes were called in the late 1790s, whereupon employers resorted to the courts. The years 1806–1842 produced a series of trials in which union members were indicted, usually upon the charge that they had conspired to raise wages.[4] Thus the pattern of union goals and the nature of the conflict with management (and sometimes, government) were fixed very early in the history of unionism.

In the years of increasing industrialization following the Civil War, American labor entered a period of expansion and frequently violent struggle against employers and government — a period marked by such explosive episodes as the Haymarket Massacre in Chicago (1886), the Homestead Massacre in Pennsylvania (1892), and the Pullman strike involving Eugene Debs' American Railway Union (1894). Two results of this long struggle were the development of broadly based and relatively stable labor organizations (the most successful of which was the American Federation of Labor, organized under Samuel Gompers in 1886), and the creation of some legal precedent favorable to union organization, which would be expanded in the thirties. Examples of the latter trend were the successful arbitration of the anthracite coal strike in 1902, following intervention by President Theodore Roosevelt; the technique of arbitration initiated by Louis D. Brandeis in the New York cloak and suit industry in 1910; the establishment, in 1913, of a federal Department of Labor.

The American Federation of Labor, in bringing together twenty-five specialized unions in one parent organization, typified an increasing tendency to broaden the base of union structure and to include more and more occupations within it. The AFL, however, was still a combination of skilled workers. Unskilled and semiskilled labor, up to the time of the First World War, were left without union representation.[5] But the tendency to reach out even to these groups was present in the labor movement of the period. The Knights of Labor, organized in 1878 and lasting until 1893, was prepared to admit all gainfully employed persons, and the Industrial Workers of the World, organized in 1905, laid particular stress on the organization of unskilled and migratory workers.[6]

Labor unions prospered during the 1917–1918 war but came on hard times during the twenties, beginning with the depression of 1921. Between that date and 1929, American unions lost roughly one and one-half million members, of whom about one million had belonged to the AFL. This drain of membership continued steadily through the years of deepest depression, until 1933.[7]

A contemporary historian comments that the National Labor Relations Act (Wagner Act), passed in 1935, was "the greatest victory gained by organized labor in American history."[8] It was certainly the most noteworthy of a number of measures passed during the first administration of Franklin D. Roosevelt, measures intended to increase employment and offer employees the protection of union membership. The effects of New Deal labor policies are apparent in union membership figures, which increased from slightly under three million in 1933 to nearly four and one-half million in 1935.[9] Although the turbulence of the Republic Steel strike, with the Memorial Day riots of May, 1937, was yet to come, this pattern of sharp expansion and growth continued; by 1944, the United States had a labor force of fifty-four million, of whom thirteen million were union members; by 1947, the unions claimed fourteen million members, or 22.6 percent of the labor force.[10]

The social theorist Kenneth Burke, in a work published in the year of the Wagner Act, employs the term *occupational psychosis*, by which he means the fixing of a successful technique for solving human problems into a formula, which is then applied in new and sometimes inappropriate areas.[11] Thus, he says, the people of a preliterate culture, such as the American Plains Indians, may solve most of their problems of survival by hunting, whereupon the methods and philosophy of hunting become psychotic (rigidly fixed) in the culture, resulting in a hunting religion, a hunter's concept of marriage, and so on.

To some extent, such a psychosis was probably created by the successful effort of unions to resolve the problems of American wage earners. As most historians agree, unions and various other labor movements were most successful when they concentrated on the business of protecting and improving the lot of workers on the job. Both the Knights of Labor and the IWW offered broad programs of social betterment, but these never interested potential members as much as the prospect of collective bargaining for higher wages, shorter hours, and the closed shop. Once the unions had demonstrated that they could successfully bargain on behalf of their members, in a favorable climate of statutory law, legal decisions, and even public opinion, their techniques and values became fixed into a formula and thereafter began to seem appropriate for solving the problems of *all* wage earners — and indeed, of all individuals in an unfavorable power position who must, in order to survive, deal with organizations of superior strength. (In this connection, it is instructive to study the current activities of black groups, dissident students, organizations of the poor, and so on, to observe the translation of the union "psychosis" into new problem areas.)

Thus it seems to have been inevitable, in the 1930s, when the unions finally achieved a strong position in the American economy, that they should have attracted and absorbed workers in a variety of previously nonunion occupations, including those in the rapidly developing broadcasting industry.

Radio: From Fad to Business

Radio offers one of the pure, classical examples of the new communication medium which, having appeared because it was technically inevitable, seems to be quite without practical function. Marconi is generally credited with the invention of wireless telegraphy in 1895; his interest in the device was apparently inspired, not by a vision of a world transformed by electronic communication, but by the experiments of Heinrich Hertz, a German physicist who in the late 1880s had demonstrated in the laboratory the validity of an earlier (1868) theoretical paper by James Clark Maxwell developing for the first time the concept of radio waves.[12] Having successfully sent and received Morse signals by wireless, Marconi offered his invention to the Italian government, only to have the device refused, as there seemed no practical use for it. Marconi then went to England, where his telegraph found immediate use in maritime communication.

Reginald Fessenden first demonstrated the transmission of voice signals in 1906, and the demonstration attracted considerable public attention, but only as an oddity of science. Not long after, Fessenden abandoned his researches in radio as unprofitable.[13]

In 1916 David Sarnoff, then an employee of Marconi Wireless Telegraph Company of America, wrote a memorandum to Edward Nally, general manager of the company, proposing the manufacture of a "radio music box" which would make radio a household utility by bringing "lectures, concerts, music, recitals, etc." into the home. The proposal was rejected.[14]

The emergence of radio as a *public* means of communication in 1920, a quarter-century after Marconi's achievement and nearly fourteen years after Fessenden's demonstration, was wildly accidental — paralleling, in some respects, the events which brought broadcasting to Great Britain.[15] During the war years of 1917–1918 the Westinghouse Electric Corporation had manufactured large quantities of radio equipment on government contracts. The war over, the contracts stopped; and by 1920 Westinghouse found itself struggling against the near-monopoly of patents and markets for marine radio equipment held by the General Electric and American Telephone and Telegraph companies, and handled through G.E.'s newly created subsidiary, the Radio Corporation of America. Caught between its investments in facilities for manufacturing wireless equipment and its obvious inferiority to RCA in patent holdings, Westinghouse desperately sought a way out.

In April, 1920, a Westinghouse engineer, Frank Conrad, resumed a long-standing interest in amateur radio and began broadcasting from his garage in Pittsburgh, using the call letters 8XK. The audience for his talks, phonograph records, and live piano solos was obviously composed of other amateurs — at least, until September of that year. At that point, the Joseph Horne department store ran an advertisement for "amateur wireless sets . . . $10.00 up." A Westinghouse executive, seeing the advertisement, envisioned a tremendous new business opportunity: simple, easy-to-operate radio receivers for the ordinary family — radio for the millions! A larger and more powerful transmitter was built by Westinghouse, a regular schedule of programs was planned, and on October 27, 1920, Station KDKA, Pittsburgh, came into being. On the evening of Election Day of that year the first KDKA program was transmitted: returns on the Harding-Cox presidential election.

New broadcasting stations appeared, many of them extensions of amateur wireless operations: WHA, Madison; WDAP, Chicago; KNX, Hollywood. But the real flood of new services came in 1922, when over five hundred stations were licensed.[16]

These broadcasting operations were amateur in all respects except, in some cases, the technical, and they continued in essentially amateur status for a considerable time thereafter. The early radio stations were all subsidized — by set manufacturers, like KDKA; by newspapers, like WGN, Chicago; by religious organizations and educational institutions; sometimes by private citizens with a message for the world, such as Dr. John R. Brinkley of Milford, Kansas, and Colonel L. K. Henderson of Shreveport, Louisiana. Performers commonly went unpaid, except for free transportation to and from the studio. When in 1924 the Kansas City local of the American Federation of Musicians demanded four dollars per musician per radio performance, consternation spread among radio station managers. The Kansas City *Star* finally appropriated $120 a week for musicians who appeared on its Station WDAF, which meant that WDAF thereafter broadcast nothing larger than a string trio.[17] The AFM demand was apparently the first ever made on radio operators by a union. If there were to be few other such demands for a long time to come, the reason was that radio was simply not a profit-making business.

AT&T station WEAF, New York, was the first to demonstrate that radio broadcasting could be turned to profit.[18] On August 28, 1922, for a fee of $50, the station broadcast a ten-minute commercial for the Queensboro Corporation, vending cooperative apartments in Jackson Heights. The experiment was successful, and WEAF began a consistent policy of selling time on the air. Some other stations followed suit, but by no means all.[19] American radio did not go wholly commercial until the networks became firmly established. Their more complex technical service and the elaborateness of the programs they offered made the subsidization of broadcasting a virtual impossibility.

But this gradual transformation of radio into a profit-making enterprise produced, to say the least of it, very uneven and unpredictable financial results for those actually involved in putting programs on the air. Writers and performers suffered most; engineers, station managers, and sometimes announcers were hired and paid, though not generously, but free-lance talent was quite another thing. Film and theater stars, vaudevillians, singers, and the like were invited to fill the endless gaps of the radio day, but in the earliest years of broadcasting they went uncompensated. Heywood Broun wrote in 1924, "These broadcasters do not pay. Instead they offer the performer publicity. It is a highly depreciated currency." [20] This was of course not always true: Will Rogers is said to have been paid a thousand dollars for a single performance on the WEAF "Eveready Hour" — and this long before the beginning of national networks.[21] Freeman Gosden and Charles Correll, when they began doing the sketches which developed into "Amos 'n' Andy," on Station WEBH, Chicago, received in exchange only free dinners at the Edgewater Beach Hotel. Shifting to WGN, as "Sam 'n' Henry," they were paid in real money, but not very much. A further shift to WMAQ, Chicago, increased their salaries to $150 a week each.[22] In 1928 the series was syndicated on transcription, and in 1929 "Amos 'n' Andy" went on the NBC network, with a salary of $100,000 a year going to Gosden and Correll.[23] The rewards of radio were variable.

The increasing reliance on sale of commercial time as a means of financing broadcasting, plus the coming of the networks (NBC Red and Blue in 1926–1927, CBS in 1928, Mutual in 1934) with all their technical expertise and sophisticated standards of production, turned radio into a big-money business and a source of enormous wealth for some who were involved in it. The development of broadcasting unions shortly thereafter confirmed and strengthened this reclassification of the new medium.

The stock-market crash, and the depression which followed it, had a rather peculiar effect on radio. As is fairly well known, radio, network radio in particular, rapidly became the primary means of public communication in depression America; it offered, almost free of charge, an excellent news service, a front-row seat in the theater of national and international politics, and a variety of exceedingly popular entertainments. The large business concerns which sponsored network programs remained reasonably solvent and had money to spend on advertising. At the network level, radio was probably more secure during the thirties than most of the competing media.

Local radio, on the other hand, was hard hit by the economic collapse. Small businesses failed, or at best came close to bankruptcy, and could pay little if anything in cash for radio advertising. For a time, many local stations received most of their income in trade: meal tickets, hotel space, groceries, and so on. This economic fact naturally was reflected in the wages paid to station employees, which were minuscule.[24] Even in large cities — San Francisco and Chicago are examples — actors were frequently paid a flat fee of five dollars per performance. And although in 1931 both NBC and CBS earned net profits of about $2,300,000, network pay for the average employee — performer, writer, director, and so on — was not really much better.[25]

There was, of course, talk among radio personnel — by now almost wholly professional and well experienced — of forming unions to improve their situation, but little action was taken until after a body of legislation designed to protect wage earners and to foster the spread of unions had been developed under the New Deal.

The Appearance of Unions in Broadcasting

When the unions finally appeared in broadcasting they did so in several ways: they were organized spontaneously by radio workers to meet current needs, as in the case of the National Association of Broadcast Employees and Technicians; they were organized within the radio industry but owed something of their structure and attitudes to older unions, as in the case of the American Federation of Radio Artists; they were already in existence, and moved into radio because the new medium was providing work for their members, as in the case of the American Federation of Musicians; or like the International Brotherhood of Electrical Workers, they were invited to organize employees of radio stations. Our hypothesis is that, although the success of the trade union movement by the early thirties had made the organization of radio workers nearly inevitable, the specific ways in which this process took place had some significance for the later development of radio and television broadcasting.

NABET and IBEW, for example, seem to have created in radio an enclave of professional electrical technicians, closely linked with similar personnel in other communications fields, such as telephone service. The immediate ancestor of NABET, the Association of Technical Employes, was organized at NBC in 1933 by a group of engineers and technicians. A contract, which became effective in January, 1934, was negotiated. The new union found itself in competition with the IBEW, but was nevertheless successful. It began to expand in 1937, adopted its present name in 1940, and affiliated with the CIO in 1951.[26] Like other unions, NABET displayed a tendency to expand its organization into marginal occupations; its inclusion of directors in the broad category of technicians is especially interesting, in the perspective of our hypothesis.

The union structures which provided for performers and writers created very different linkages. In 1937, the first radio performers' union was organized, simultaneously and independently, by two groups. In New York, the Actors Equity Association set up a committee to organize radio artists; the first meeting, which drew one hundred and twenty-three performers, took place on July 11, 1937. A few days earlier, in June, over three hundred performers had met in Hollywood for the same purpose. When each group had learned of the existence of the other, a joint meeting was held, and AFRA, the American Federation of Radio Artists, was formed. Its charter was granted on August 16, 1937, by the Associated Actors and Artistes of America (the Four A's), a union which included Actors Equity as one of its branches.[27]

Unionization of writers in broadcasting followed much the same pattern as the unionization of performers; the television writer today is linked firmly to his print colleagues, by way of radio, film, and drama. The chronology of this organization is interesting. The Authors League of America was organized in 1912, originally to represent the interests of book and magazine writers; dramatists were later admitted, and in 1926 the Dramatists Guild was founded as a separate branch of the league. In the late thirties, the Screen Writers Guild and the Radio Writers Guild were added to the league structure. The increasing importance of television toward the end of the 1940s provoked lengthy discussion on the most suitable way to include workers in the new medium within the union structure. The final result was the creation, in 1954, of the Writers Guild of America, East, and the Writers Guild of America, West, to represent radio, television, and motion picture writers.

The American Federation of Musicians was founded in 1896 in consequence of the breakup of an earlier association, the National League of Musicians, and was chartered by the AFL. As we have noted above, the AFM made its first demands on broadcasters in 1924. By the end of 1967 its most important arrangements in broadcasting were with television; the union had agreements with the three networks, TV, film, and videotape agreements with production companies, and local agreements with some TV stations.[28]

The emergence of TV as a commercial, public medium after 1945 meant, of course, that the unions already active in radio extended their sphere of influence to the new medium. At the same time, other unions previously concerned with theater and motion pictures made their appearance; an example is the International Alliance of Theatrical Stage Employes and Moving Picture Machine Operators of the United States. IATSE was founded in 1898 to include stage carpenters, property men, and electricians. During the 1920s it expanded to cover technicians in the Hollywood film studios, film exchange employees, and film projectionists. By a natural extension in the late 1940s it organized video and audio engineers, transmitter engineers, and other technicians in television.[29]

A Concluding Note

In general, then, our examination of the history of American unions and broadcasting has directed attention to the phenomena described, in slightly variant forms, by the terms "occupational psychosis" and "cultural lag." The common theme which seems to relate these two terms is that men do not escape their successes. The phrase "occupational psychosis" reminds us that a useful technique for dealing with *some* continuing problems will often be generalized and extended into new problem areas; thus, a "technological psychosis" may lead to the "scientizing" of business, art, human relations, religion. "Cultural lag" suggests that once-successful techniques tend to become rigidly institutionalized, and so persist long after they have become obsolete.

In using these terms, we would not claim that the rigidities imposed on radio and television by unionization involved obsolete or even inappropriate techniques for dealing with the condition of labor in broadcasting, or for developing the content and styles of the media. But there can be little doubt that the unions helped to shape radio and television as we know these media today. A popular stereotype of unionism follows roughly the Marxist concept of the class struggle: the worker opposed to the capitalist, management at war with labor. We would argue instead that the union movement, by concentrating heavily on collective bargaining over hours, wages, and working conditions, has contributed powerfully to the "business psychosis" in the United States. Specifically, we claim that the unionization of broadcasting workers confirmed the status of radio and television as commercial enterprise.

As for the lesser psychoses derived from their individual histories, it seems likely that the broadcasting unions, as a sort of side effect, influenced considerably the forms of radio and television programming, and perhaps even their content. AFRA's ancestry in Actors Equity, for example, must certainly have worked to identify radio actors with their colleagues in the theater, rather than encouraging the creation of a "new breed" in radio. When the radio unions, like NABET, moved to television, their existence in the new medium must surely have reinforced the basic resemblances between the two media and made it much less likely that television would develop its own idiosyncrasies. IATSE technicians surely brought to television techniques and a tradition derived from theater and films, which must have influenced television styles and forms. In general, it is hard to imagine television developing a highly imaginative, idiosyncratic style where the workers who produced it were most likely to force it into a resemblance to the media with which they were most familiar. The influence of the unions may well provide some documentation for McLuhan's view that the content of a new communication medium is an old medium — or, as in the case of both radio and television, a variety of old media. Here, as always, our social structures bind us to the past.

NOTES

1. C. W. Ceram, *Archaeology of the Cinema* (New York: Harcourt, Brace, & World, 1965), p. 195 ff.
2. The *New York Times*, November 21, 1925; December 26, 1926.
3. John R. Commons and associates, eds., *A Documentary History of American Industrial Society*, 10 vols. (Cleveland: Arthur H. Clark, 1940), 3:62.
4. *Ibid.*, p. 106.
5. This issue was still a matter of controversy in the AFL in 1933; see Philip Taft, *Organized Labor in American History* (New York: Harper and Row, 1964), p. 463 ff.
6. Terence V. Powderly, *Thirty Years of Labor* (Philadelphia: T. V. Powderly, 1890), p. 74; Taft, *Organized Labor*, pp. 296–97.
7. Richard B. Morris, ed., *Encyclopedia of American History* (New York: Harper and Brothers, 1953), p. 525.
8. Taft, p. 451.
9. Morris, *Encyclopedia*, p. 525.
10. *Ibid.*, p. 526.
11. *Permanence and Change: An Anatomy of Purpose* (Los Altos, California: Hermes Publications, 1954), pp. 37–49.
12. Degna Marconi, *My Father Marconi* (New York: McGraw-Hill, 1962), p. 12.
13. Lloyd Morris, *Not So Long Ago* (New York: Random House, 1949), p. 412.
14. Gleason Archer, *History of Radio to 1926* (New York: American Historical Society, 1938), pp. 112–13.
15. The following account of the Conrad broadcasts and the establishment of KDKA is based on material drawn from Archer, *History of Radio*, pp. 190–204, and Erik Barnouw, *A Tower in Babel* (New

York: Oxford University Press, 1966), pp. 61–74. For the analogous British history, see R. H. Coase, *British Broadcasting: A Study in Monopoly* (London: Longmans, Green and Co., 1950), ch. 1, "The Origins of the Monopoly."

16. Archer, pp. 393–97, lists some 225 stations which were on the air as of May 1 of that year.
17. Barnouw, *Tower in Babel*, p. 134.
18. For a detailed account, see William Peck Banning, *Commercial Broadcasting Pioneer: the WEAF Experiment, 1922–1926* (Cambridge: Harvard University Press, 1946).
19. By the end of 1925, 1492 broadcasting licenses had been issued by the government, 562 stations were then actively broadcasting, and of these, 100 were "broadcasting for hire." *Ibid.*, p. 285.
20. Quoted in Barnouw, p. 134.
21. *Ibid.*, p. 159.
22. *Ibid.*, p. 226.
23. *Ibid.*, p. 229.
24. *Ibid.*, p. 235.
25. *Ibid.*, p. 237.
26. The above details are from literature issued by the union, as well as John Gardiner's "Television Unions: a Tide of Rising Expectations Swells Up from the Ranks," *Television* 24 (October 1967), p. 29 ff.
27. Allen E. Koenig, "A History of AFTRA," *NAEB Journal*, July–August 1965, pp. 48–58.
28. "You Are Your Union" (New York: AFL, 1961), p. 7.
29. Gardiner, "Television Unions," p. 32.

2 The Effects of Unionism on Broadcasting: A Mythmatical Analysis

by ROBERT L. COE
with DARREL W. HOLT

Nearly everyone who has even nibbled at the history of organized labor in America has come across the story told of Samuel Gompers in the early days of his American Federation of Labor. Asked what his union *really* wanted, Gompers allegedly confided, "More!"

Having sat on both sides of the negotiation table during some forty-five years in the broadcasting industry, I've come to the conclusion that both management and labor have played the same game — called "More!" In St. Louis during the early twenties, for example, I was an early member of broadcasting's first technical union. A few years later, having been named chief engineer of a St. Louis radio station, I sat on the other side of the table. After the war, in 1948, I became most closely involved in labor negotiations as general manager of a television station in New York City. In most recent years, as a vice-president of the ABC television network, I've been able to spend more time watching than participating in labor matters. Over the years, needless to say, there has been a good deal of labor-management maneuvering to watch. From what I've seen — if we want to cast it in television terms — most of it has been a sophisticated remake of the same old plot. More.

I suppose that this kind of background explains my being asked to contribute to this volume: my own maturation in the broadcasting industry nearly coincides with that of the industry itself. The hope is, therefore, that I can discuss some of the effects of unionism on the industry, that I can isolate and describe some of those industry aspects which may be traced to the fact that broadcasting unions have existed. Now, *there's* a challenge!

Rather, let me simply share some relevant experiences which have grown out of those forty-plus years of negotiation table-hopping. The focus, of course, will be on the earlier circumstances which I believe correlate somehow with the industry as it is now constituted. Probably the most suitable form for this account is that of a case history.

My first experience with a broadcasting labor organization was from the sidelines in early 1926. Let me set the stage.

I was employed by KSD, one of the pioneer radio stations in St. Louis, as one of three technicians on the staff. The licensee was the Pulitzer Publishing Company, a fine organization which published the *Post-Dispatch*. By the standards of the day we were treated very well, despite the fact that there was no broadcasting union available to us. Granted, a six-day week was standard for most of us, and twelve- or fourteen-hour days were not uncommon. On these occasions, I recall, the company granted me a dinner allowance of seventy-five cents in lieu of overtime pay. Inasmuch as I could enjoy an excellent dinner for fifty cents, I realized a little cash profit as well.

My weekly salary was something like sixty dollars, a fairly substantial amount for the time. But at KSD there was something more — something intangible and elusive — that offered a reward over and above satisfactory wages and treatment. Perhaps it was simply being a part of *the* prestige station in the area. Perhaps it was the general thrill of playing a significant part in a new and exciting medium. Whatever it was, it contributed to the stability, loyalty, and more-than-usual contentment of the KSD technical staff.

It was into this kind of "happy family" market that the first "super power" radio station went on the air in St. Louis. Boasting a new 5,000-watt Western Electric transmitter, KMOX had begun programming on Christmas Day, 1925 — the newest and most powerful station in the area. Naturally, we at KSD were curious about the experiences of those people who enjoyed this modern electronic equipment. Just as naturally, KMOX technicians were curious as to how their circumstances of employment compared with those of their peers in the more established stations.

The comparison, it turned out, annoyed them. Some of them were working a seven-day week, with no overtime, and a maximum salary of perhaps thirty dollars per week. In addition, one of the rules of the United States Department of Commerce (this was before the creation of the Federal Radio Commission) dictated that super-power transmitters must be located outside the city of principal service, so that the signal would not "blanket out" those of the local stations. Therefore, the KMOX transmitter was located some fourteen miles outside St. Louis, in what was then an isolated rural area. It was a matter of some concern to their technicians that, at any given time, only one of them would be on duty at the transmitter. To explain this concern, I must jump ahead a year or so.

For a time, I became engineer-in-charge of this same KMOX transmitter. Though modern for its time, it still was a bulky conglomeration of wires, tubes, and metal cabinets which took up most of the floor area of a rather large building. Components were so awkward and scattered that it was difficult for one man to locate a malfunction (they occurred rather frequently in those days) and make repairs. My particular problem arose in connection with the storage batteries — a good many of which were necessary to operate the transmitter. Moreover, two sets of batteries were required in order that one set could be charging while the other was in use.

On this particular morning I was in the battery room leaning over a battery which had been on charge during the night, when a spark ignited the gas given off by the charging battery. The explosion blew off the top of the battery and splattered acid over my face. Fortunately, I closed my eyes in time, but if, by this time, there had not been a second man on duty who could lead me out of the room and promptly help clean the acid off my face, the consequences could have been serious.

A year or so earlier, however, the lack of a second man at the transmitter combined with wages and hours dissatisfactions to create a labor problem at KMOX. Within a month or so of the station's going on the air, KMOX technicians began talking to the International Brotherhood of Electrical Workers.

IBEW had been established in the late nineteenth century, largely for the purpose of organizing electrical construction workers. Local No. 1 of that organization had been chartered in St. Louis, and the electricians and electrical maintenance men at the *Post-Dispatch* were among the many members of that local. But up to that point in 1926 there was no substructure of Local No. 1 to accommodate radio technicians.

Following talks with KMOX technicians, though, the union created a new classification for such people — Class E, as I recall — and took them into the fold. Shortly thereafter, the union called on the management of KMOX to negotiate. I cannot recall management's reaction to the suggestion, but in any case, a strike resulted when the technicians walked out.

To the best of my knowledge this was the first organization of broadcast employees in the country, and therefore the first organized strike in the history of broadcasting. It is my recollection that, despite the walkout, the station did get back on the air after some difficulty; the strike lasted little more than a week; and IBEW won recognition as the bargaining agent for the KMOX technicians.

There are at least three correlations to be suggested at this point. Consider, for example, that the strikers achieved rather easily some improvement in wages, hours, and certain working conditions at a time when improvement was certainly in order. These goals, of course, generally persist today, although it must be granted that they were not peculiar to the new union. Rather, such goals were simply a perpetuation of the reasons for the organization of labor in the first place.

Moreover, immediately before the walkout the technicians made certain that management would clearly understand their importance to the orderly operation of the station: they loosened a wire here, reversed a circuit there, and in other ways altered the equipment so as to render it virtually inoperable. Although, as I have said, management did get the station back on the air, when I joined KMOX more than a year later we were still trying to restore the equipment to its prestrike condition. But again, this method of "physical negotiation" did not originate with the broadcasting union, but was inherited as a technique which had worked successfully for other industry negotiations earlier, and would continue to be employed in the future.

To emphasize this point: Not long after KMOX technicians joined IBEW, some of us from KSD were in a business agent's office one evening, listening to his explanation of how powerful and persuasive his union was when negotiating with management. "Of course," he said pointedly, "if our negotiations on a normal basis are not successful, we can always take *this* route." Reaching under his coat, he extracted a snub-nose revolver and slapped it on the table. That he was quite serious may be borne out by the fact that, some years later, this same business agent was shot dead in the lobby of his own office building.

Finally, for the moment, I believe that the success of this early IBEW radio technicians organization explains an otherwise curious fact: although the National Association of Broadcast Employees and Technicians (NABET), with few exceptions, represents technicians at both NBC and ABC, IBEW represents those at CBS. Recall that KMOX became a CBS affiliate not too long after that network's formation in 1927, and became a wholly owned-and-operated CBS property in 1931. There was, of necessity, close contact between the technicians at KMOX and those of CBS from the beginning of the station's affiliation with the network. Certainly, as I recall it, the KMOX technicians at that time privately took credit for their CBS brothers' swinging to IBEW when it came time to choose the union to represent them.

It is only fair to note that Bill Lodge, CBS vice-president for engineering and affiliate relations, does not agree with this theory. On the other hand, as I recall my last conversation with him on this subject, he admitted that he was not with CBS at the time in question, and furthermore he can offer no alternative explanation for the fact that IBEW has represented CBS technicians from the beginning.

After KMOX had recognized IBEW in early 1926, we three technicians at KSD were not strongly motivated to join the union, for the simple and understandable reason that we had always been treated very well at KSD. Moreover, the wage scale finally established for radio technicians in St. Louis was still below the salaries we enjoyed at KSD. The union's business agent, however, offered a most persuasive argument to the newspaper licensee of the station: If KSD radio technicians did not become members of IBEW, the union would establish a picket line around the *Post-Dispatch* building.

In those early days, we must recall, and to some extent even later, many newspaper licensees considered their investments in radio stations and their promotional budgets in much the same light. A publisher could use his station, as well as gimmicks connected with the electronic novelty, as a means to increase newspaper circulation. I recall, for example, that one such circulation booster for the *Post-Dispatch* was an "antenna kit," consisting simply of a coil of wire, a couple of insulators, and lightning arresters. Later, they offered a much more sophisticated premium — a crystal set.

The daily newspaper, however, remained far and away the publisher's principal concern. At the *Post-Dispatch*, as at most newspapers in the larger cities, employees performing the various mechanical crafts were already pretty well organized. Electricians and electrical maintenance men were already members of IBEW. In short, a picket line by any affiliated union would inevitably halt the printing of the newspaper — a consequence which publishers of that day would try to avert at almost any cost. Accordingly, nearly any union policy or demand which did not totally obliterate the bounds of reason, and which facilitated the uninterrupted publishing of the paper, was accepted with minimum fuss by the publisher-licensee.

It was not surprising, therefore, that the business manager of the *Post-Dispatch* called the three of us into his office and pointedly explained that the station owners would not think any the less of us if we joined IBEW. It should be emphasized that, although we were not highly motivated, we did recognize the overall value of the organization to the industry. Certainly, the KMOX technicians had received worthwhile and well-deserved benefits. We joined. Shortly, all the technicians in all the St. Louis radio stations were members of IBEW.

America's young broadcasting industry marveled at the speed with which all St. Louis radio technicians were organized — not to mention the extensive power they were able to exert when necessary. As an outgrowth of this latter fact, St. Louis rapidly developed a country-wide reputation as (depending on your point of view) a trouble spot for certain kinds of broadcast operation.

If, for example, plans called for a remote broadcast from the St. Louis Municipal Auditorium — or from several other theatres, as I recall — the producer immediately felt the effects of the less-than-cordial relations between IBEW and the International Alliance of Theatrical Stage Employees (IATSE). Backstage at these particular theatres, at least, the stagehand members of IATSE were in complete control. Even though both IATSE and IBEW were affiliated with the American Federation of Labor, the former was able to enforce a requirement that at least one IATSE member must be hired by any St. Louis radio station which wished to broadcast from any one of those theatres. If the radio station's IBEW crew was self-sufficient, then the IATSE man must be hired as a standby.

Similar problems were posed, however, by IBEW. Suppose that the fledgling national network, NBC, should wish to originate a network feed from St. Louis. They could send their technical crews in only if they agreed to hire at least one local IBEW technician to work with the out-of-town crew.

This fact leads to one of several possible correlations which we might consider at this point: I believe that the obvious success and power of IBEW in St. Louis provided at least some of the impetus for NBC technicians to organize their own Association of Technical Employees (later to became NABET) in 1933. Any NBC technician in town for a network origination would have to have been unusually imperceptive to fail to notice the alacrity with which network officials complied with the demands of the IBEW local.

Furthermore, although all unions traditionally have sought to retain jurisdiction over all work which falls within their respective areas of dominance, the fact remains that adding extra men to technical crews increases the cost of the program. It stands to reason that NBC would be well aware of this fact when, on occasion, it weighed the pros and cons of originating a program from St. Louis.

If the easily observable success of IBEW in St. Louis motivated the organization of radio technicians elsewhere, it is not too great a logical leap to suspect that this same success encouraged, to some degree, the organization of employees in other areas of broadcasting, and perhaps encouraged existing unions to attempt to enter this potentially lucrative field.

Certainly, word of what was happening in St. Louis was disseminated rapidly enough. The pioneering nature of many of the policies and activities of the St. Louis local invited close surveillance by many of the nation's foremost union leaders. At the same time, executives from Local No. 1, as their duties carried them around the country, did their part to see that no one was deprived of this information.

In any case, the organization of radio technicians spread fairly rapidly from St. Louis into other parts of the Midwest. The fact that the initial growth was in the Midwest, instead of the larger cities in the East, seems especially significant.

Perhaps the most important correlation of all is the role of management — especially the newspaper licensee — in early labor negotiations. Consider that radio was a new medium, exhibiting characteristics and posing problems which were in several respects different from those previously encountered. One might suppose, then, that the attitudes, policies, and techniques of the new broadcasting union might also depart in some respects from those of traditional unionism. On the contrary, the new union seemed to buy the entire package of traditionalism, and attempted to knead and shape the new industry until it fit the pattern.

It is not profitable, now, to crystal-gaze the outcome, had management successfully resisted this approach, and instead worked with the organization to create new, compromise patterns more suitable to the new medium. Suffice to say, management did not successfully resist. The *Post-Dispatch*, in fact, unwittingly encouraged the traditional pattern and helped to give it permanent stature. By the time other new broadcasting unions came into being, the nonbroadcasting tradition had become the broadcasting tradition.

Explanation of two other events, or sets of circumstances, seems in order at this point. One of them is important because it describes one of those rare instances in which a direct cause-effect relationship is obvious, and because it illustrates one of the ways in which union activity clearly resulted in well-defined values for an entire station. The second is important because it describes one of the ways in which a few labor leaders were able to employ their union's power as a weapon for personal retaliation.

Although it is hardly necessary for most readers, we will place the first situation in perspective by recalling that, since the beginning of broadcasting, music has been a staple in most programming diets. Indeed, the relations between broadcasting stations and music sources — as well as the organizations which control these sources — is worthy of a study in itself. Suffice to say that, since the National Association of Broadcasters was conceived in late 1922 as one means of combatting the royalty demands of the American Society of Composers, Authors and Publishers (ASCAP), relations with the music industry have both soothed and riled the savage breast of broadcasting.

The most mercurial of those relationships, in the early days, were with what was probably the strongest union in any way connected with broadcasting — the American Federation of Musicians. Long and firmly established in movie theatres, hotels, and night clubs, the AFM moved rather quickly into broadcasting. In fairly short order the union adopted and successfully enforced a quota system: each radio station must employ a specified number of musicians on its full-time staff, the number varying from station to station according to criteria applied by the union.

A few stations were able at first to remain exempt from the quota system. KSD, St. Louis, for example, had completely closed its studio in 1926 and remained content to relay all the network programs available. Now and then, of course, an important event might motivate a remote origination, but KSD programming was almost entirely network. Station breaks and other occasional bits of live copy were delivered by the engineer at the transmitter, then located on the roof of the *Post-Dispatch* building. The station maintained no sales staff, and the only commercial business resulted from infrequent announcements requested by one or another of the newspaper's advertisers. At such times, the announcements were also delivered by the lone transmitter engineer.

Even so, KSD was an immensely prestigious station, owned by a prominent newspaper, and the AFM could no longer ignore the station's escaping a required quota. As far as anyone could tell, the union initiated action to require KSD to employ a specified number of union musicians. There is reason to believe, however, that the invitation to initiate action was actually extended by KSD competitors and by some of the *Post-Dispatch*'s own staff who wanted to see the radio station become more active. In any case, a representative of AFM called on the *Post-Dispatch*. With the newspaper's traditional sensitivity to possible labor problems, the KSD staff soon blossomed forth with a small orchestra. Interestingly, as full-time employees of KSD, these union musicians outnumbered the rest of the full-time staff.

A chain reaction took place almost overnight. The musicians were on the payroll, and so we began to build some programming around them. But a crowded transmitter shack on the roof was hardly an appropriate place; therefore, we reactivated the studio. Moreover, a sequence of tunes, interrupted only by a topside engineer's "The next selection is . . ." hardly constituted an award-winning program; additional talent was brought in. As our local live-programming expertise increased, however, so did our overhead. That situation was effectively remedied by the addition of an efficient sales force.

The cause-effect relationship in this illustration is clearly evident. KSD, as far as programming was concerned, had been little more than a repeater station for the network. With AFM activity as a catalyst, however, it rapidly came to life and assumed a fully competitive commercial position in St. Louis.

The second event did not enjoy an equally pleasant and positive denouement. Quite the contrary, it illogically and unnecessarily widened the communications gap between the technicians and management. In my experience, this is a condition which exists generally throughout industry and is no better (and is probably worse) today, when genuine and effective intracompany communication is so vital.

At any rate, during the mid- and late-thirties I was chief engineer and supervisor of operations for KSD, and therefore no longer a member of IBEW. A man who is responsible for the smooth and trouble-free technical operation of a radio station tends to become edgy when the station suddenly goes off the air. That's what happened! It was only after I saw our transmitter and studio engineers assembled in the lobby of the building that I realized equipment failure was not the problem. Rather, the engineers had "pulled the plug." No advance warning; no statement of grievances; no attempt to negotiate; nor, for much longer than it took me to wish that tranquilizers had already been invented, any explanation.

That explanation, when it finally came, was incredible. It seems that the IBEW business agent was in court that day to testify in reply to charges which had been brought against him. I no longer remember details of those charges, but they were newsworthy enough to warrant coverage by a *Post-Dispatch* photographer. As the photographer prepared to take a picture of the business agent, the latter warned that he would shut down both the newspaper and the radio station if the picture were taken. The photographer, of course, took the picture, and immediately one of the business agent's assistants phoned the technicians at KSD and the electricians at the *Post-Dispatch*, ordering them off the job.

As I recall it, at that very moment the newspaper presses were grinding out one of the several daily editions. Nonetheless, being loyal union men, the electricians prepared to comply with the order. It's just that they weren't very energetic about it, and by the time they walked off the job, the job was completed. The edition hit the street as scheduled. The radio technicians, though equally loyal union men, were considerably less experienced in the ebb and flow of a business agent's blood pressure. Therefore, when the order came to "shut 'er down," that is what they did — right now!

There was no point to the short-lived walkout; the union achieved nothing. In fact, the only observable consequence I noticed was that the KSD management never quite forgave the technicians for what seemed to be an immediate and unreasoned compliance with an irrational and unwarranted order.

Even though television had not yet arrived in St. Louis as 1946 dissolved into 1947, I received a forecast of some of the labor problems that loomed over the new medium's horizon. Again, let's set the stage.

As chief engineer of KSD, I was working toward a target date of February 8, 1947, to put KSD-TV on the air. Inasmuch as KSD-TV was the first independent station to go on the air after World War II, and there was no other TV station in St. Louis, our technicians knew little or nothing about the medium or its equipment. Therefore, in the fall of 1946 I had arranged with RCA to deliver two field cameras and associated equipment, together with a few home receivers, so that we could prepare for the February sign-on. My thought was that we could dry-run some programs as a means of familiarizing our men with TV equipment and techniques. At the same time, we could pipe these practice programs to receivers installed in our studio building, and thereby demonstrate the new medium to various invited guests. The promotional value of this plan seemed evident.

As the highlight of our practice programming, we conceived the idea of "televising" what was probably *the* outstanding public social event in St. Louis each fall — the annual Veiled Prophet Parade and Ball. According to plan, we would install the receivers in a special viewing room within the studio building, and would invite a number of prominent citizens, including potential advertisers, to join us for the demonstration.

Fortunately, the television pickup of the parade would be no problem, for the parade route passed right by our building; erecting a camera stand over the sidewalk would be a simple matter. Covering the ball, however, would be another matter. As I recall, it was to be held in the Municipal Auditorium, some ten or twelve blocks away. But here we had the complete cooperation of the local telephone company, which provided a video circuit between the two buildings. Incidentally, this was the first such circuit to be installed in any city between Chicago and the Pacific Coast.

Early on the morning of the ball, our KSD technicians and I arrived at the auditorium, loaded with TV cameras and assorted paraphernalia. Recognizing the realities of life, I had arranged for an IATSE standby man for the day and evening, even though televising the event was not "for real." Just inside the door I was met by a good and longtime friend, the head stage electrician. Interspersed with the usual amenities, his greeting informed me that an IATSE business agent was on his way down from Chicago to insist that all cameras be operated by members of that union.

Soon the Chicago business agent bustled in to advise me that he had several IATSE cameramen following him from Chicago, and they would have to be employed if we were to televise the ball that night. I assured him, naturally, that this was not to be a genuine telecast, but only a closed-circuit demonstration to a few receivers in a room about a dozen blocks away. Furthermore, I pointed out, if this demonstration were a success and television really got going in St. Louis, quite a number of jobs would be created. All this was fine with him, but if we wanted to cover the ball that evening, IATSE men must run the cameras.

While we were discussing the matter, I was called to the telephone. My caller was the IBEW business agent, warning me that only our regular IBEW men could handle the cameras that evening. As a regretful alternative, he would be forced to call all our technicians off the job.

This verbal ping-pong went on all day long. By 8:00 P.M., when the ball started, the matter was still unresolved. But resolution was on the way: it wasn't too long before the public address system went silent. Next, the lights, which played an important part in the spectacular and beautiful staging of the ball, began to fade. At that point the general manager of KSD, who was on the scene, frantically wig-wagged my attention. One of the officials of the ball, he explained that we could not be a party to ruining that justly famous event, and that I should order our men to shut down the cameras and get out as quickly as possible.

This we did. Fortunately, I had kept our cameras on during all of the activities preliminary to the ball itself, and so the demonstration was not a complete failure.

Several months later, as we neared the sign-on of KSD-TV, that same IATSE business agent apologized for his unwavering stand that night, explaining that he had not realized that only closed-circuit practice was involved. Suffice to say that KSD-TV went on the air with our own IBEW men operating the cameras, but with one IATSE stagehand in the studio and another one of their men operating the film projector. Time has mercifully erased the memory of how many hours of negotiation with both unions were required before we all agreed on this division of jurisdiction

I suppose that, even today, most young people in television see themselves ultimately as doing Big Things in the Big City. Back in the late forties, of course, not only was TV new and novel, but network radio still retained a good deal of its Golden Age glitter. Therefore, the appeal of New York City was especially strong. My chance came when I was invited to put another TV station on the air.

Arriving in Manhattan on January 2, 1948, I was the new vice-president and general manager of WPIX, a TV station licensed to the New York *Daily News*. At that moment, however, WPIX existed mostly as printed capital letters on a construction permit, even though our target date was June 15. Being asked to plan, organize, build, and test a commercial television station in five and one-half months seemed like being asked to build the Pyramids with a slingshot.

I was rather unnerved, then, to discover that staffing the station properly required my negotiating with some twenty different unions and locals. Happily, I discovered this early through numerous telephone calls and visits from legions of business agents, whose unions either already represented, or hoped to represent, employees in that new and not-very-well-charted field of TV.

Consider, for example, that TV programming requires the services of several kinds of talent — artists who may perform in the studio or in a variety of remote locations. This fact throws one into contact with the American Federation of Television and Radio Artists (AFTRA), the American Guild of Variety Artists (AGVA), Actors Equity, the Screen Actors Guild, and the AFM — to mention the most active. Providing much of the material for many of these artists are the writers, who are also well organized. At the same time, many supporting services are required: costumers, costume designers, scene painters, scenic designers, and more. And central to our concern, of course, are the technicians.

Very early, IBEW entered the front door of WPIX through my hiring of a chief engineer. Clearly, one of my most important first needs was that of a chief who would supervise the technical planning of the station, while also starting to assemble a competent technical staff. Experienced TV chiefs were extremely difficult to locate in 1948, though, and I had to import from St. Louis an engineer who had been my assistant at KSD-TV. Already an IBEW member of several years, he naturally built a technical staff which consisted mostly of IBEW technicians.

Just as naturally, NABET and IATSE were disenchanted by that turn of events. NABET, as previously mentioned, was strongly entrenched at the NBC television station; IATSE was the authorized representative of technicians at the DuMont station, WABD. Accordingly, each group felt a preexisting, proprietary right to represent WPIX technicians. Hour after countless hour of negotiation followed, bringing us much nearer to our June 15 sign-on date than to a solution of the jurisdictional problems.

Finally, the matter was laid before the National Labor Relations Board, which led to many more time-consuming discussions with a federal mediator, and then to an NLRB election in the station. The outcome of the election gave representation of studio, remote, and transmitter engineers to IBEW, stage hands and projectionists to IATSE. And speaking of remotes, members of the Teamsters' local already were driving *Daily News* trucks, and so there was no jurisdictional dispute at all: we readily agreed to their suggestion that their members should drive our remote units.

We had planned to rely rather heavily on remotes in our program schedule, for we were an independent station and believed that we could not only handle such programs somewhat more easily than the network affiliates, but also that such programs would provide suitable competition to network fare. On our opening night, for example, two of our most prestigious programs were to be night club remotes — one from the famous Latin Quarter, the other from the Versailles. At the former, the show would be emceed by *Daily News* columnist and sportswriter Ed Sullivan, while the show at the latter would be emceed by *Daily News* columnist and critic Danton Walker.

A day or so before our opening night, some talent unions suddenly awoke to the fact that there were to be telecasts from these two clubs. AGVA, AFM, and, as I recall, Actors Equity pointed out to me that we had no agreement with their respective unions; therefore, we could not put their people on television. This problem could be solved easily, of course, if we would agree to certain conditions. Although these conditions were a little fantastic, it is only fair to point out that inexperience lay at the root of them. The TV industry was so young, nobody really knew what was "right" or "fair."

In any case, the shows did go on, although the rather sizable additional payments demanded — notably by the AFM — forced WPIX to shelve plans for subsequent remotes from those locations. From then on, whenever Ed Sullivan performed for WPIX, he did so either from our studios or from some other location equally suitable to 1948 program budgets. Incidentally, those shows that Ed Sullivan did for us were the forerunner of the

"Toast of the Town," which, as "The Ed Sullivan Show," remains on CBS as one of television's oldest programs.

Again, it should be mentioned that, with additional experience, the unions might have moderated their demands. As it was, WPIX had to pay prohibitively heavy additional fees, even though the managements of both clubs helped out to a degree. Recall that, in mid-1948, there were relatively few TV receivers out in homes; most of the sets were in taverns and other public places. Because advertising rates and therefore sponsor interest related directly to audience potential, there were only about two hundred business firms in the entire United States who chose to advertise on television. Consequently, we at WPIX could only quaveringly guess at how long it would be before income would approach outgo.

Another WPIX approach to programming warrants mention. We very early began to build a television newsreel organization — the first TV-based operation, certainly, in America, and as far as I know, in the world. During the eighteen- to twenty-four-month life of this organization we accepted a great deal of expense, trouble, and time-commitment to build a world-wide news team of contacts and stringers in most of the world's important cities. For our visuals, we made agreements with, or hired outright, individual photographers or organizations in most major capital cities.

On the local scene we were equally ambitious, with something like fifteen cameramen and, when appropriate, accompanying sound crews to cover New York City. To handle all this film from home and abroad (there was no video tape in 1948), we set up rather extensive film processing facilities. Our procedure was to prepare a "white paper" each day from all this footage. We would then use all of it, or clips from it, on our own programs, while syndicating it to other stations around the country. The size of this undertaking, of course, brought with it another group of unions.

It is not my intent at this point to suggest that all union demands were unreasonable. They were, however, significant; and, in combination with other costs, our world-wide newsreel pioneering proved too costly to maintain. After nearly two years, then, we turned the operation over to one of the new firms which had recently entered the field solely to produce visual news for whoever wanted it.

As 1948 faded into 1949, New York City television service consisted of the four stations owned and operated by ABC, CBS, DuMont, and NBC, as well as two independents, WOR and WPIX. Of these, ABC and WOR were the last to sign on, and their arrival occasioned several joint negotiations with some of the unions. Growing out of a few of these sessions were contracts which covered all the TV stations then existing in New York City.

Over the years it has become apparent that what we did in New York tended to establish many of the ground rules with which the television industry has had to live ever since. Not all elements of that legacy were equally desirable, however, for both management and labor committed some unfortunate errors. From a management point of view, for example, we erred by agreeing too readily to some of the unions' demands.

In retrospect, I believe that it was inevitable that we would commit certain errors. I account for this by reemphasizing the vulnerability of certain categories of licensees. Consider WPIX, for example. Not only was it licensed to the *Daily News*, but it was also located in the same building. Any serious labor dispute, even though concerned solely with WPIX, would result in a picket line around the entire building. In that case, the work stoppage would undoubtedly include the newspaper.

The position of the networks was only slightly better. For ABC, CBS, and NBC, television still was a sideline, an investment in the future. Their radio networks remained the principal source of income, and it was quite possible that any disturbance in TV could produce considerable sympathy on the radio side. DuMont, of course, had no radio network, but their executives joined those of the other networks in the vision of sight-and-sound as *the* medium of the foreseeable future. Whatever the motivation, the networks — especially NBC — seemed particularly reluctant to risk a quick fade to black because of labor problems.

That rather succinctly states the most important proposition: broadcasting stations simply cannot afford to go dark. More than many industries, broadcasting suffers a nearly irretrievable loss when work stoppage occurs. The time lost and the programs not played can be made up only to a negligible degree. Accordingly, broadcast management usually cannot remain adamant to the bitter end. It is to the credit of broadcasting unions, too, that they have infrequently forced management into that kind of position.

Nonetheless, it has happened, and so one management practice is to try to ensure that supervisory personnel are trained to some extent in the various operating and announcing functions. Then, if a walkout does occur, these people can at least keep the station on the air. In the past, I've found myself sometimes in the newsroom, sometimes running a camera.

In looking for other correlations, I've discovered that no matter how I've approached them verbally, the substance of each can be simply stated — cost. This is not to say that unions alone have contributed to the constantly increasing costs of broadcasting; nor, despite the focus of this paper, have the technical unions deserved special censure. It is certain, though, that the continual drive on the part of all unions to improve the salaries and other financial benefits of their members has been a major factor.

Actually, it is my contention that craft unions — all the so-called below-the-line unions — were forced psychologically into occasional aggressive demands by at least two policies of program management. That is to say, since audiences began to demand glamorous stars in broadcasting, just as they had earlier begun to idolize certain motion picture performers, management has been tempted to pay prices for talent and program rights that have been unrealistic in relation to the economic condition of the country.

Granted, the talent of a given performer may be unique and therefore highly appealing. In view of the rigorous competition for audiences, programmers often bid astronomically for the services of a proven audience-getting star — this after paying a fabulous price for rights to the vehicle in which he is to appear. Sometimes the price of those two factors, the star and his vehicle, will each be several times that of the total income to *all* the below-the-line people who have contributed to the success of the program. One cannot be surprised, then, when at contract renewal time these people apply considerable pressure on their business agents to "sweeten the pot."

But along with this I can point to a large number of instances when desirable programs died in the idea stage, or, having been produced once, were canceled. In those instances, restrictive labor demands made the programs financially prohibitive. Conversely, we can see evidence all around us today that suggests that cost is wholly ignored in the production of several TV series and many special events.

It is even possible that costs combined with changing advertising strategy to send the single-sponsor TV program into near oblivion. In radio's Golden Age, as well as in the early days of television, advertising strategy placed considerable value on one sponsor's acquiring a psychological "title" to a given series and its star. Today, the typical advertiser's television dollars are spread over several program types, either as spot announcements which involve no sponsorship whatsoever, or as participating sponsorships with other advertisers. Granted, this approach may well expose a larger and more varied audience to the message, but no matter what his philosophy, it is a rare advertiser who cares to underwrite the entire cost of today's typical television series.

If this cost notion is valid, then the wheel has come full circle, because cost is a function of the labor-management game called More. No matter how many high-sounding phrases slither across the negotiation table, no matter how beneficial are the by-products of the ultimate agreement, both have been playing to achieve their respective objectives.

Generally, of course, the adversaries' objectives are different. Labor wants more income and fringe benefits, both of which add to the industry's cost of doing business. Management usually wants additional net profits, which are most obviously obtained by reducing the cost of doing business, while retaining or increasing gross sales. It's a game which, in one sense, both sides win. Labor normally achieves most of what it wants; management sometimes maintains or improves its income-to-cost ratio by increasing efficiency in production and distribution, but often by passing the added costs along to the consumer. Inasmuch as all employees and most industries are also consumers of other industries' goods and services (and *they* have been playing the same game!), the victory may be more psychological than economic.

Now, this is not intended to be a negative opinion. In fact, as we look at the kind of competitive capitalism which contributed to America's growth, we can hardly expect labor-management relations to be otherwise. If anything negative is implied, it's that their positions have been too extreme on occasion. Either management has exploited employees, or the union has exerted its power to a point where we can't be certain "who's running the shop."

What often happens, then, is this: one side acts, which "causes" the other side to overreact. The "effect" of the overreaction becomes a "cause" of retaliatory overreaction, and so on. And so, causes produce effects which become additional causes of additional effects to a point where cause and effect seem interchangeable.

That's why this essay concerning the effects of unionism on broadcasting is called "a mythmatical analysis."

3 Broadcasting Unions: Structure and Impact

by GREGORY SCHUBERT
and JAMES E. LYNCH

The major movement towards the unionization of broadcast employees began with the passage of the National Labor Relations Act (Wagner Act) in April of 1935. Until that time only a few minor labor organizations involving broadcasting personnel had been in existence. The combination of a national administration in Washington interested in protecting the workingman and the rapid development of network radio in the 1930s provided necessary impetus for union growth. In the ten years that followed, other unions were formed and given jurisdictional control over radio performers, writers, directors, and technicians. These controls were carried over into television, and the result was the gradual emergence of eight major labor organizations which now represent approximately three hundred and twenty-five thousand employees in the broadcasting industry.

Broadcast unions can be separated into the categories "creative" and "technical." Involved in the control and jurisdiction of personnel in the creative area are the American Federation of Television and Radio Artists, the Screen Actors Guild, the Writers Guild, East, and the Writers Guild, West, the Directors Guild of America, and the American Federation of Musicians. The technically oriented unions are the International Brotherhood of

Electrical Workers, the National Association of Broadcast Employees and Technicians, and the International Alliance of Theatrical Stage Employees.[1]

These organizations — their structure, impact, and history — will be briefly examined here in the context of contemporary broadcasting and labor-management relationships.

The American Federation of Television and Radio Artists (AFL-CIO)

On August 16, 1937, the American Federation of Radio Artists received its charter from the Associated Actors and Artistes of America, commencing a long and checkered bargaining career by a union organization representing creative broadcasting personnel.[2]

Radio performers, long subjected to harsh working conditions, low pay, and long hours, saw the Wagner Act as a means of rectifying past inequities. In two separate meetings held in Los Angeles and New York, radio personnel decided to band together and secure for themselves rights being demanded generally by labor. The result was the formation and chartering of AFRA.

The fledgling union's first successful negotiations, held in 1937, were with radio station KMOX in St. Louis, Missouri. Management at KMOX, feeling that the quality of their personnel might be compromised by free-lance talent, refused to recognize AFRA as the bargaining agent for station announcers. An election to determine bargaining rights, as prescribed by the National Labor Relations Act, was held at KMOX. The resulting vote, in AFRA's favor, was its first union-station victory, one that quickly introduced network-wide negotiation and contract acceptance.[3]

AFRA's success with the networks was followed closely by negotiations with advertising agencies and sponsors for jurisdiction over those performers who worked in broadcasting. Letters of union recognition were soon signed, and AFRA's role as the negotiator for broadcasting talent gained further acceptance.[4]

The union continued to expand its jurisdiction, adding individual stations as well as smaller regional networks. Seventy percent of live broadcasting (both sustaining and commercial shows) was under the jurisdiction of collective bargaining agreements at the time of AFRA's second national convention.[5]

Following World War II, television began to emerge from the restrictions imposed on its development during the war. By the late 1940s, it had grown to such an extent that it had become a sizeable force in the broadcast industry.

The first television network personnel contract was ratified, effective December 8, 1950. It was negotiated not by AFRA, but by the Television Authority. The Television Authority, composed of representatives from the American Guild of Variety Artists, the American Guild of Musical Artists, Actors Equity, and Chorus Equity, had been formed on May 22, 1934, and had at that time been granted jurisdiction over television. It was not until 1950, however, that it received authority from the "four A's" to negotiate a code.[6]

In 1951, members of the Television Authority voted 101 to 42 to merge with AFRA. With a resolution from the four A's endorsing the action, a *T* was added to AFRA on September 20, 1952, and a new union, the American Federation of Television and Radio Artists, emerged.[7]

AFTRA scored an important first for a talent union in its 1954 contract with the networks. The agreement called for establishment of a network-supported pension and welfare plan, and the inclusion of an industry-supported major medical policy covering union members under network contracts. It was the first time in the history of broadcast union negotiations that this type of provision received network approval.[8]

The union continued to improve wage and supplemental benefits for its members with each contract signing. The only serious problems encountered by the union during this period involved jurisdictional control, and merger discussions with the Screen Actors Guild, an organization representing performers in both television and feature films. At issue was the role of the filmed

TV performer and the question of which union could claim jurisdiction over him. In the dispute, the Screen Actors Guild was successful in maintaining itself as the bargaining agent for performers in filmed television programs. The only major victory won by AFTRA revolved around the use of video tape recordings of programs. SAG claimed that this new method of program reproduction was, in essence, an improved film technique, while AFTRA maintained that video-taped programs were essentially live. After prolonged negotiations, it was resolved that video tape recording was a live medium and that performers who appeared on taped programs would fall under AFTRA's jurisdiction.[9]

An AFTRA-SAG merger had been suggested in 1960 as a method of strengthening the bargaining position of both unions, but SAG membership rejected the proposal.

The early and mid-1960s were uneventful years for the union and its members. Some conflicts arose, notably the attempt by AFTRA to organize performers appearing on WNDT, New York City's noncommercial television station. WNDT agreed to recognize AFTRA jurisdiction in representing announcers and other professional performers, but it resisted efforts to unionize teachers or professors appearing on non-instructional television programs. The dispute was resolved in April, 1963, when AFTRA lost its bid to represent TV teachers on the issue of residuals (pay for repeat performances), and to bargain for free-lance professors — voted down by the educators themselves.[10] It was also in 1963 that AFTRA negotiated an agreement with the networks calling for a minimum fee and residual payment formula for appearances on programs originating in this country and simultaneously or subsequently broadcast in foreign areas by satellite or cable.[11]

In March of 1967 the union began its first national network walkout. The strike was prompted for the most part by network reluctance to accept AFTRA's proposed fee and salary schedule for newsmen at network-owned-and-operated stations. AFTRA was joined in its walkout by sixteen other broadcast-oriented unions and guilds.[12]

However, the strike highlighted intense intraunion strife, exemplified by the strike-breaking news broadcasts of NBC newsman Chet Huntley. For most of the thirteen-day strike Huntley, without partner David Brinkley, continued to perform his news chores for the network. He claimed support from his colleagues, but he was joined on the air by only a few other NBC newsmen. At the heart of internal dissension was the issue of AFTRA representation of news personnel. In the minds of some, AFTRA was primarily an entertainer's union and therefore not the propei bargaining agent for newsmen.

In the fall of 1967 AFTRA, in support of an NABET strike against ABC, called on its membership to honor the picket lines set up by NABET. The sharp division between the newsmen in AFTRA and their fellow members was again highlighted; the news staffers at the owned-and-operated network stations refused to cooperate with AFTRA's request. The union, in retaliation, fined the recalcitrant performers who had kept the stations operating. (The fines were later suspended after pressure from ABC and NABET.) However, it was this refusal which many believed to be the reason for AFTRA's subsequent withdrawal of its NABET strike support.

Because of the diversity of its membership the future of AFTRA is somewhat clouded. As jurisdictional problems are resolved, the union will have more of an opportunity to expand its representation and provide a more resilient and responsive service for its members. It has begun to reflect financial strength, and showed in the latter part of 1967 a pension fund whose book value was over twenty-six million dollars, and assets on January 1, 1968, of over one million dollars.[13]

Screen Actors Guild (AFL-CIO)

The Screen Actors Guild wields considerable power over the broadcasting industry because of the more than 60 percent of television programming done on film. Since its inception in

1933, the guild has been a dynamic and guiding force in the organization and support of performance personnel. Originally it was formed as an attempt to curb the alleged abuse of actors and actresses by motion picture producers. At issue in the early days were problems of long hours, poor working conditions, and even poorer pay — the same issues which rallied workers in all labor unions.

SAG's first and most important jurisdictional battle in broadcasting came in 1950 when the TV Authority was given complete control over television broadcasting talent, both in film for TV and in live performance. SAG, which had always been the sole bargaining agent for film personnel, rejected this idea. Both unions approached the National Labor Relations Board for a jurisdictional ruling. The board sided with SAG and awarded it control over film personnel, thereby providing the existing delineation in jurisdiction between SAG and AFTRA. This separation has been further reinforced by the fact that SAG won twelve out of thirteen similar jurisdictional disputes with AFTRA in the early 1950s.[14]

Although the union had established a firm policy regarding salaries and working conditions for actors and actresses, television was able to provide it with a secondary source of income — the residual.

In 1952 the guild negotiated and established the principle that actors in television motion pictures must be paid, along with their original compensation, additional fees for domestic reruns of television entertainment films. Since then this contract has been renegotiated several times, each bringing gains for the actors, including higher residual payments. The guild also negotiated for and obtained additional payments to actors for domestic and foreign pictures, and in 1964 was successful in gaining special fees for actors appearing in television programs distributed in foreign markets.

In a related field, after a six-week strike in 1960, the guild won a formula for payments to actors for their television rights when theatrical features were sold to television. The guild was not satisfied with this original arrangement and in a progressive departure from ordinary collective bargaining aims, it in 1965 devised and secured producer approval of a totally new formula for payment. The formula sets for each actor in the cast of a theatrical picture an irreducible minimum for his television rights. As television earnings of the picture increase, the actor's minimum fee rises.[15]

The guild also negotiated a television-commercials contract which in addition to setting minimum fees and working conditions for actors making commercials, established a unique system of use and reuse fees, with payments to the actor continuing as long as the commercials are broadcast. This provision has been expanded and reshaped several times to include foreign use, transmission via cable, and satellite broadcasting.[16]

Financially, the Screen Actors Guild has played an important role in the lives of its members by collecting and distributing a total of $72,400,000 in domestic residuals from 1953 to November, 1967. From January, 1967, to November, 1967, the guild members received $2,918,283 in foreign residuals and $1,571,681 for motion pictures shown on television. SAG's total revenue for fiscal year 1966, less producers' contributions to the pension fund, was $104,753,000.[17]

The guild has used its right to strike only three times, and in each case the issue was television. In all three instances the union was successful.[18]

At the moment, however, the union's biggest concern is runaway productions. SAG and its members are unhappy about the rash of producers who are filming abroad and using foreign actors at lower wages. The union is attempting to arrange agreements with sister organizations in other countries to establish a more standard wage scale on an international level. It is also lobbying in Washington for subsidies to producers in order to make it more attractive and less expensive for them to film in the United States.

The Writers Guild of America (Ind.)

The history of the Writers Guild can be traced to the early 1900s when the Authors Guild was first established. The Authors Guild was designed primarily as a protective organization for writers of books, short stories, articles, and miscellaneous materials. It was during this period that the writers of dramatic material also formed an organization, the Dramatists Guild, which subsequently joined forces with the Authors Guild to form the Authors League. With the development of the motion picture industry another medium of expression for the creative writer emerged, and with it a new organization to protect his needs — the Screen Writers Guild. The guild quickly became a branch of the Authors League.[19]

From 1921 to 1936, the Screen Writers Guild served primarily as a professional and social organization for its members. Members met periodically to stage and view plays and to exchange information of a professional nature.[20] But as events developed, the guild leadership and members became increasingly aware of needs much the same as those of other unions within and without the entertainment industry: in their case, respect for the rights of the writer, protection for him in the pursuit of his livelihood, and the need for some economic guidelines to provide him with a degree of financial security. As a result, the guild was reincorporated in 1936 as an affiliate rather than a branch of the Authors League. With the passage of the Wagner Act and its subsequent support by the U.S. Supreme Court, the Screen Writers Guild had the opportunity to call for an election and gain eventual certification. The reincorporated guild became the sole collective bargaining agent for writers in the motion picture industry.[21]

In 1939, collective bargaining with film producers commenced, and the first contract, signed in 1942, covered writers for seven years.

Because of the vast quantity of written material used in radio broadcasting, a new branch of the Authors League was formed.

This new group was known as the Radio Writers Guild, and would serve as the jurisdictional umbrella for radio writers.[22]

With the advent of television and its use of writing, a move was made in 1950 by the Screen Actors Guild, which had helped earlier to create the Radio Writers Guild, to organize a group of television writers within its own membership. The move was made to protect the writer-actors and the union from jurisdictional problems, but envisioned eventual autonomy for the writers group.

However, the endless proliferation of branches representing facets of the entertainment industry became burdensome to the Authors League, and, as Erik Barnouw describes it, "Commencing in 1949, meetings took place in New York between representatives of the Authors League, Dramatists Guild, Radio Writers Guild, Television Writers Group and Screen Writers Guild trying to devise a simpler and stronger form of unification."[23]

The Authors League, because of the continuing and bothersome overlapping of union organizations, decided in 1954 to form the Writers Guild, whose new membership would include members of the old Screen Writers Guild, the Radio Writers Guild, the Dramatists Guild, and others. Within this new organization was a solidarity and homogeneity of representation for writers employed in radio, television, and motion pictures.[24]

As it is constituted now, the guild is divided into two units: the Writers Guild, East, and the Writers Guild, West. The Mississippi River is the geographical dividing line, but there is close cooperation between the two segments, especially during contract negotiations. The division came about as a result of the merger in 1954 between the Screen Writers Guild and the western branch of the Radio Writers Guild; the Screen Writers then became the Screen Branch of WGAW, the television and radio writers became the TV-Radio Branch of WGAW.

The WGAW is run by a council of twenty-three members under a president, first vice-president (also president of the Screen

Branch), second vice-president (also president of the TV-Radio Branch), secretary (also vice-president of the TV-Radio Branch), and treasurer (also vice-president of the Screen Branch). Eighteen other members — nine from each of the branches — make up the balance of the governing body.

In the East, the midwestern and eastern branches of the Radio Writers Guild became the radio branch of the Writers Guild of America. There are also twenty-three members on the council of the WGAE, with five officers; its branch officers, however, are designated separately, and the eighteen other members are elected directly by the guild membership from a cross section of writing classifications.

Guild TV and radio contracts cover staff writers, news writers, and free-lance writers, including those for live television and documentary television. No one needs to be a member to place a first script; however, a nonmember must apply within thirty days of script acceptance and pay a membership fee of $50.[25] In addition to acting as the writers' representative before management, the union checks on individual contracts, prepares occasional market reports, and studies problems relevant to its members.

Contracts for members of the guild in radio and television and motion pictures are inclusive and specific. The majority of contracts are designed to protect the free-lance writer in singular or multiple program production and in films. The guild reserves the right to waive wage minimums, but the individual writers can negotiate for wages higher than those sanctioned by the union.

An important guild-negotiated contract provision concerns residuals and residual rights. As is the case with other "creative" unions, the Writers Guild has attempted to protect its more than four thousand members by adopting codes covering additional payment to members for re-use of their materials. Writers Guild of America, West, which represents writers in film, television, and radio on the West Coast, earned more than $5 million in television residuals in 1968. This was an increase of 19 percent over 1967.[26]

Other provisions of Writers Guild contracts concern wording of credits: "teleplay by," "story by," "special material by," "written especially by," etc. In addition, there are contractual codes which cover the position of the writer's credit on the screen, the size of the type used, and the duration of the credit. Contracts do not allow contingent employment; that is, they provide that writers should be paid, whether or not their work is used. Contracts provide for the right to rehearsal attendance by the writer in live television and protect his right to view a rough cut of a finished television or motion picture film. These are but a few of the normal contractual provisions.[27]

The Directors Guild of America (Ind.)

The present structure of the Directors Guild of America, as in many of the broadcast unions, is a result of an amalgamation, in their case of several radio-television and screen directors' groups. From 1915 to 1935 the Motion Picture Directors Association functioned as the first directors' representative. In 1935, the Radio Directors Guild was formed as a unifying force for more solid and productive negotiation of the problems of creative freedom, working conditions, and better wages.

The present organization, the Directors Guild of America, came about with the merger in 1960 of the Radio-TV Directors Guild and the Screen Directors Guild. The merger was an expedient by which both sides (unions) increased their membership and thus improved their bargaining positions.[28]

The guild received a further membership boost in 1964 when unit managers of Hollywood, following the lead given by the Assistant Directors local 161, New York, merged with the organization. In 1965, the Screen Directors International Guild also joined the guild.[29]

This broad membership, involved in virtually every phase of

directing, has served to provide the guild with impressive strength and recognition on the national level as an effective and dynamic organization. At the present time, the guild is spokesman for more than three thousand individual directors, assistant directors, and stage managers in most phases of radio, television, and motion picture production.[30] In addition, it has over five hundred separate contracts in effect with production agencies. This multiplicity is a result of the complex nature of the motion picture and broadcasting industries and the need to negotiate individual contracts for each classification of director.

Contract negotiations with the many agencies involved have been successful both in establishing a creative atmosphere for the director and in improving wages and working conditions.

The first television contract negotiations were carried out by the Radio and Television Directors Guild in 1950.[31] Included in the codes were provisions for a minimum wage scale and improved working conditions. However, the guild did not press the fledgling television industry in its financial requests. There was a sense on the part of most of the unions and guilds who dealt with the infant industry that too much financial pressure could conceivably retard television's promising development. In order to allow it to prosper, the guild made only modest wage and fringe-benefit requests. One provision, however, in that first contract foreshadowed a policy of reimbursement that many other unions would take up — the payment of residuals. The contract included a promise by the networks to study the feasibility of the request once television had begun to show a profit.

In 1960, following the merger of the Radio and TV Directors Guild and the Screen Directors Guild, another union-network agreement was reached. Provisions of this contract insured guild members a 10 percent wage increase, enlarged residual payments for film and taped material, insured payment for use of material on pay-TV or broadcast by satellite, and more creative freedom.[32] By 1964 wages, though important, were overshadowed by the Guild's determination to provide its membership with even more comprehensive creative responsibility in the production of motion picture and television films. In a contract with the Association of Motion Picture and Television Producers, the guild demanded and received the right to include a "Director's Bill of Rights" which provided a clear definition of the director's creative responsibility. Included in the bill were provisions which gave the director the right to screen film shot at the end of each day; to a "director's cut" following completion of shooting; to consultation on music and dubbing; to screen credit equal in size to 30 percent of the title of the production; and to the inclusion of the director's name in any paid advertisement for the film.[33]

Most recent conflicts and successes indicate that the guild is maintaining a vigil over the creative freedom of its members. Directors of motion pictures have demanded and are beginning to receive the cooperation of networks in the editing of feature length films to fit the television time limitations and for commercial insertions. The guild has also begun to expand its sphere of influence through an international approach. Exchanges of personnel with other countries have already been made and steps have been taken with the British Association of Cinematography, Television and Allied Technicians for mutual cooperation and exchange of working privileges for members of the two groups in both countries.

The Directors Guild of America has prided itself on being as concerned about the creative rights of its members as it is about wages. Perhaps it is this approach which accounts for the guild's apparent success and for the professional esteem it has gained for its membership.

The American Federation of Musicians
of the United States and Canada (AFL-CIO)

The foundations of the American Federation of Musicians were laid in the mid-1800s. The first trade organization for musicians was formed in 1863 in New York under the leadership of Henry D.

Beissenharz. In 1871, several similar trade groups banded together and formed the National Musical Association, which functioned as a quasi union for the next ten years.[34]

In 1886 the National League of Musicians was organized in opposition to the National Musicians Association, and in ten years the membership had grown to nine thousand. With labor beginning to band together, it was natural that in 1896 the American Federation of Labor should ask the National League of Musicians to join in a united front. When the league refused, the AFL started a separate union, the American Federation of Musicians, which was chartered in that same year as a counter-union.[35]

By 1904, the National League of Musicians could no longer compete with the stronger American Federation of Labor–supported musicians' union and it was dissolved, leaving the American Federation of Musicians one of the strongest associations in the AFL.[36]

The union's earliest association with broadcasting was in the early 1920s, when its members performed on radio for the publicity that the new medium afforded them. By 1922 the picture had begun to change: the president of the Chicago AFM local, James C. Petrillo, demanded that local radio stations pay musicians for their performances and services. To fight this demand, the stations used prerecorded music and disguised it as live performance, starting a long court battle in which Petrillo asked that recorded material be restricted to home and noncommercial use. In 1940, a federal court ruled that the musicians' rights to music performed and recorded ended with the sale of the record.[37]

In retaliation Petrillo, who had become president of the national organization, led the AFM in an industry-wide recording boycott. This lasted for twenty-seven months and ended only after the American Federation of Musicians had secured from the networks a trust fund and royalties for all recordings and live transcriptions.[38]

Still concerned over the availability of work for musicians in broadcasting, Petrillo continued to battle for the use of standby musicians for live programs and against use of music recorded in foreign countries. In 1946 Congress passed the Lea Act, ending another of Petrillo's quests—for a quota of musicians at each station based on market size, station size, and amount of local live-programming.

AFM contracts in television, like radio, have been concerned with wages, vacation periods, and the establishment and maintenance of a pension fund. Gains have been steady but unspectacular. The biggest gains have been in reimbursement for re-use of kinescoped or video-taped programs. Before 1959 the union-network contract allowed for only one re-use of a recorded program, and specified that union musicians receive their original fee for the replay. In 1959 the union relaxed somewhat and agreed to allow networks more than one repeat, with a lessened residual demand.[39]

Musicians do not receive residuals for music performed in motion pictures shown on television, but musicians performing in or for a film do divide equally among themselves a 1 percent fee based on the rental price of the film.[40]

Because the union membership is so well defined, the American Federation of Musicians has seldom been involved in disputes of a jurisdictional nature. The only exceptions were cases in which the union attempted to organize announcers and other nonmusicians at broadcast operations.

The structure of the AFM is weighted heavily toward national control. Most powerful and largest locals are those in Los Angeles, Chicago, and New York, and they are closely watched and tightly run by the national officers. The national also sets up criteria and bylaws which regulate all seven hundred and twenty-five chapters in the United States and Canada. Broadcasting is affected by the union primarily on the network and group-owner level, with only a few stations organized at a local level.

The American Federation of Musicians has always been a

strong and relatively effective union, serving a creative group of people through efficient and powerful bargaining. Under President Herman Kenin, who replaced James Petrillo upon his retirement from union leadership, the union has continued, but in a less militant manner, to bargain successfully for its members.

The National Association of Broadcast Employees and Technicians (AFL-CIO)

The forerunner of the National Association of Broadcast Employees and Technicians was the Association of Technical Employees, formed in 1933. It was small, with only seven locals, but had the distinction of being the first organization formed solely to represent broadcasting employees. In 1934, the association negotiated its first network contract with NBC.[41]

In 1937, with radio already an important and growing medium and television in the not-too-distant future, the association began an expansion program and by 1940 had changed its name to the National Association of Broadcast Engineers and Technicians. As the union's scope and jurisdictional influence expanded to include nontechnical personnel, the organization dropped the classification "engineers" and replaced it with "employees."[42]

When NBC was forced to divest its interest in and control of the Blue Network, NABET found itself with jurisdictional control in a new network. The network, the American Broadcasting Company, had been formed from the ex-NBC owned network.[43] The union was therefore in a position to continue as the bargaining agent at both networks.

During the 1940s NABET, because of frequent and bitter jurisdictional battles with the International Brotherhood of Electrical Workers (IBEW had also begun organizing technical personnel in broadcasting), sought protection against continual raiding. In 1951 the organization affiliated with the Congress of Industrial Organizations. With a more secure position, NABET successfully organized employees at a number of local stations, thus adding to its total membership and providing the union with a broader base from which to negotiate.

The union has been involved in numerous jurisdictional disputes, in part due to its largely technical membership. In 1951, NABET and the IBEW skirmished over representation of CBS technicians. The problem was settled by a National Labor Relations Board election which prevented the NABET take-over. In a later dispute the union lost control of television lighting crews to IATSE.

In addition to interunion problems, the union has been involved in bitter disputes with both NBC and ABC. In 1959 NABET struck the National Broadcasting Company because some nonunion personnel were hired to do work ordinarily done by NABET technicians during an overseas production of the "Today" show. Although the network had flown nine union members to Paris for the program, the union stood firm on principle that as many men as needed should have been sent by the company. The walkout lasted three weeks and ended after the union withdrew its charge.[44]

Another abortive NABET strike occurred in January, 1967, against KABC-TV, Hollywood. It lasted one day, after which ABC obtained a restraining order forcing members back to work. The decision was based on a no-strike clause in the master agreement between NABET and KABC-TV. This issue generated a mass of charges and countercharges which led to a complete investigation by the international executive committee of NABET. Two key regional officials were removed by the IEC and what followed was described by international president Eugene Klumpp as "the most unpleasant internal crisis in our history." Involved were New York Local 11 and Hollywood Local 53, who were fighting for local autonomy and less interference from the international office. A peace package was presented to the dissidents by the IEC in April, 1967, and accepted by the membership of both locals a month later. Radical changes in the internal structure and method of operation of the union took place. Concessions were made to the network locals, and a great deal of local autonomy resulted. Scars from the crisis still exist within the union.

In the fall of 1967, following a "no acceptance of contract" vote by NABET membership at the NBC-ABC owned and operated stations, the union struck ABC and in a move unpopular to many members assessed nonstriking NBC employees one-half of their pay for strike support. The union had the support of AFTRA and the International Brotherhood of Teamsters, with partial help from the Writers Guild, East. At issue were wage increases and contract length, as well as the amount of the network contribution to the pension fund.

Early in October NABET and NBC reached accord on the proposed contract. However, strike-bound ABC filed a one-million-dollar suit against the union for statements implying that the network had been found guilty of unfair labor practices. In addition, the network approached the National Labor Relations Board and charged that NABET was picketing a sponsor and was itself practicing unfair labor procedures. (The NLRB later ruled in favor of the network.)[45]

The problem was settled in November of 1967 with acceptance by the union and ABC of a new four-year pact covering wage increases, a shortened work week, and a provision allowing the network to instigate grievance proceedings.

At present, NABET represents about eighty-five hundred broadcast employees and has contracts with NBC, ABC, and some fifty-seven local stations throughout the country.[46] As with the other unions discussed thus far, the motivating agent in its contract negotiations has been the desire for higher wages, better working conditions, and job security.

Much of the union's present concern is about its faulty internal structure. Future success depends to a great extent on the ability of its leadership to blend all parts of the union into a more cohesive whole.

The International Brotherhood of Electrical Workers (AFL-CIO)

In 1876, telegraph workers were a part of the Knights of Labor. An unsuccessful strike in 1883, however, convinced them that they should break away and become the United Order of Linemen. When the St. Louis Exposition of 1890 opened, a new group, The Wiremen and Linemen's Union, emerged. The exposition, with a major emphasis on the use of electricity, had attracted a number of technicians, as well as telephone employees already members of the Wiremen's Union. With jurisdictional control extended to electricians, the union in 1891 became the International Brotherhood of Electrical Workers and had ten participating locals.[47]

In 1931 IBEW began to organize engineers in radio. Locals in Chicago and St. Louis both had broadcasting members, and an all-broadcasting local was formed in Birmingham, Alabama. Early in the 1940s the union adopted an organizational plan for some twenty-five local broadcasting unions scattered across the country, in order to service the members in stations where IBEW had organized.[48]

This strong emphasis on local autonomy has carried through to the present time. Even though the International has titular control of the locals, rarely does it exercise its power; for the most part it allows locals self-government.

The International Brotherhood of Electrical Workers' primary network contract is with CBS. The union has set a standard wage scale for radio and television technicians, and CBS employees are all paid according to this scale. As mentioned earlier, the locals serving each organized CBS outlet draw up proposed union-demand packages. Each local then presents its requests to the International, which in turn combines and adjusts all contracts into one single contract used by the national organization in its dealings with the network.

Only a fraction of the total IBEW membership of 950,000 is associated with the broadcast industry. The 12,000 members who are involved with either radio or television are divided among

CBS Sports Network, Incorporated, and 176 local stations.[49] The IBEW, like the two other technicians' unions, is protected from interunion raiding and jurisdictional problems by its membership in the AFL-CIO nonraiding agreement. The agreement prohibits member unions from invading each other's jurisdiction and encourages fair play in new and open areas.

The union has maintained good relationships with management and has seldom been involved in jurisdictional disputes.

International Alliance of Theatrical Stage Employes and Moving Picture Machine Operators of the United States and Canada (AFL-CIO)

The International Alliance of Theatrical Stage Employes had its roots of development in the theatrical traditions of the late 1800s. The first local groups were organized to protect theatrical craftsmen from abuse by employers in the late 1870s. They were formed, in part, to protect local workers from employment exclusion by road companies. Organization was haphazard and fragmented, and it was not until 1893 that a unified effort at building a national stage employees' organization was begun. In July of 1894, the fledgling Alliance of Stage Employees received a helping hand when it was admitted to membership in the American Federation of Labor.[50]

By 1902, the union had become an international organization with the addition of chapters in Canada, whose protective functions were the same as their American counterparts. In 1913, the growing craft union established its permanent headquarters in New York City.

The early years were growth years for the union, as its membership increased from 1,500 in 1893 to 31,500 by 1932. The number of locals also increased substantially from a total of 11 in 1893 to 699 in 1932.[51] Membership in the union was at first restricted to carpenters, electricians, and propertymen in theatrical productions. Later the jurisdiction of the union expanded to include calcium light operators, property cleaners, and motion picture operators.

For the major part of its history IATSE has been committed to a policy of home rule. In essence, this has meant a hands-off attitude by national officers toward local IATSE bargaining units. The union allows the individual unit to bargain with management over wages, benefits, and working conditions. But the union has tightly controlled hiring practices giving members from other of its locals the first opportunity at available positions before opening the door to members of sister unions.

The union has been involved in several major jurisdictional disputes, most of which have ended in compromise settlements between the differing factions. Jurisdictional problems arose from the union's highly quasi-industrial membership and a conflict of interest which often came into play with many of the predominantly craft-oriented unions in the parent American Federation of Labor.

The first major dispute began in 1914 when the International Brotherhood of Electrical Workers attempted to obtain jurisdiction over motion picture projectionists. By 1918 IATSE, which had beaten back the IBEW threat, began a massive attempt to take over all motion picture industry craftsmen. This resulted in fierce competition between IATSE and its fellow AFL craft locals in Los Angeles.[52] By 1924 some of the conflict had reached a compromise, and a pact was signed with the IBEW and the carpenters' organization. This temporary peace ended in 1933, when the union called a general strike of all major motion picture studios. In order to combat the work stoppage, the other AFL craft organizations stepped into the vacated positions, breaking the strike and forcing IATSE to retreat.

The next three years were spent rebuilding a somewhat shattered image. Rebuilding was aided by the National Recovery Act and the codes in the act which allowed the union to regain control of motion picture projectionists. By 1935 the union was again strong enough to challenge the film producers, and in a show of power closed the Paramount theater chain in Chicago. The producers capitulated, and the union received jurisdictional control over film craftsmen.

In 1937 the scenic artists broke away from IATSE and formed their own union, the first time a craft union had left the fold to contract with management separately. The jurisdictional disputes simmered until 1946, when IATSE became embroiled in a new series of disagreements. At odds with the union were painters, decorators, paper hangers, the IBEW plumbers, steam fitters, building service employees, machinists, carpenters, and joiners.

Following an investigation by the American Federation of Labor and the House Education and Labor Committee, the unions agreed to honor all past commitments and to arbitrate for new agreements between the dissonant elements.

Since then the union has engaged in bargaining for improved wages, better working conditions, continued jurisdictional control and expansion, and maintenance of existing organizations. Most serious of recent problems has been the defection of seventeen hundred Canadian Broadcasting Corporation employees. In a 1966 dispute Canadian IATSE members voted to withdraw from the union, largely because of the union-imposed contractual codes curtailing overtime employment.

The present international-union membership is over sixty thousand, represented by some one thousand local organizations. Of this total, only about twelve thousand are directly involved in television operations or production, and only 10 percent of the broadcasting stations employ IATSE personnel.[53]

The present IATSE jurisdiction in TV covers stagehands, make-up artists, wardrobe attendants, graphic artists, technicians, and remote lighting crews. TV film coverage includes members in production positions: grips, make-up artists, set designers, scene artists, cameramen, soundmen, film editors, electricians, and screen cartoonists.

The union has long been regarded by the industry as an accomplished and steady organization. Members are under constant union scrutiny and must perform their jobs efficiently and quickly.

The future may have a great impact on IATSE and its membership, as it may on all technical unions. Changing technology and improved production techniques will understandably press the union into a constant reevaluation of its goals and bargaining procedures.

Conclusion

The rise of unions in broadcasting and their impact has closely paralleled the development of the industry. Union-management contract negotiations, though often marked by bitter exchanges and feeling on both sides, have proven to be of mutual benefit. Union members have gained wage and fringe benefits that are often above those of nonindustry workers. Management has gained a highly skilled and for the most part highly dedicated group of professional broadcasting technicians and employees.

Of the unions and guilds discussed in this chapter, all but two were formed for purposes other than the protection and representation of broadcasting employees. The American Federation of Television and Radio Artists and the National Association of Broadcast Employees and Technicians are the only groups whose roots can be traced directly to the broadcasting industry, and historical evidence would suggest that AFTRA, more than any of the others, has faced a precarious balance and fight for survival within broadcasting.

This is perhaps a significant factor in the often minor gains made by AFTRA. It lacks the diversification and wide-based economic force for prolonged strike efforts, as well as the ability to call upon allied forces within the union membership for strike support and additional power.

With rapid technological advance in the industry and the increasing use of filmed material by it, all of the broadcasting unions will have to face a reevaluation of objectives and goals. The spiraling costs of production involving technicians and talent are also going to have some effect on television as a potent advertising force.

Only the future can show with any degree of accuracy the eventual face of the broadcasting unions and their impact upon the industry which they serve. The unions and management have a long history of successful negotiation, because both sides were responsive to each situation and its implications. If this attitude of responsiveness continues as the industry develops and changes, if management and labor are willing to recognize that growth and flux are inevitable, then there is every indication that the unions and the industry that they serve will continue to prosper.

NOTES

1. Only the eight major unions are treated in this chapter. There are, however, other labor organizations, such as the International Brotherhood of Teamsters (Ind.), the Screen Extras Guild (Ind.), the Screen Cartoonists Guild (Ind.), the Producers Guild of America (Ind.), the Composers and Lyricists Guild of America (Ind.), and the United Scenic Artists, Local 829 (AFL-CIO), operating within the broadcasting industry.
2. Allen E. Koenig, "A History of AFTRA," *NAEB Journal*, July–August 1965, p. 50. The Associated Actors and Artistes of America was a loosely knit umbrella organization of various entertainment labor organizations, including Actors Equity Association, Chorus Equity Association, American Guild of Musical Artists, American Guild of Variety Artists, Screen Actors Guild, Screen Extras Guild, Brother Artists Association, Hebrew Actors Union, and the Italian Actors Union.
3. *Ibid.*, p. 58.
4. *Ibid.*
5. *Ibid.*, p. 50.
6. "Authority, Networks Reach Agreement," *Broadcasting*, December 15, 1950, p. 27.
7. "New Trade Organization to Represent R-TV Personnel," *New York Times*, September 21, 1952.
8. Koenig, "History of AFTRA," p. 54.

9. Morris Gelman, "The Above-the-Line-Unions," *Television*, November 1967, p. 47.
10. Koenig, p. 47.
11. "Transocean Broadcasting to Pose Problems," *Sponsor*, October 14, 1963, p. 4.
12. "When 100,000-A-Year Men Go on Strike," *U.S. News and World Report*, April 17, 1967, pp. 98–99.
13. Gelman, "Above-the-Line Unions," p. 70.
14. *Ibid.*, p. 42.
15. Herbert T. Silverberg, "Authors' and Performers' Rights," *Law and Contemporary Problems* 23 (Winter 1950): 63.
16. *Ibid.*
17. Screen Actors Guild, *Screen Actors Guild Balance Sheet*, April 1968, pp. 19–20.
18. Gelman, p. 42.
19. *Ibid.*
20. *Ibid.*
21. *Ibid.*
22. *Ibid.*, p. 47.
23. *The Television Writer* (New York: Hill and Wang, 1962), p. 241.
24. *Ibid.*
25. Gelman, p. 44.
26. "Residuals Keep Mounting," *Broadcasting*, January 13, 1969, p. 59.
27. Barnouw, *Television Writer*, p. 241.
28. Gelman, p. 44.
29. *Ibid.*
30. *Ibid.*
31. "New Contracts Boost Film Director's Pay," *Broadcasting*, May 16, 1960, pp. 27–29.
32. *Ibid.*, p. 28.
33. Directors Guild of America, *Basic Agreements with the Motion Picture Producers Association*, 1964.
34. Robert D. Leiter, *The Musicians and Petrillo* (New York: Bookman Associates, 1953), p. 13.
35. *Ibid.* pp. 14–15.
36. *Ibid.*
37. *RCA Mfg. Co., Inc. v. Whiteman*, 114 F.2d 86, CCA2 (1940); affirmed by the U.S. Supreme Court, 311 U.S. 712 (1940).
38. Leiter, *Musicians and Petrillo*, p. 140.
39. Lawrence D. Hinder, "A Study of the Relationship Between the

AFM and the Producers of Network Television Programs between 1948 and 1963," (Master's thesis, Ohio State University, 1963), p. 68.

40. Gelman, p. 45.
41. John Gardiner, "The Below-the-Line Unions," *Television*, December 1967, p. 45.
42. *Ibid.*
43. *Ibid.*
44. "NBC, NABET Agree and TV Tape Dispute Ends," *Broadcasting*, May 18, 1959, p. 9.
45. "NBC and ABC Final Offers Draw a Fat Ixnay from NABET Membership," *Variety*, September 20, 1967, p. 27.
46. Gardiner, "Below-the-Line Unions," p. 45.
47. Florence Henderson, *Handbook of Labor Unions* (Washington: Fraternity Press, 1944), p. 106.
48. Gardiner, p. 46.
49. *Ibid.*
50. *Ibid.*
51. *Ibid.*
52. *Ibid.*
53. *Ibid.*

Part II

FEDERAL ACTION AND
ARBITRATION IN BROADCASTING

4 Broadcasting and the National Labor Relations Board

by THOMAS C. WARNOCK

The National Labor Relations Board was established July 5, 1935, by the National Labor Relations Act. The act has had a history of substantial revision in twelve-year intervals. The 1935 act called upon the NLRB to remedy only the employer's unfair labor practices, such as interference with employees' freedom to organize and bargain collectively, domination of unions, antiunion discrimination, and refusal to bargain.[1]

In 1947 the Taft-Hartley Act, formally titled the Labor Management Relations Act, overhauled the National Labor Relations Act, broadening its coverage to make it unfair and unlawful for unions to engage in such practices as the intimidation of employees, restraint or coercion of employers, and refusal to bargain collectively.[2]

In 1959 the Labor Management Reporting and Disclosure Act, again, substantially amended the original act. Restrictions were placed on organizational and recognitional picketing; secondary boycott provisions were strengthened; and steps were taken to eliminate the issue of federal versus state jurisdiction in labor disputes.[3]

The National Labor Relations Board functions as an independent federal agency established to administer the law as stated in that act. In this capacity it has two primary functions. First, to attempt to prevent or remedy unfair labor practices by unions or by employers. Second, to determine, by conducting secret-ballot elections, whether workers wish to have unions represent them in collective bargaining. The board cannot act upon its own initiative in either function. It handles only those unfair-practice charges and petitions for employee elections which are filed by labor or management.[4]

NLRB Structure

The National Labor Relations Board has five members and a general counsel, each appointed by the President with approval of the Senate. The board members are selected for five-year terms, with the term of one member expiring each year. The general counsel is appointed to a four-year term.[5] Reappointments may be made, and four of the six present officials are serving second or third terms.[6]

The NLRB has its headquarters in Washington, and thirty-one regional offices and eleven smaller field offices throughout the country. The total staff numbers about twenty-three hundred.[7]

The agency's judicial functions are separate, by law, from its prosecuting functions. Its members serve as the judicial body, and the general counsel is responsible for the issuance and prosecution of formal complaints and for the prosecution of cases in the courts. He also supervises the activities of the regional offices.[8]

Although the NLRB has no official legal power to enforce its orders, it may seek enforcement through the United States courts of appeals. Likewise, groups affected by the decisions of the board have the right to appeal.[9]

When an unfair labor practice charge is filed at one of the regional offices, members of the staff conduct an investigation. Following the investigation, the regional director works with the parties involved to attempt to reach a voluntary settlement. If such a settlement cannot be achieved, formal complaints are issued, and the case is set before the trial examiners. Trial examiners have the power to conduct formal hearings and issue decisions. These decisions may be appealed to the board. If they are not appealed, they become orders of the board.[10]

Decisions affecting the broadcasting industry have been made by the NLRB in seven major areas: NLRB jurisdiction, certification, scope of bargaining units, unfair labor practices by management, unfair labor practices by labor, union jurisdictional disputes, and grievances. First we shall examine representative NLRB cases in each of these areas. Then we shall deal with the right to appeal NLRB decisions in circuit and district courts.

NLRB Jurisdiction

Perhaps the most important, and certainly the first, major question we should examine is the board's decision to assert jurisdiction over employers and bargaining representatives in broadcasting. The NLRB has always assumed, and most broadcasters have accepted the assumption, that the National Labor Relations Act is sufficiently broad in terms of coverage to include all commercial broadcasting stations. Generally, the law includes all businesses engaged directly in interstate commerce, engaged in the production of goods or services for interstate commerce, or engaged in activities affecting interstate commerce.[11]

In the past, NLRB jurisdiction has been unsuccessfully contested by small stations on a number of occasions. Station KCOR in San Antonio, Texas, for example, claimed the board should have no jurisdiction, because only six employees were involved and that six did not constitute a "substantial number." The board asserted jurisdiction and stated in its decision that two or more persons would be considered a substantial number for NLRB purposes.[12]

Even though a station may not send an audible signal outside the state where it originates, the board has based jurisdiction on other factors: interstate network affiliations, national wire-service connection, use of out-of-state recordings, and sales to national advertisers, for instance.[13]

In 1951, as part of its policy of limiting its activities to the most important aspects of interstate commerce, the board decided that it would no longer take jurisdiction over radio and television stations doing a gross volume of less than $200,000 per year.[14] This figure was later reduced to $100,000.[15]

In another typical case involving the question of jurisdiction, the board asserted its right to certify a group of cameramen who were employed by a station on a free-lance basis. Here the board was providing the employee with the right to union representation even though he was not on the regular payroll.[16]

In a rather unusual case, the board established its jurisdiction over station KPAC in Port Arthur, Texas, a station owned and operated by Port Arthur College, a nonprofit organization. The board held that even though the institution did not make a profit, the gross volume of business done by KPAC was such that it did affect commerce.[17]

As a rule, the NLRB has asserted its jurisdictional right over all of the larger, and consequently more significant, employers in the industry.

Certification

In order for a representative of the employees to be recognized or "certified" by the board he must be clearly proven the choice of a majority of the employees he will represent. Such certification can be accomplished by presenting a petition to the board, or, if there is some question as to who the representative should be, a request can be made that the board conduct representation elections.[18]

The following is a good example of the vast majority of such cases. In 1940 the American Federation of Radio Artists petitioned the board for certification as the talent representative at WCPO in Cincinnati, Ohio. The board ordered elections, which established AFRA as the choice of a majority of the employees participating. Accordingly the board certified AFRA and instructed the owners to recognize it as the bargaining agent in the negotiations in progress.[19]

In some cases management merely wants the representative to obtain certification. In a few instances, however, management has contested this right. WTCN in Minneapolis, for example, refused to recognize a union, claiming that the bargaining unit it represented was too limited. Upon determination by the board that the unit was not too limited, the union was certified.[20]

A third variation involves the petitions of more than one union for certification of the same bargaining unit. When more than one bargaining agent is involved, a majority is still required. If it is not obtained, a runoff election is held. If it is still not obtained, no union is certified.[21] Likewise, when only one union is involved, failure to obtain a majority will result in denial of the petition for certification.[22]

Appropriate Bargaining Units

The term bargaining unit has two different, but related, meanings. One is the contract unit, which identifies those who may vote as a group in an NLRB election. When a union wins an NLRB election, the subsequent contract unit usually coincides with the original election unit. The election unit is based either on an agreement of the parties in a consent election, or on a board determination of the appropriate unit in a board-ordered election following a hearing.

In determining what constitutes an appropriate unit, the board has built up a series of principles which it uses as a guideline in determining each new case. Generally an attempt is made to put together voting groups composed of employees who seem to have common interests. Taken into consideration are such factors as the relationship of skills, homogeneity of wages, hours, working conditions, and supervision, bargaining history, industry practice, company organizational structure, and union membership patterns. Each new case is determined on its own merits, often resulting in a new and different interpretation of old guidelines.

In the early years most decisions followed the patterns of collective bargaining which have persisted in the larger cities. The American Federation of Musicians was interested only in musicians, the International Brotherhood of Electrical Workers in technicians, and so on. When some of the smaller stations began to organize, the simple guidelines became considerably less useful.

Bargaining in local broadcasting has usually been on a single-employer and single-station basis, while multiple-employer bargaining is the rule in many negotiations at the network level. For example, the NLRB has sanctioned a multiple-employer bargaining unit for performing talent on live network television programs.[23]

Group-owned stations are usually handled on a single-station basis. As a rule the board considers the differences in working conditions from one station to the next far too great to permit group-wide certification. An important exception has been the allowance of network negotiations on a system-wide basis, covering not only network programming, but also employees at the networks' owned and operated stations.

Most bargaining units in broadcasting group employees according to skill—announcing or technical ability, for example— often corresponding closely to the departmental structure set by the employer. Some units have been established on a plant-wide basis, covering all, or almost all, nonsupervisory employees.[24]

Larger stations may have from two to five contract units, the two most important of which cover announcers and technicians. Most stations with any collective bargaining at all have either their announcers and their technicians represented, or at least their technicians.

Network labor relations are much more complex. Each of the three networks has contracts with more than a hundred separate bargaining units. In this area the NLRB has been forced to operate on a case by case basis, since little or no precedent has been established. The variety of situations brought before the board seems limitless. In 1945, for example, the board approved a petition IATSE filed to have television clerical workers at CBS included in the same bargaining unit as radio.[25]

In contrast to the general rule of local representation, the board denied a petition by technicians at CBS to leave the national unit and form a local New York City unit on the grounds that such a unit would not be appropriate to the national network situation.[26]

In a third example the board held that news desk men at NBC were not supervisors, even though they assigned stories to news writers. As a result, the news desk men were allowed to form their own unit and be represented by NABET.[27]

The most obvious problems with bargaining units at the local level are caused by the overlapping of jobs: the announcer who operates his own controls, the announcer who is also a salesman, or the engineer who also works in sales. While most stations where such positions exist are so small that they have only one bargaining unit anyway, there are times when such personnel must be arbitrarily placed in one unit or another by the board. Whenever possible, the system of self-determination is used to aid the board in making a decision.

Unfair Labor Practices (Management)

Unfair labor practices on the part of an employer are the subject of section 8 (a) of the Taft-Hartley Act. This section protects the employee from three types of possible action on the part of his employer. It is deemed unfair for the employer:

(1) to interfere with, restrain, or coerce employees in the exercise of the rights guaranteed in section 7; (right of self-organization, to form, join, or assist labor organizations, to bargain collectively through representatives of their own choosing, and to engage in other mutual aid or protection; also the right to refrain from any or all such activities except to the extent that such right may be affected by an agreement regaining membership in a labor organization as a condition of employment)

(2) to dominate or interfere with the formation or administration of any labor organization or contribute financial or other support to it: *Provided*, that subject to rules . . . an employer

shall not be prohibited from permitting employees to confer with him during working hours without loss of time or pay;
(3) by discrimination in regard to hire or tenure of employment or any term or condition of employment to encourage or discourage membership in any labor organization. . . .
(4) to discharge or otherwise discriminate against an employee because he has filed charges or given testimony under this act;
(5) to refuse to bargain collectively with the representatives of his employees. . . .[28]

Of the five, the first and last are most important. The first prevents the employer from interfering in the organizational process, while the last forces him to bargain with the union once it has been formed.

The first provision has often been used to support the last, as in a case involving the American Communications Local 16 and the Greater New York Broadcasting Company. Management refused to bargain with the union, stating that Local 16 had unjustifiably called a strike during negotiations. The board ruled that refusing to negotiate was, under the circumstances, equivalent to failure to recognize a certified bargaining agent (an unfair practice under section 8 (a) (1)).[29]

Another important area affected by section 8 (a) is that of employment. Sections 8 (a)(1) and 8 (a)(3) combine to prohibit the employer from using his right to hire, promote, and fire as a weapon against labor. In a case filed by the International Brotherhood of Electrical Workers, for example, the board ordered management to rehire a supervisor on the grounds that he had been discharged solely because he had failed to report the union activities of nonsupervisory personnel to his superior. In addition to being rehired, the board ordered that he receive full benefits of his tenure and all back pay.[30]

In one example of an NLRB decision under section 8(a)(2) a station owner threatened to close his station if the employees voted to become unionized. While the owner was charged with many other violations, this act alone was sufficient to convict him of unfair labor practice.[31]

As stated at the outset, the provisions of section 8 (a) were a part of the original act of 1935. Section 8 (b), added in 1947, deals with unfair practices on the part of labor, the next area to be examined.

Unfair Labor Practices (Labor)

While section 8 (a) protects the employee and the labor organization, section 8 (b) protects the employee and the employer. Some of the provisions in section 8 (b) are almost identical to those in section 8 (a), merely confirming the fact that such practices are also considered unfair when labor engages in them. In addition, section 8 (b) prohibits excessive initiation fees or dues, featherbedding, and secondary boycotts.[32]

Section 8 (b)(5) was used recently by ABC, which charged NABET with asking excessive initiation fees in order to prevent the hiring of nonunion summer replacements. The NLRB agreed with ABC and ordered NABET to return to its old rate scale.[33]

Section 8 (b)(6), which deals with featherbedding, stems from the Federal Act of 1946 amending the Communications Act of 1934, otherwise known as the Lea Act. The Lea Act made it a criminal offense to use pressure upon a licensee to employ persons "in excess of the number of employees needed by such licensee to perform actual services."[34] The first test of the Lea Act came almost immediately as James C. Petrillo was charged with its violation for forcing, by threat of a strike, a radio station (WAAF, Chicago) that used no live musicians to hire double their number of American Federation of Musicians affiliated employees. In December of 1946 the U.S. District Court, Northern District of Illinois, found the Lea Act unconstitutional and dismissed the charges against Petrillo.[35] This decision was reversed by the U.S. Supreme Court in June of 1947.[36] Following the Supreme Court reversal, a district court decision absolved Petrillo on the grounds that no evidence supported the contention that he was aware of the fact that WAAF needed no more musicians. Petrillo's defense rested on the fact that he had never said the musicians were not to be used.[37]

The exact wording of the Lea Act has also been incorporated in the Labor Management Relations Act as section 8 (b)(6). It protects broadcasting, as well as other industries, from the boldest form of featherbedding; but it cannot prevent featherbedding guised as the performance of services, no matter how useless or inefficient they may be.

Section 8 (b)(7) prohibits secondary boycotts and in broadcasting is most important where labor's relationships with sponsors are concerned. The secondary boycott provisions were used against NABET in its 1967 strike against ABC, to prevent picketing outside a large local sponsor's store.[38]

An unusual application of the secondary boycott provision in broadcasting involved WCKY, Cincinnati, which charged AFTRA with unfair labor practice for requiring members to have local record-producers fill out questionnaires stating whether or not records were intended for use on WCKY (or other struck local stations). WCKY charged that the information was used to pressure union members into refusing to make transcriptions which were for use on the struck station. The board decided in favor of WCKY and issued a cease and desist order to AFTRA.[39]

Section 8 (b)(7) also protects the employer against certain types of illegal picketing, including picketing by an uncertified union.

The unfair labor practice clauses are essentially designed to eliminate the unfair advantages which the act creates for both labor and management. While it is only partially successful in protecting all those concerned, it does manage to protect the individual worker quite well.

Jurisdictional Disputes

Jurisdictional disputes can be conveniently subdivided into those involving representation of workers, and those involving the type of work to be performed by workers already represented. Disputes involving representation of workers by a given bargaining agent can usually be solved quite easily by a method already described: the holding of NLRB-supervised representation elections. There are cases, however, which have exceptional circumstances. What happens, for example, when workers wish to change their affiliation, but a legal and binding contract already exists between management and the present union? As a rule, the board has held that new representation elections cannot be held until the old contract expires.[40] An interesting case which carried this dilemma one step further was the case of NABET vs. IBEW at station WSPR in Springfield, Massachusetts. In that instance, IBEW had a contract with management which renewed automatically each year unless one of the parties gave thirty days notice of intention to terminate the agreement or change the conditions. NABET contended that a representation election should be allowed at renewal time, while IBEW held that the contract was permanently binding unless actually cancelled. The board held that IBEW's notice of its intention to request an increase in salaries at contract renewal time was a change. They considered the contract no longer binding and ordered representation elections at that time.[41]

Another jurisdictional case involved WHN in New York, owned and operated at the time by Loew's Incorporated. The Theatrical Protective Union (AFL) claimed they should represent WHN engineers even though the American Radio Telegraphers Association (CIO) had just won an NLRB election because TPU represented most other Loew's employees (Loew's Theatres) and hence they were a more appropriate bargaining union. The board ruled in favor of ARTA on the grounds that TPU had made no attempt before the elections to organize WHN engineers.[42]

The second type of jurisdictional dispute is covered under section 10 (k) of the act. It provides a ten-day period for the parties concerned to settle the dispute themselves. After that time it is the duty of the board to hear and determine the dispute, which usually involves unfair labor practices on the part of one or both of the unions competing for the same work.[43]

A typical case in broadcasting was the dispute between NABET and IATSE in which NABET members refused to work unless their members were assigned to operate the new special-effects projectors which NBC had assigned to IATSE. The board ruled that IATSE should continue to operate the projectors, since the operation was more mechanical than electrical. The board further declared the strike illegal, since it was in violation of an existing NABET-NBC contract.[44]

Grievance Disputes

While most are handled through procedures established by and involving only labor and management, there are occasions when matters involving grievances are brought before the NLRB. Since there is no specific provision for the handling of grievance procedures within the Labor Management Relations Act, such cases are generally brought before the board as unfair labor practice suits. Often the board merely reviews the finding, or orders compliance.[45] (Details of the unfair labor practices provision have been described earlier in the chapter.)

Powers of the NLRB

To enable the NLRB to perform its duties under the act, Congress delegated to it certain powers. These have to do principally with investigations and hearings, and are contained in section 11 of the act. This section authorizes the board to examine and copy pertinent evidence, issue subpoenas, administer oaths, examine witnesses, receive evidence, and obtain a court order requiring production of pertinent evidence.[46]

Section 11 (3) of the act is especially interesting, in that it denies a witness the right to refuse to give testimony even if it tends to incriminate him. To avoid violation of the Constitution, the act goes on to guarantee that evidence given in such circumstances cannot be used against the witness unless he commits perjury in making the testimony.

Section 12 provides penalties up to a $5,000 fine or one year's imprisonment, or both, for persons resisting or otherwise interfering with procedures of the board.[47]

Additional powers of the board include the right to issue cease and desist orders, reinstate employees, and effectuate the policies of the act.[48] Section 10 (j) allows the board to petition for an injunction in connection with any unfair labor practice after a complaint has been issued. Section 10 (e) empowers the board to petition the U.S. Court of Appeals for a court decree enforcing the order of the board, while section 10 (f) guarantees the right of appeal in the appropriate circuit court to anyone "aggrieved by an order of the Board." As with any matter decided in the courts, decisions are ultimately subject to appeal and review by the U.S. Supreme Court.

The various court decisions in the case of WAAF vs. Petrillo discussed earlier are typical of the actions permitted under section 10.[49] The power of the court to overrule the board is demonstrated in the case of NLRB vs. Inter-City Advertising Company. In that instance the board had certified a union after representation elections, but the majority representation had been lost by the time the board acted upon the results of the election. The employer had made a change in personnel which left less than a majority in favor of any union at all. The final decision of the board was in favor of certification on the grounds that the change in personnel was a deliberate attempt to prevent certification. The fourth U.S. Circuit Court of Appeals reversed the decision and ruled that the employer had not violated the unfair practice provisions.[50]

The examples used in this chapter, while representative, in no way indicate the tremendous volume of decisions and settlements made by the board which have affected the broadcasting industry, not to mention the many other industries. Since its establishment the NLRB has handled more than two hundred and fifty thousand cases charging unfair labor practices. The board has also conducted more than one hundred and fifty thousand secret-ballot elections in which more than twenty-five million workers have participated.[51] The total flow of cases filed with the NLRB has nearly doubled in the last ten years.[52]

As the relationship between labor and management changes, so does the role of the NLRB in that relationship. Such appears to be the present situation in the broadcasting industry. At this point, most stations which are going to organize have already done so. Those that have not, with a few exceptions in the still-developing UHF markets, are not likely to do so in large numbers in the future. According to NLRB member Sam Zagoria, future labor-management negotiations will tend toward a consolidation of union forces which will be encouraged by management, and deal with increased problems caused by automation.[53] As Zagoria points out, these problems can be solved by labor's and management's willingness to assist one another rather than fight.[54] If this is what develops, the NLRB will take a less active role in broadcasting labor relations, although expansion of the industry will continue to hold the level of broadcasting's demands on the board relatively constant.

NOTES

1. *National Labor Relations Act*, 29 U.S.C. §§ 141–68 (1935), pp. 1, 3–6.
2. *Labor Management Relations Act*, 29 U.S.C. § 158 (b) (1947).
3. National Labor Relations Board, *Statements of Procedure*, rev. Jan. 1, 1965. 30 F.R. 15918, pp. 2–4.
4. National Labor Relations Board, *Layman's Guide to the National Labor Relations Act* (Washington, D.C., 1966), p. 1.
5. *Labor Management Relations Act*, 29 U.S.C. § 153 (1947).

6. John Fanning, Howard Jenkins, Jr., Frank McCulloch, Samuel Zagoria, Gerald Brown (unpublished biographical sketches).
7. NLRB, *Summary of the National Labor Relations Act, 1967* (Washington, D.C., 1967), pp. 27–28.
8. *Labor Management Relations Act*, 29 U.S.C. §§ 153–56 (1947).
9. NLRB, *Layman's Guide*, pp. 47–48.
10. NLRB, *Rules and Regulations, 1965* (Washington, D.C., 1965), pp. 2–7.
11. *NLRB vs. Jones and Laughlin Steel Corporation*, 301 U.S. 1 (1937).
12. "Sunshine Broadcasting Company," *Labor Relations Reference Manual* 24 (1949): 1236.
13. WDXB, *Labor Relations Reference Manual* 24 (1949): 1469.
14. KXLR, *Labor Relations Reference Manual* 35 (1954): 1333.
15. NLRB, *Layman's Guide*, p. 40.
16. "Pulitzer Publishing Company," *Labor Relations Reference Manual* 31 (1952): 1158.
17. "Port Arthur College," *Labor Relations Reference Manual* 27 (1950): 1055.
18. NLRB, *Layman's Guide*, p. 10.
19. "Scripps-Howard Radio," *Labor Relations Reference Manual* 6 (1940): 494.
20. "Minnesota Broadcasting Company," *Labor Relations Reference Manual* 2 (1938): 359.
21. "Interstate Broadcasting Company," *Labor Relations Reference Manual* 5 (1939): 389.
22. "WGAL Incorporated," *Labor Relations Reference Manual* 7 (1940): 75.
23. "ABC," *NLRB* 96 (1951): 815.
24. "Los Angeles Broadcasting Company," *Labor Relations Reference Manual* 5 (1939): 389.
25. "CBS," *Labor Relations Reference Manual* 18 (1946): 1114.
26. "CBS," *Labor Relations Reference Manual* 2 (1938): 130.
27. "NBC," *Labor Relations Reference Manual* 63 (1966): 1143.
28. *Labor Management Relations Act 1947*, as amended by Public Law 86–257 (1959): § 8 (a).
29. "Greater New York Broadcasting Company," *Labor Relations Reference Manual* 12 (1943): 132.
30. "Inter-City Advertising Company," *Labor Relations Reference Manual* 26 (1950): 1065.
31. "WEAM," *Labor Relations Reference Manual* 28 (1951): 1393.

32. *Labor Management Relations Act*, 1947, as amended by Public Law 86–257 (1959): § 8 (b).
33. "ABC," *Labor Relations Reference Manual* 65 (1967): 1134.
34. "U.S. District Court vs. Petrillo," *Labor Relations Reference Manual* 19 (1947): 2088.
35. *Ibid.*
36. "U.S. Supreme Court vs. Petrillo," *Labor Relations Reference Manual* 20 (1947): 2254.
37. "U.S. District Court vs. Petrillo," *Labor Relations Reference Manual* 21 (1948): 2205.
38. "ABC Wins One Over NABET," *Variety*, Nov. 15, 1967, p. 29.
39. "AFTRA," *Labor Relations Reference Manual* 45 (1960): 1202.
40. NLRB, *Layman's Guide*, p. 13.
41. "WSPR," *Labor Relations Reference Manual* 16 (1945): 58.
42. "Marcus Loew Booking Agency," *Labor Relations Reference Manual* 1-A (1937): 138.
43. NLRB, *Layman's Guide*, pp. 46–47.
44. "NBC," *Labor Relations Reference Manual* 31 (1953): 1542.
45. "WRAC vs. IBEW," *Labor Relations Reference Manual* 47 (1961): 1366.
46. *Labor Management Relations Act, 1947*, § 11.
47. *Labor Management Relations Act, 1947*, § 12.
48. *Labor Management Relations Act, 1947*, § 10.
49. "U.S. District Court vs. Petrillo," *Labor Relations Reference Manual* 19 (1947): 2088; "U.S. Supreme Court vs. Petrillo," *Labor Relations Reference Manual* 20 (1947): 2254; "U.S. District Court vs. Petrillo," *Labor Relations Reference Manual* 21 (1948): 2205.
50. "Inter-City Advertising Company," *Labor Relations Reference Manual* 17 (1946): 916.
51. NLRB, *25-Millionth Vote Observance*, March 2, 1967, (u.p.), pp. 3–4.
52. NLRB, *Annual Report to Congress, 1967*. Washington, D.C., p. 2.
53. Sam Zagoria, "Labor News and Labor Relations," mimeographed (Chicago: NLRB, 1968).
54. *Ibid.*, p. 7.

5 What Has To Be Arbitrated in Broadcasting?

by ROBERT COULSON

Labor grievances in most industries tend to be symptomatic of underlying labor relations difficulties. The broadcasting business is no different. Rapid changes in techniques have swept the industry, and as jobs have changed, stress has been placed upon unions to protect their members' employment security, pay rates, and job content. During the term of collective bargaining agreements, such problems appear as unresolved grievances which must be determined by a labor arbitrator, a professional problem solver who is brought in by the parties involved to resolve the dispute over contract interpretation.

Almost all collective bargaining contracts in the United States contain some form of grievance procedure, generally terminating in final and binding arbitration. The broadcasting industry follows the general pattern. In contrast, few collective bargaining contracts contain a commitment to arbitrate disputes that may arise in connection with the negotiation of renewal contracts. This too is the broadcasting pattern.

A recent Bureau of Labor Statistics survey of arbitration procedures in 1,717 contracts indicated that in the communications industry 77 contracts out of 80 included grievance arbitration. Only 3 contracts, covering 19,900 workers, contained no grievance arbitration; in contrast, there were 481,400 workers covered by some form of grievance arbitration.[1]

The communications industry is more likely than others to limit the issues that may be arbitrated. Eighteen of the contracts reported in this industry permitted binding arbitration of any kind of grievance, whereas 59 excluded some grievance issues from arbitration. In industry generally, 7 out of 10 agreements permit any dispute not resolved in the last step of the grievance procedure to be referred to arbitration. The tendency to exclude certain issues from arbitration is also found in the chemical, machinery, electrical equipment, and transportation equipment industries.[2]

In the broadcasting industry, the arbitrator or the neutral chairman of an arbitration panel is generally selected on an *ad hoc* basis. Although some collective bargaining contracts provide for a three-man panel with party-appointed representatives, the requirement is sometimes waived by the parties. The awards I have encountered in the broadcasting industry customarily involve only one arbitrator. Use of a single *ad hoc* labor arbitrator is increasingly the pattern in all industries, as the party-appointed system, with its additional expense and latent ambiguities, is gradually eliminated.

Most contracts in the broadcasting industry provide for selection of the *ad hoc* arbitrator from a list submitted by the American Arbitration Association, with the result that many of the arbitrators on the AAA national panel have accumulated extensive experience in broadcasting cases. The opinions written by these arbitrators often contain insights into the underlying reasons for disputes, and hint at how such differences can be resolved. More than that, they are a unique source of information on labor relations problems.

The selected cases reported here concern various broadcasting controversies: program competition, management decisions involving program production, jurisdictional disputes, and issues involving pay rates and job content.

Program Competition

One of the facts of life in the broadcasting industry is the cutthroat competition for the attention of an audience and for resulting advertising revenue.

The impact of competitive program-rating upon production personnel is unique to television and radio. This competition will often affect individual employees. An arbitration under the voluntary labor arbitration rules of the American Arbitration Association before Los Angeles arbitrator Edgar A. Jones, Jr., involved such a situation. The grievant, a radio disc jockey and member of the American Federation of Television and Radio Artists, claimed that he had been discharged without cause.[3] The employer alleged that the grievant's ratings had faded, and that he was no longer "capturing the fancies . . . of the listening public."

As Jones pointed out, the epitaph "Who lives by the ratings, dies by the ratings" has an ominous currency among those whose talents are precariously airborne. Failure to produce an audience may justify a discharge. But the employer must show cause. To uphold such a discharge, there must be adequate proof of failure. AFTRA claimed that the employer had failed to meet the test and that, in fact, the grievant had been fired because he participated in a 1961 strike.

At the hearing, the arbitrator required the employer to submit an analysis of comparative ratings between the grievant and his disc jockey competition in the same time slot. The company's proof failed to justify the discharge, and this failure was considered crucial by the arbitrator.

The program director who fired the grievant had served as a replacement for striking disc jockeys during the strike, and had been expelled from AFTRA. The grievant had been a shop steward in the radio station during the strike, and when dismissed was one of two remaining ex-strikers. The arbitrator concluded that the discharge had been for union activity and ordered the grievant reinstated on the air, with full back pay and no loss of seniority. Here one finds a competitive standard asserted by the employer to justify a discharge, but a failure to meet the standard. Only the use of program ratings to attempt to prove cause makes this case unique. Poor performance on the job is frequently hard to prove in other industries.

In another case, Philadelphia arbitrator Lewis M. Gill, in reinstating a radio and television newsman who had been discharged for alleged incompetence, quoted the company's brief to the effect that "The determination of whether a newsman's work is unsatisfactory depends, in almost every instance, upon management's evaluation of the man's work based upon subjective standards."[4]

As Gill pointed out, his problem was "to strike a fair balance between the company's right to reasonable leeway in determining competence, and the employee's right not to have his career dealt a near-fatal blow without convincing proof that he was in fact incompetent." Here again, the employer failed to sustain the burden of proof.

The emphasis on competition has an impact on job security in other ways. Seniority provides one case in point. Management may question whether reliance upon seniority rights, which might be appropriate in less competitive industries, is feasible in the production of broadcasting programs.

For example, during a layoff, technicians such as film editors must be retained in accordance with seniority provisions of the collective bargaining contract. Arbitrator Israel Ben Scheiber ruled in favor of the employer in one case.[5] A layoff of some technicians had to be made from among a group of employees with equal seniority as technicians. The Columbia Broadcasting System retained some of the employees from within the group on the basis of ability. The union urged that service with the company in other jobs should determine the matter. Scheiber found for the employer on the basis that the contract expressly defined *seniority* in terms of the "date employed as a technician," and that among technicians with equal seniority the CBS yardstick was not unreasonable.

Management Rights

In the broadcasting industry, employers have tried hard to defend their managerial rights to change production methods in order to take advantage of improvements in technology and marketing, while the unions have attempted to impose job security restrictions upon those rights.

A number of cases have involved definition of the geographical area within which an engineer must be assigned to tape live broadcasts. For example, one arbitrator held that such a requirement did not apply when a recording was made of taped news received over the telephone.[6] The arbitrator, Thomas Knowlton, rejected what he called a "rather involved and strained definition" maintained by the union, and upheld the employer's right to receive such material without an engineer standby.

In another case, Louis Yagoda held that an employer was not required to pay for a standby engineer when it obtained tapes of a U.S. Army briefing session of West Berlin mayor Willy Brandt.[7] He held that such a program was not originated by the employer, despite the fact that the interview was held within fifty miles of the station and the employer may have counted on obtaining the tape from another source.

Similarly, Harry Dworkin held that in a case in which the contract permitted an announcer to record program inserts, an engineer need not be present when an announcer recorded a fifty-minute interview with an author at the station's administrative offices. The tape was later transcribed and edited by engineers to constitute twenty-nine minutes, twenty-three seconds of a fifty-five minute program. Dworkin held that this interview constituted an insert rather than the "main body" of the program, being one of sixteen parts, although the longest.[8] In another case, the union claimed pay for six engineers assigned for standby time at the studio during a live interview of Premier Khrushchev that for security reasons had to be telecast from the United Nations.[9] The arbitrator ruled that the engineers' union could not unreasonably withhold permission to accept "feed" and that the employer did not have to pay the six engineers for standby time.

The installation of new, more automated equipment often leads to grievances. In Taft Broadcasting Company v. the International Brotherhood of Electrical Workers, Local 253, the union challenged the employer's right to install remote control apparatus at a radio station.[10] This grievance went to court to determine whether the employer was required to arbitrate the issue. The contract included a broad arbitration clause. The U.S. Court of Appeals, Fifth Circuit, ordered the employer to arbitrate the dispute. (There is no record of the final outcome. Presumably, it was settled.)

In another case involving NABET, the issue involved a contractual requirement that the company notify the union thirty days in advance of making any change in a procedure "which increases or makes more difficult the duties or job of the employee," and negotiate as to the methods for and limitations thereon.[11] After reviewing the facts of the case, the arbitrator determined that the work change involved did not fall within the contract definition.

Another management rights case concerned Station KQED.[12] The arbitrator held that the educational television station had not violated its collective bargaining contract by subcontracting certain video tape work which it had no equipment to do itself. The arbitrator, Adolph Koven, pointed out that in the absence of a specific provision prohibiting subcontracting, the test of management's right to subcontract was one of good faith and reasonableness. Here the employer showed that its own equipment was inadequate, that it had ordered new equipment to eliminate the need to subcontract but that the new equipment had not yet arrived, and established that it had not intended to discriminate against the union in its actions.

These cases indicate that skirmishes on the grievance line in the broadcasting industry often concern management rights intimately connected with the complex nature of broadcasting production.

Jurisdictional Disputes

Complicating the management rights battlefield is the craft structure of the unions in the broadcasting industry. Unions must jostle each other for jobs in the changing employment picture. Frequently it is difficult for the employer to determine the lines delineating the job jurisdiction of contesting unions.

In one case, the representative of TV electricians claimed that its jurisdiction over "equipment and apparatus by means of which electricity is applied" should extend to the erection and handling of a platform which would be used as a mount for a camera to film a series of seminars to be televised.[13] The employer had assigned the work to the theatrical stage employees, who had also claimed it. The arbitrator upheld the employer on the ground that an objective reading of the contract would limit jurisdiction to apparatus which was actually connected to electricity. The fact that the employer intended to use the platform for such an application in the future was not sufficient to bring the work within the contract terms.

Only one year before, another arbitrator, Herman Gray, had held in favor of the union, where the employer had assigned jurisdiction to stage employees to handle apparatus that would ultimately be used in connection with electronic equipment.[14] He held that such equipment should be assigned to stage employees only when it is used as a prop, and granted jurisdiction to the electricians.

Sometimes the contest involves the right to represent an entirely new unit, and in these situations there may be less of a craft flavor to the dispute. Under the AFL-CIO internal disputes procedure, the permanent umpire, David L. Cole, considered a case where NABET was seeking to organize the employees of an experimental UHF television station which had been purchased by Central Broadcasting of California.[15] The previous owner of the station had an established bargaining relationship for its radio station employees with the IBEW, but not for its TV employees. Cole held for NABET because the UHF television station was new, and Central had no previous bargaining history with TV employees.

Central's decision to make the technological leap from radio to television had created an organizational vacuum and provided an opportunity for jurisdictional expansion. This case reminds one of situations in other industries where an employer acquires or establishes a new installation for which there is no established collective bargaining relationship. The internal disputes procedure permits third-party review of the jurisdictional scramble.

An organizational split between radio and TV bargaining units came to the fore in another case. The union contested the discharge of a news announcer who was a full-time employee of the employer's radio station. The union's contract was solely with the broadcaster's TV station, where the announcer sometimes worked part time. The court ordered arbitration of the question of whether the employer had to "show cause" to fire a part-time employee.[16] (Here again the dispute was later settled.)

Job Content and Pay Rates

Almost every industry that employs craft-union workers finds that problems arise when job content must be changed. Prickly jurisdictional and pay rate issues spring up on all sides. And craft unions have learned a variety of responses with which to accommodate to the need for change. Because the technology of broadcasting guarantees a changing job content, there is a constant source of potential grievances.

Craft unions in the broadcasting industry sometimes submit such issues to arbitration. They were among the early sponsors of voluntary arbitration, and they continue to believe in it. In general, these unions try to find some way to resolve their differences with the employer without using the strike, but strikes are not unknown, and may even be increasing.

The widespread use of arbitration in broadcasting may be encouraged by yet another factor, not always present in other industries. In broadcasting, if the message does not go out on the air at the minute it was scheduled it may be lost forever. A strike can eliminate all live production. There can be no stockpiling of live inventory, although taped shows and motion pictures can be used in the event of a strike of production facilities. There can be no delay in selling the fresh product, and both parties recognize this fact.

Furthermore, broadcasting unions have been able to negotiate high wage levels. The industry has been profitable in recent years, partially because rapid technological development has made it possible to resolve cost problems by automation and efficiency, and partially because the industry has been surfing on a marketing ground swell.

If and when the broadcasting industry loses its ability to expand its market, to lift its profits, and to manipulate technological change, then one should anticipate new stresses upon labor relations in the industry. Will the unions' desire to engage in resistant behavior increase dramatically? Will functional jurisdictions be more seriously challenged? Will there be increasing warfare between unions? In the words of the soap opera, "Watch next week's show!"

Whatever may be the future of labor organization in the broadcasting industry, its use of arbitration will probably continue. Strikes over grievances have occurred infrequently. When they have occurred they have proved expensive to both parties, and to other employees in the industry.

Furthermore, many broadcasting grievances have limited application. Indeed, they sometimes concern only one employee. Arbitrator Peter Seitz in 1965 decided a case in point, involving

Radio Buffalo.[17] The grievant was an announcer of commercials who had decided to "jump" to a competing station, not yet in operation. A newspaper article announced his departure and his new affiliation. He was discharged a few months later. His union filed a grievance. Seitz held that the publicity given the job change had so completely destroyed the grievant's usefulness as an employee as to constitute just cause for discharge. This case involved only the employment rights of one enterprising individual.

Other cases involve more typically group rights but may involve very small groups. For example, Metromedia required all employees to sign a memo acknowledging that they were aware of a rule against unauthorized visitors on company premises.[18] Eight employees refused to sign. Two were discharged. Six were not. Arbitrator Harry J. Dworkin sent the two discharged employees back to work. Unlike the other six, these two happened to be union stewards. Dworkin found discrimination against them. Such a case could arise in any industry, since it does not involve uniquely broadcasting issues.

On the other hand, the broadcasting industry and its craft unions frequently engage in wage controversies much like those which occur in the construction industry, but involving particularly complex pay provisions in the employment contract. For example, in one recent case James Altieri struggled with trying to interpret the 1957 AFTRA staff-announcer agreement.[19] The introduction for the host of "Movie Greats" was switched in 1961 from a live format to a video-taped recording. Neither the announcer, the executive producer, or various union or management officials seemed able to agree upon the appropriate rate provisions in the agreement. For over three years the wrong rate was paid. Finally, early in 1965, a grievance was filed. The arbitrator reviewed the entire matter and determined that the company should pay the higher "host" rate, but only from the date the grievance was filed. The award was rendered in March of 1966, after many man hours had been invested by AFTRA and the employer in straightening out the confusion.

Other cases involve "standby" requirements, another provision which is peculiar to the industry and troublesome to the employer. A case in point was recently decided by Abram Stockman.[20] It arose under an AFTRA contract which permitted a member of management to appear on the program "provided . . . there shall be assigned and present, a member of the staff who might otherwise make such appearances." The news director, a supervisor under NLRB standards, had been appearing on an early morning television news broadcast, usually with a staff announcer, in a "Huntley-Brinkley" format. AFTRA claimed that in addition to the staff announcer who appeared on the show, another member of the staff should be paid as "silent standby." After a careful analysis of the contract and its bargaining history, the arbitrator determined that the employer did violate the contract by not providing a standby staff member. Stockman added, "We recognize, of course, the implications suggested by a silent standby. But it is not for us to pass judgment on the economics of the practice."

In fact, the economic pressure of increased competition will probably be the ultimate judge of such provisions, as they become too expensive for broadcasting employers.

Television and radio continue to grow, both in the United States and elsewhere. Many thousands of employees, executives, and investors are personally concerned with the economic health and expansion of the industry. Furthermore, broadcasting plays an ever increasing role in providing news and entertainment to the public.

Therefore, the task of protecting the flexibility of management while at the same time safeguarding the important interests of employees is increasingly important. The collective bargaining agreements between employers and the various broadcasting unions will be the vehicles for accommodating these conflicting social needs.

The general issues which lead to grievances in the broadcasting industry — discharge, management rights, assignment of personnel, and union jurisdiction — are common to other competitive industries that are undergoing technological change. But the broadcasting dispute takes on a unique character because the industry itself is unique; the use of competitive rating standards to justify discharge or reassignment may be unique to broadcasting; questions such as use of standby personnel may concern one-time decisions to produce programs in a particular fashion but may become perennial problems for the industry; issues of job jurisdiction may constitute a well established line of conflict between competing unions, with the employer pinned in the role of the middle-man. How can such issues best be resolved? Most, of course, will be handled through informal accommodation or in the early stages of grievance procedure.

Arbitration, as exemplified by the cases discussed above, will continue to dispose of the most difficult day-to-day contract disputes, particularly those which turn upon an interpretation of contract provisions. By having a body of experienced arbitrators who are particularly familiar with broadcasting problems, the industry can continue to resolve most of its labor problems without suffering expensive work stoppages.

It is probable that technological and marketing changes will continue to create disputes that management and union leadership have not yet anticipated. But even here the grievance and arbitration procedure will provide an early-warning system, making it possible for the parties to come to grips with their problems, even though some of them will ultimately have to be resolved in the collective bargaining process. Therefore, labor arbitration seems to be serving a useful purpose in the broadcasting industry, as it does elsewhere in the economy.

NOTES

1. U.S. Bureau of Labor Statistics, *Major Collective Bargaining Agreements: Arbitration Procedures*, nos. 1425–26 (June 1966), p. 7.
2. *Ibid.*
3. American Arbitration Association, unpublished opinion and award, 1965.
4. American Arbitration Association, unpublished opinion and award, 1965.
5. International Brotherhood of Electrical Workers, Local 1212, and Columbia Broadcasting System. *Labor Arbitration Reports* (Washington: The Bureau of National Affairs, 1962), 37:330.
6. International Alliance of Theatrical Stage Employes and Moving Picture Machine Operators of the United States and Canada and RKO General, Inc. American Arbitration Association, "Summary of Labor Arbitration Awards," mimeographed (New York, 1963), no. 54–5.
7. IBEW, Local 1212, and Metropolitan Broadcasting Division of Metromedia, Inc. (Radio Station WNEW). American Arbitration Association, "Summary of Labor Arbitration Awards," mimeographed (New York, 1962), no. 45–3.
8. NABET, Region 4, and Storer Broadcasting Co. American Arbitration Association, "Summary of Labor Arbitration Awards," mimeographed (New York, 1967), no. 110–6.
9. IBEW, Local 1212 and National Telefilm Associates, Inc. *Labor Arbitration Reports* (Washington: The Bureau of National Affairs, 1962), 38:437.
10. Taft Broadcasting Company v. IBEW, Local 253. *Labor Arbitration Reports* (Washington: The Bureau of National Affairs, 1962), 37:1073. Arbitrability was determined by the U.S. Court of Appeals Fifth Circuit (New Orleans) with opinion in *Labor Relations Reference Manual* (Washington: Bureau of National Affairs, 1962), 49:2572.
11. American Arbitration Association, unpublished opinion and award, 1966.
12. National Association of Broadcast Employees and Technicians and Station KQED. *Labor Arbitration Reports* (Washington: The Bureau of National Affairs, 1963), 40:638.
13. IBEW, Local 1212, and Educational Broadcasting Corporation.

American Arbitration Association, "Summary of Labor Arbitration Awards," mimeographed (New York, 1966), no. 88–3.

14. IBEW, Local 1212, and Educational Broadcasting Corporation. American Arbitration Association, "Summary of Labor Arbitration Awards," mimeographed (New York, 1964), no. 75–9.

15. IBEW v. NABET. *Labor Arbitration Reports* (Washington: The Bureau of National Affairs, 1964), 41:873.

16. Taft Broadcasting Company v. American Federation of Television and Radio Artists. *Labor Arbitration Reports* (Washington: The Bureau of National Affairs, 1962), 37:778. Arbitrability was determined by the U.S. Court of Appeals Sixth Circuit (Cincinnati) with opinion in *Labor Relations Reference Manual* (Washington: The Bureau of National Affairs, 1962), 49:2572.

17. NABET and Radio Buffalo, Inc. *Labor Arbitration Reports* (Washington: The Bureau of National Affairs, 1966), 44:428.

18. NABET and Metromedia, Inc. *Labor Arbitration Reports* (Washington: The Bureau of National Affairs, 1966), 46:161.

19. American Arbitration Association, unpublished opinion and award, 1966.

20. American Arbitration Association, unpublished opinion and award, 1965.

6 Decisions Affecting the Networks and Unions

by CHARLES G. BAKALY, JR.

The labor problems confronting management in the broadcasting industry are, as a rule, extremely interesting. Perhaps the most important reason for this is that the industry is in a constant state of change caused by new developments in automation and technology. As soon as one set of problems is resolved, new problems are presented. In the Warnock and Coulson chapters the reader has been exposed to many of these problems. In this chapter problems faced primarily by the networks will be examined, especially those which have been resolved by arbitrators or the National Labor Relations Board. The chapter will stress relations with the craft unions rather than relations with the talent guilds, since the former have more traditionally been concerned with automation.

In our environment of technological change, it is not surprising that management has encountered resistance from the unions in the industry, who are very much concerned with the possible loss of bargaining unit work resulting from automation. This concern for work preservation is magnified by the existence of a number of different unions in the broadcasting industry, each representing a different classification of employee. Coulson has observed that as the content of jobs is changed by technological innovation, the jurisdictional lines of these unions may become blurred, and interunion problems may often develop.

Establishment of Union Jurisdiction Through National Labor Relations Board Representation Proceedings

As noted before, the jurisdiction of unions is often established by National Labor Relations Board elections. A frequently crucial aspect of such proceedings is the determination of the appropriate bargaining unit or units. Such a determination may have operational repercussions for management if it results in the proliferation of small bargaining units. Often, when one union petitions for a specific unit, another union will intervene in the proceeding and petition to represent separately only a portion of that unit. In such cases, assuming that both units would be appropriate, the board will often leave the determination of whether there will be one or more units to the employees themselves.

For example, in one case both NABET and IBEW sought to represent a system-wide unit of the technical employees of CBS.[1] IATSE sought to carve out of this unit a separate unit of motion picture cameramen, film cutters, and editors. In its decision and direction of elections, the board found that the film cutters and editors at Los Angeles could constitute a separate appropriate unit. However, the ultimate decision of whether such employees would have a separate bargaining unit or be part of the system-wide unit was left to the employees. The board held that if a majority of the film editors and cutters at Los Angeles voted for the IATSE, the IATSE would be the exclusive bargaining agent in a separate unit. On the other hand, if IATSE did not receive a majority of the votes in the separate unit, the film editors and cutters would be made a part of the system-wide unit and their votes would be pooled with the other members of the system-wide unit.

Other examples of such self-determination elections in the broadcasting industry are common. In a second case, the Brotherhood of Painters, Decorators, and Paperhangers, AFL, sought to represent a unit composed of scenic designers and decorators at CBS.[2] IATSE intervened and claimed that the decorators should be a separate bargaining unit. The board found that there was sufficient community of interest between the designers and decorators to justify their inclusion in a single bargaining unit. At the same time, the board found that the decorators had a distinguishable function and somewhat different working conditions. The board, therefore, concluded that a self-determination election should be held so that the decorators themselves could decide whether they would be in a separate bargaining unit represented by IATSE or in the broader unit represented by the Painters.

In a third case, IATSE sought to sever a unit of six motion picture film cameramen from a broader unit represented by IBEW.[3] The board found that the film cameramen constituted a separate and functionally distinct group and met the severance criteria established by the board in the American Potash and Chemical Corporation decision.[4] It therefore directed a self-determination election to determine whether the employees desired a separate unit represented by IATSE, or to remain in the broader unit represented by IBEW.

Although bargaining units in the broadcasting industry have often been narrowly drawn by the board to allow separate representation for differing classifications, the geographic scope of such units has often been broad. Thus company-wide and multi-employer bargaining units have been common. For example, in one case the Television Writers of America sought to represent a unit of all freelance writers employed by the networks for television programs produced in Los Angeles.[5] At the same time, the Authors League of America sought a unit of all freelance writers and composers employed by the networks or advertising agencies for network television programs originating from New York, Chicago, or Los Angeles, and for syndicated programs regardless of origin. In rendering its decision, the board was greatly influenced by the previous collective bargaining history for writers and for similar groups of employees and by the integration of the networks' operations. Based upon these factors, it approved the multiemployer, nationwide unit sought by the Authors League of America, excluding, however, composers and advertising agency employees. The unit sought by the Television Writers of America limited to Los Angeles was found inappropriate.

Bargaining history was also important in a second case.[6] Here, the board also found only a broad geographic multiemployer unit appropriate, but only after prolonged litigation. In this case, the Musicians Guild of America petitioned for separate units of all musicians who prepared and recorded soundtracks used in television films and who were employed by CBS, ABC, and NBC in Los Angeles County. The petitioner was opposed by the incumbent American Federation of Musicians, who claimed that its nationwide, multiemployer contract barred an election, and even if it were not a bar, the previous bargaining history compelled a nationwide, multiemployer unit. The board, however, refused to consider either the contract or the bargaining history because, in its opinion, the contract contained an illegal union-security provision. It then found a nationwide, but not a multiemployer, unit appropriate and directed separate elections at ABC and CBS, where the Musicians Guild had made a sufficient showing of interest. The Musicians Guild subsequently won the election at ABC and was certified. In an effort to test the legality of the board's decision, ABC refused to bargain with the Musicians Guild. By the time the unfair labor practice case reached the board, the Supreme Court had held in a different case that the type of union-security provision which the board had previously found objectionable was in fact lawful.[7] The board, therefore, admitted that its unit determination had been in error, vacated the election, and found only a nationwide, multiemployer unit appropriate.

Jurisdictional Disputes
Not Involving the Establishment of Bargaining Units

Election and unit determinations, however, do not put an end to all jurisdictional disputes. Some disputes, such as those over the assignment of specific job functions, may arise which are not susceptible to resolution in NLRB representation proceedings. Such disputes frequently present troublesome problems for management.

Especially during the early years of television, jurisdictional disputes concerning the assignment of specific job functions frequently erupted into strikes and threats of strikes. Some relief was provided by section 8(b)(4)(D) of the National Labor Relations Act, as amended, which made it an unfair labor practice for a union to strike or threaten to strike with the object of forcing an employer to assign particular work to one labor organization rather than to another. A statutory exception was provided, to cover cases in which the employer was failing to abide by the union's certification. The section, however, was unique in that before the board could issue a complaint under 8(b)(4)(D), it was first required to hold a hearing under section 10(k) of the act to "determine" the dispute out of which the unfair labor practice arose. For a considerable period of time after the enactment of these sections in 1947, the law relating to jurisdictional disputes, especially the meaning of a board "determination" under section 10(k), was subject to a considerable amount of confusion. Interestingly enough, much of the important case law in this area was forged in cases relating to jurisdictional disputes in the broadcasting industry.

A dispute between NABET and IATSE over the lighting of staged shows from remote locations was the subject of one of the first important cases.[8] When NBC assigned the work in question to IATSE, NABET stopped work and was subsequently charged under section 8(b)(4)(D). In the section 10(k) proceedings, the board first found that the disputed work was not within

NABET's certification so as to fall within the specific exclusion found in the statute. The board did, however, find that the disputed work had been awarded to NABET in its collective bargaining agreement with NBC. The board stated:

> The Board is persuaded that to fail to hold as controlling herein the contractual preemption of the work in dispute would be to encourage disregard for observance of binding obligations under collective-bargaining agreements and invite the very jurisdictional disputes Section 8(b) (4) (D) is intended to prevent.[9]

The board thereupon awarded the work to NABET in the 10(k) proceeding and in effect upheld the legality of NABET's work stoppage. The case established that not only is a certification a defense to an 8(b)(4)(D) charge, but so is a collective bargaining agreement in which the employer has awarded the disputed work to the charged union.

The assignment of remote lighting was also the cause for a later dispute at CBS which was to eventually reach the United States Supreme Court. In this case, it was the International Brotherhood of Electrical Workers which struck for the disputed work.[10] The board held in the 10(k) proceedings that as neither IBEW's certification nor contract covered the work in question, IBEW was not entitled to strike for the work involved. When IBEW refused to comply with this decision, the board proceeded under section 8(b)(4)(D). IBEW, however, defended on the ground that the 10(k) determination was invalid because the board had not made an affirmative award of the work, but had simply determined that IBEW was not entitled to strike for the work due to the lack of a certification or contract awarding it the work.

The Supreme Court held, contrary to the board, that the board was required to make an affirmative award of the disputed work under section 10(k).[11] According to the Court, the legislative history of the Taft-Hartley Act revealed that Congress intended the board to resolve the dilemma faced by employers in such situations. By making an award only in cases where the work was covered either by the certification or the contract, the board left the vast majority of disputes unresolved. The Court then proceeded to reject the arguments advanced by the board. As to the board's contention that it had no standards upon which to base its awards, the Court simply expressed confidence in the board's ability to formulate its own standards based upon its experience and upon the standards used by arbitrators and joint boards. The Court also rejected the argument that an award by the board would discourage private settlements of disputes. The Court found that this was a policy question which Congress had already settled in enacting section 10(k). Lastly, the Court rejected arguments that affirmative awards would create conflicts with sections 8(a)(3), 8(b)(2), and 303 of the act.

There have been numerous other board cases involving jurisdictional disputes in the broadcasting industry which, unlike the two preceding cases, have not involved the establishment of new legal principles. For example, in one case NABET cameramen refused to pick up a cloud-effect scene because the special effect projector used was manned by an IATSE electrician.[12] In its determination of the dispute, the board held that the operation of the special effects projector was within the certification of IATSE. Similarly, in a second case, IBEW engaged in a work stoppage over the assigning of the operation of the front and rear screen projectors to members of IATSE.[13] The board found that the operation of such projectors was related more to the work performed by the stagehands and stage electricians than to that performed by the technicians. The board, therefore, concluded that the disputed work was within the IATSE certification. In a third case, IBEW technicians refused to run a film sequence for the "Mama" program because the scene was filmed by a member of IATSE.[14] Unlike the two preceding cases, the board found that the charged union was entitled to the work in question and could therefore strike for the purpose of obtaining this work. According to the board's analysis, the disputed work was covered by the IBEW's collective bargaining agreement with the employer.

As Coulson has pointed out, disputes between unions over job jurisdiction have not been limited in their determination to proceedings before the National Labor Relations Board. They have also been decided in a second forum — arbitration. While the board proceedings under section 10(k) can be initiated only if one of the unions strikes or threatens to strike, arbitration has the advantage of not requiring such coercive action for its initiation. On the other hand, arbitration of jurisdictional disputes has one very fundamental defect. A jurisdictional dispute is by its very nature a three-party matter; participation in an arbitration, however, is usually limited to the union whose contract is being arbitrated and the employer. Seldom will the second union join in the arbitration proceedings under the other union's contract and thus become voluntarily bound by the result. Management therefore faces a possible dilemma. It is conceivable that one union may arbitrate under its contract and receive a favorable award, while the second union may do likewise and receive an award in its favor. The employer may thus be faced with conflicting awards. In spite of this difficulty, the United States Supreme Court has held that such disputes must be arbitrated, unless clearly excluded by the arbitration clause. The Court reasoned that even if all parties would not be bound by the arbitrator's decision, the arbitration might nevertheless have a "curative effect." [15]

A number of jurisdictional disputes in the broadcasting industry have gone to arbitration. An interesting example involved a dispute between NABET and IATSE over the handling of a camera and monitors on "The Les Crane Show." [16] The camera in dispute was suspended by ropes from the ceiling grid and had been installed by NABET personnel. ABC, however, assigned the job of adjusting the ropes before, during, and after the show to members of IATSE, who made the necessary adjustments upon cue from the stage manager. In addition, IATSE personnel were assigned the task of raising and lowering the monitors, which were likewise suspended by ropes. NABET's claim before the arbitrator was that the raising and lowering of both the camera and monitors by IATSE members during the show violated its master agreement.

In his discussion of the case, the arbitrator first noted that the resolution of NABET's claim must be determined on the basis of the NABET master agreement alone and not on the basis of ABC contracts with other unions over which NABET had no control and over which the arbitrator had no authority. The arbitrator then focused on section 6.1 of the NABET master agreement, which essentially provided that ABC would not transfer out or subcontract bargaining-unit work except to the extent it had done so in the past. He noted that in the past, members of IATSE had raised and lowered microphones during a show by a similar arrangement. He found that the latter task was essentially the same as the disputed work, and therefore concluded that the raising and lowering of the camera and monitors was in fact a type of work that had previously been transferred out of the bargaining unit. Thus NABET's claim was accordingly denied by the arbitrator, and the possibility of conflicting arbitration awards was thereby avoided.

"The Les Crane Show" also provided another interesting arbitration case involving a similar issue.[17] During his show, Les Crane frequently used an Electrovoice 642 microphone mounted on a gun stock. This microphone was directional in nature and was used by Crane to pick up responses from the audience. The gun stock would be aimed by Crane at the person speaking and the entire device was thus referred to as the "shotgun mike." NABET claimed that it was improper for Crane to use the shotgun mike and that only NABET members had handled such directional equipment in the past. However in his decision, the arbitrator pointed out that talent had frequently used a second microphone for interviewing purposes. He found that the function served by the microphone was a more important factor than its directional or nondirectional nature. He therefore concluded that the use by talent of a directional microphone for interviewing purposes was a type of work that had in the past been performed by individuals outside the bargaining unit. Accordingly, he found that section 6.1 had not been violated.

Although Crane was probably a member of AFTRA, it is interesting to note that the latter dispute involved little likelihood of an active jurisdictional controversy between AFTRA and NABET. The handling of the shotgun mike by NABET might well have created greater work opportunities for NABET members, but, conversely, the handling of the microphone by Crane would not have increased the work opportunities for AFTRA members. Crane's interest was one of dramatic effect and in no way affected the institutional interests of AFTRA. Even if NABET prevailed in the arbitration, it would be unlikely that AFTRA would then have attempted to arbitrate the matter under its contract.

The question of union jurisdiction over microphones was also the center of controversy in another arbitration case.[18] In this case NABET claimed that NBC was violating the NABET master agreement by permitting talent, who were members of AFTRA, to put on and take off lavalier microphones, "off-camera," without the assistance of NABET technicians. These microphones were suspended by a string around the neck of the performer. Section A2.1 of the master agreement provided that only technicians could "operate and maintain technical equipment." In reaching his decision, the arbitrator found that the above contractual language was ambiguous with respect to the disputed work. He therefore examined the past practice in New York City, where the grievance arose. Here, he found this practice mixed and thus not determinative. He was therefore compelled to base his decision on the past practice under the master agreement in other cities, where he found that NABET had allowed performers to pick up and place on themselves lavalier microphones without the assistance of technicians. The grievance was therefore denied.

In another jurisdictional dispute, involving NBC in New York City, past practice at other locations was not found controlling.[19]

Here the work dispute centered on a new practice of placing metallic tabs on film for the purpose of automatically stopping a film projector at the desired time. Previously, the projector had been manually stopped by a NABET projectionist, who received his cue from a white leader spliced into the film at the appropriate location. Although this innovation did not displace the NABET projectionist, who was still required to start the projector, NABET claimed that the work of attaching the tabs should be performed by its members rather than by the IATSE film editors who were then doing it. In support of its contention NABET cited the practice at Buffalo and Washington, where NABET technicians handled projector-activating tape and tabs. The arbitrator found the Washington practice not controlling, in that the editors and technicians in Washington were both represented by NABET, and NBC had left to the NABET local president the selection of the group which would perform the work. Similarly, he found the practice in Buffalo was not controlling presumably because it involved tape rather than tabs and because the arrangement there was reached under a threat of strike. Rejecting these practices, the arbitrator based his holding simply on the finding that the application of the tabs did not involve bargaining-unit work of NABET. He reasoned that the tabs had simply replaced the white leader, which had always been applied to the film by the film editors. He accordingly denied the grievance.

A past practice was also distinguished in a jurisdictional dispute involving CBS. In this case, CBS maintained in the San Fernando Valley of California a motion picture production facility known as Studio Center.[20] The employees at Studio Center were represented for the most part by IATSE. CBS also maintained a broadcasting facility in Los Angeles known as TV City, where live, video tape, or kinescope programs were produced. Employees there were, with a few exceptions, represented by IBEW. It had been the practice at Studio Center for the producers and others to review the motion picture film shot the previous day (known as "dailies") by means of projectors located at the Center and operated by members of IATSE. Beginning in 1965, however, the "dailies" were sent to TV City and were transmitted back to Studio Center for review by means of a closed circuit television system. The resulting signal received at Studio Center was transmitted through a distribution rack to various monitors located in the offices of the reviewers. Under this new arrangement, the distribution rack at Studio Center was operated by a member of IATSE. IBEW, however, protested this assignment and claimed that the operation of the distribution rack fell within its jurisdiction. In denying the IBEW's claim, the arbitrator found that the IBEW's contract excluded from its scope the production of motion picture film, and found that a review of such unfinished film fell within this exclusion. A past practice of assigning the closed circuit distribution rack in New York to IBEW members was distinguished, in that completed films there were transmitted over the system.

Subcontracting

The discussion to this point has been concerned with work preservation disputes in which two unions representing employees of the same employer were involved or at least potentially involved. A similar dispute can arise where work is subcontracted or transferred to another employer, or where an independent contractor rather than an employee is used. In the latter situation an arbitrator uses the same general form of contractual analysis, but management is not faced with the possibility of conflicting arbitration awards. This type of dispute will now be considered.

There are generally three different types of remedies which unions have sought in such situations. The most common remedy is an arbitration award requiring that the individuals doing the work in question be replaced by bargaining unit personnel. An interesting example where such an award was obtained involved the use by NBC of leased tractors which were operated by em-

ployees of the lessor and which were used for the purpose of haul-
ing NBC-owned mobile trailers.[21] The past practice revealed that
NABET drivers had consistently driven NBC-owned self-
propelled mobile units. On the other hand, non-NABET personnel
had driven self-propelled mobile units which were leased, and
mobile units where both the tractor and trailer were leased. The
case, involving leased tractors and NBC-owned trailers, fell between these two areas of past practice. In deciding it the arbitrator first determined that NABET personnel were indeed capable
of driving the tractor-trailers. He then turned his attention to
section A2.4(a) of the master agreement, which provided essentially that where new equipment was introduced by the company,
it would be operated by bargaining unit employees, provided the
equipment replaced or supplemented had been operated by such
employees. The arbitrator found that the leased tractor and NBC-
owned trailer were a substitute for the NBC-owned self-propelled
mobile unit and therefore held that NABET drivers were entitled
to drive the leased tractors.

In a second case, NABET was unsuccessful in its efforts to
obtain such a remedy.[22] Here, an independent contractor had
been used to prepare a documentary on the Chicago sanitary district. NABET claimed that news and special events writers under
the contract should have been used instead. The arbitrator first
noted that similar programs had been subcontracted in the past
and that the degree of such subcontracting had not increased. He
also observed that the clause defining the duties of news and
special events writers referred only to "news programs or audi-
tions" and not to documentaries. He therefore denied the
grievance.

A second type of remedy involves not an attempt to replace a
person with a bargaining unit employee, but rather an attempt to
extend the collective bargaining agreement to cover the person
actually performing the work. Such a remedy is usually sought
only when the individual in question cannot be readily replaced.
The following case is an example.[23] A reporter from a Cleveland

radio station had, together with other reporters, questioned the parents of John Glenn after Glenn's first orbital flight. Part of the interview was later used by NBC in a one-hour "special" about the orbital flight. AFTRA thereupon demanded that the Cleveland reporter be compensated by NBC under the AFTRA contract for his performance in the interview, and that payments also be made for the reporter to the AFTRA pension and welfare fund. The theory propounded by AFTRA was that the reporter had become an employee of NBC by means of an "implied" contract. The arbitrator, however, disagreed. He could find no contract, either expressed or implied, and thus denied the grievance on the ground that the reporter was not an employee under the AFTRA contract.

A somewhat different approach involving the same remedy was taken by a second arbitrator.[24] Here, the question before the arbitrator was whether guests on "The Gypsy Rose Lee Show" were covered by the AFTRA contract. He held that the determining factor was the nature of the activity in which the guests engaged and not the existence of a written or oral contract of hire. He reasoned that the interview of a guest and activities merely incidental thereto would not result in the guest's being covered by the AFTRA contract. However, if the interview became a performance by the guest, the guest would be covered by the contract whether such a performance was originally intended or not.

A third remedy is sometimes sought when work is transferred or subcontracted. This remedy is usually the result of collective bargaining rather than arbitration, and involves "make-work" performed by bargaining unit employees to compensate for the work done by individuals outside the unit. A good example can be found in section A2.3 (a) of the 1961 NABET master agreement. This section provided that video tapes received by mail, air express, or messenger and recorded by persons not covered by the collective bargaining agreement must be checked in their entirety before use. The precise meaning of the section was the subject of a subsequent arbitration case.[25] In the case, the arbitrator held that the checking of the tapes referred to in the section required an independent check of the video tapes separate and apart from any playback required for dubbing, viewing for continuity acceptance, editing, or any other reason.[26] He also held that the section applied to all video tapes recorded by non-NABET personnel whether or not the company had the underlying property right to the program involved. He found that these make-work provisions were a compromise resulting from NABET's demand for jurisdiction over the recording of all video tapes used, including the recording of programs for which the company did not own the underlying property rights.

Job Consolidation

An entirely different aspect of the automation problem is introduced when the job content of certain job classifications is reduced because of technological improvements. In such instances management frequently attempts to consolidate into a single job classification the work previously performed by several classifications. Such combinations, however, are often contested by unions in an effort to prevent the elimination of jobs. The following two arbitration cases are an illustration.

The first case involved three changes made by NBC in Chicago.[27] First, the duties previously performed by the TV-MCR (TV-Master Control Room) from 12:30 A.M. to sign-off were assigned to the film studio technical director. Secondly, the work of the audio man and the film studio technical director was combined by assigning the automatic audio board to the latter. Lastly, the duties of the MCR in setting up the relay for the incoming feed to and from the Tape Room and in checking levels in the Tape Room were transferred to the video tape room operator and the film studio technical director. When the case was brought to arbitration, the arbitrator upheld NBC on all three combinations. He first found that the general right of NBC to combine jobs had been established in a previous arbitration case. He then examined NABET's primary argument that section A4.2 of the master agreement, which specified the duties of the technical director but did not enumerate these newly assigned duties, was intended to be an all-inclusive listing. He found the listing not to be inclusive and thus denied the grievances.

A different result was reached in another arbitration case.[28] Here the question was whether NBC could combine the jobs of projectionist and video control engineer. In this case there had been a previous award, known as the color arbitration award, which, among other things, regulated the staffing for video control engineers and projectionists. This award had resulted from the inability of the parties to resolve such issues through collective bargaining, and therefore involved an "interest" as opposed to a "rights" arbitration. The arbitrator found that the staffing provisions of the color arbitration award precluded the combination in question. In fact, he found that the company had previously made a proposal to amend the color arbitration award so as to permit such combination, but that such proposal had been rejected by NABET. He therefore sustained the grievance.

Premium Compensation

One interesting problem not directly related to technological change and work preservation has involved "golden time." Under the NABET master agreement an employee who works ten consecutive days without a day off receives additional compensation equivalent to his straight-time rate of pay for all days in excess of ten. Such time worked over ten consecutive days is commonly referred to as "golden time." There is also a separate clause in the agreement which defines the regular work day and provides that a tour of duty starting on one day and continuing into the next shall be considered one tour of duty and attributed to the first day. An arbitrator was called upon to construe these provisions with respect to an employee who had worked nine continuous days and on the tenth day had worked a long tour of 55¼ hours followed by six more days of work.[29] NBC conceded that overtime would be payable for most of the 55¼-hour tour and that golden time would be payable for the following six days. There was a dispute, however, whether golden time would also be payable for any of the 55¼-hour tour. NBC contended that it was not due in that this time should be attributed entirely to the tenth day. The arbitrator disagreed. He found that "days" in the golden time clause referred to calendar days, and that the clause defining the regular work day related only to overtime for a long tour. According to the arbitrator, the golden time and overtime provisions each served to compensate for a separate type of scheduling infringement and were thus completely independent of each other.

In a second case involving golden time, an employee had been given a time-off period of approximately thirty hours.[30] The arbitrator was asked whether this period would constitute a day off so as to avoid the accrual of golden time. NABET contended it would not and pointed to the "turnaround" provision in the master agreement. This provision provided that a day off shall consist of thirty-six hours, and specifies a penalty of $3.50 for each hour of encroachment. The arbitrator, however, disagreed with NABET's contention. He found that the two provisions were independent and provided separate penalties. He held that the thirty-hour period was sufficient to avoid the accrual of golden time and that the employee could only collect under the turnaround provision.

Strikes

Perhaps no discussion of labor problems would be complete without mention of the economic weapons available to the parties involved. There has been one interesting development in this area which had its genesis in the broadcasting industry. In September, 1960, AFTRA and NABET commenced a strike against KXTV in Sacramento, California. As part of their strike activity, the unions distributed handbills to the public naming the companies which were then advertising on KXTV and asking the public not to patronize these advertisers. As a result of this handbilling activity, some of the advertisers did cancel their contracts with KXTV. Unfair labor practices were subsequently filed against the unions, alleging that they had violated the secondary boycott provisions of the Taft-Hartley Act.

Section 8(b)(4)(B) of the act makes it an unfair labor practice for a union to threaten, coerce, or restrain any person with the object of forcing that person to cease doing business with any other person. The section does, however, contain a proviso that reads as follows:

Provided further, That for the purposes of this paragraph (4) only, nothing contained in such paragraph shall be construed to prohibit publicity, other than picketing, for the purpose of truthfully advising the public, including consumers and members of a labor organization, that a product or products are produced by an employer with whom the labor organization has a primary dispute and are distributed by another employer, as long as such publicity does not have an effect of inducing any individual employed by any person other than the primary employer in the course of his employment to refuse to pick up, deliver, or transport any goods, or not to perform any services, at the establishment of the employer engaged in such distribution.

When the case reached the board, the primary issue was whether the unions' activities were protected by the proviso. It was conceded that no picketing was involved, that the handbilling was truthful, and that the handbilling had not caused a work stoppage. However, the proviso refers only to advising the public that certain "products are produced by an employer with whom the labor organization has a primary dispute and are distributed by another employer." Here, KXTV did not produce a product, and even if it did, it was certainly not distributed by the advertisers.

The board nevertheless concluded that the proviso covered the activity in question and that therefore an unfair labor practice had not been committed.[31] It reasoned that the products mentioned in the proviso referred, in this case, to the beer, automobiles, or bread sold by the advertisers. It then took the next step and held that KXTV "produced" the beer, automobiles, or bread by enhancing their value through its advertising.

The case was appealed to the U.S. Court of Appeals for the Ninth Circuit, which rejected the board's reasoning.[32] The case was thereupon remanded to the board for further consideration. However, before the board reconsidered the case, the United States Supreme Court handed down its decision in *NLRB* v. *Sevette, Inc.*[33] In the latter case, the Supreme Court declared that there was "nothing in the legislative history which suggests that the protection of the proviso was intended to be any narrower in coverage than the prohibition to which it is an exception. . . ." Based on this language, the board adhered to its original decision.[34] When the case reached the Court of Appeals for the Ninth Circuit for the second time, the court found it necessary to agree with the board in light of the intervening Supreme Court decision.[35] It found the Supreme Court's language broad enough not only to protect the handbilling of advertisers who handle physical products, but also the handbilling of advertisers who deal exclusively in services.

One can say in conclusion that the labor problems faced by management in the broadcasting industry have been varied and extremely interesting. If there is a unifying theme to them it is generally the unions' concern for work preservation, a concern which results from a rapidly developing technology. Such problems will probably continue to be the center of interest in the future. However, there does appear to be a trend toward peaceful solution and away from the jurisdictional strikes which were common in past years. It is submitted that this is a healthy trend, and it is hoped that it will be a hallmark of the future.

NOTES

1. *Columbia Broadcasting System, Inc.*, 97 NLRB 566 (1951).
2. *Columbia Broadcasting System, Inc.*, 102 NLRB 1255 (1953).
3. *Columbia Broadcasting System, Inc.*, 110 NLRB 2108 (1954).
4. 107 NLRB 1418 (1954). The criteria for craft severance established by this case have recently been revised by the board in *Mallinckrodt Chemical Works*, 162 NLRB No. 48 (1966).
5. *National Broadcasting Company, Inc.*, 104 NLRB 587 (1953).
6. *American Broadcasting Company*, 134 NLRB 1458 (1961).
7. *International Typographical Union* v. *NLRB*, 365 U.S. 706 (1961).
8. *NABET, Hollywood Chapter*, 105 NLRB 355 (1953).
9. 105 NLRB at 364.
10. *Local 1212, IBEW*, 119 NLRB 594 (1957).
11. *NLRB* v. *Radio & Television Broadcast Engineers, Local 1212*, 364 U.S. 573 (1961).
12. *NABET*, 103 NLRB 479 (1953).
13. *Local 1212, IBEW*, 103 NLRB 1256 (1953).
14. *Local 1212, IBEW*, 114 NLRB 1354 (1955).
15. *Carey* v. *Westinghouse Electric Corp.*, 375 U.S. 261 (1964).
16. *Matter of Arbitration between ABC and NABET*, Grievance No. AN 64–31, February 1, 1965, by Benjamin C. Roberts.
17. *Matter of Arbitration between ABC and NABET*, Grievance No. AN 64–24, June 9, 1965, by Benjamin C. Roberts.
18. *Matter of Arbitration between NBC and NABET*, Grievance No. NY 60–9, June 11, 1965, by Benjamin C. Roberts.
19. *Matter of Arbitration between NBC and NABET*, Grievance No. NY 61–16, October 20, 1961, by Lloyd H. Bailer.
20. *Matter of Arbitration between CBS and IBEW*, January 21, 1966, by Thomas T. Roberts.
21. *Matter of Arbitration between NBC and NABET*, Grievance No. AN–65–14, October 8, 1965, by Benjamin C. Roberts.
22. *Matter of Arbitration between ABC and NABET*, Grievance No. AC 63–12, January 12, 1966, by Ronald W. Haughton.
23. *Matter of Arbitration between NBC and AFTRA*, L-42369, NY-L-366-64, October 4, 1964, by Aaron Horvitz.
24. *Matter of Controversy between AFTRA and ABC*, March 7, 1967, by Sam Kagel.
25. *Matter of Arbitration between ABC and NABET*, Grievance No. NY 61–33, January 25, 1963, by Benjamin C. Roberts.
26. It should be noted that section A2.3(c) of the 1967 NABET-ABC

master agreement now provides that "such check may be in conjunction with another use."

27. *Matter of Arbitration between NBC and NABET*, Grievance Nos. CG 61–11, NC 62–7 and 62–9, June 3, 1963, by Benjamin C. Roberts.
28. *Matter of Arbitration between NBC and NABET*, Grievance No. NC 62–4, October 16, 1962, by Benjamin C. Roberts.
29. *Matter of Arbitration between NBC and NABET*, Grievance No. NN 64–34, December 20, 1966, by Benjamin C. Roberts.
30. *Matter of Arbitration between ABC and NABET*, Grievance No. AN 65–34, December 20, 1966, by Benjamin C. Roberts.
31. *AFTRA, San Francisco Local*, 134 NLRB 1617 (1961).
32. *Great Western Broadcasting Corp.* v. *NLRB*, 310 F. 2d 591 (9th Cir. 1962).
33. 377 U.S. 46 (1964).
34. 150 NLRB 467 (1964).
35. 356 F.2d 434 (9th Cir. 1966).

Part III

PROBLEMS IN LABOR
AND BROADCASTING

7 Crossing National Boundaries Labor-Management Problems

by RICHARD N. GOLDSTEIN
and BARRY G. COLE

It is estimated that about one hundred million dollars will have been earned by American distributors in 1969 from the sale of American films and television programs to foreign television.[1] In fact, from 15 to 20 percent of all television programming shown overseas in 1969 will have been American produced. Overseas sales volume is expected to increase during the 1970s, due to the rapid growth of color television abroad and America's pre-eminence in color programming as well as to the trend toward commercialization of television channels in many foreign countries.[2]

This chapter will trace the attempt by various unions to share in the income earned by American television programs in the foreign market. It will also describe some of the particular labor relations problems which have resulted from that involvement and from the growth of overseas television. The chapter will only indirectly deal with the problems of selling American programs abroad. However, these problems will be summarized here because they influence the size and composition of the foreign market and thereby the revenues that accrue to the distributor and the performer. Moreover, the actions taken by other countries in limiting the number and kinds of overseas programs help put in some perspective the actions taken by some American unions in attempting to limit the foreign personnel who can be engaged on American television programs.

In an increasing number of countries, a quota has been implemented specifying the percentage of total programming which must be produced and originated in a country, or conversely, the percentage of total programming which may be foreign. Among English-speaking countries, there is a 55 percent requirement of Canadian originated programming, a stipulation that only 14 percent of prime-time programming in the United Kingdom can be of foreign origin, and a recent increase to 50 percent in Australian content requirements. But the practice of quotas is by no means limited to the English-speaking countries; in some non-English-speaking areas, for example Venezuela, 50 percent or more of the programs must be domestically produced.

Nor are quotas limited to the number of programs that can be imported. They sometimes stipulate that particular kinds of programs will not be permitted. Mexico, which represents 25 percent of the Spanish-speaking foreign market, forbids foreign feature films to be shown on Mexican television. Japan now permits such showings, but only in non-prime time. Occasionally, as in Italy, quotas are placed on the number of years a series can run. Foreign laws relating to quotas are in a constant state of flux.

Foreign barriers to American products have also included dubbing legislation in South America, dollar-exchange restrictions in Japan and Italy, and price ceilings on individual tele-films and, more recently, on total imports in Japan. Various methods of establishing de facto legal barriers to the collecting of funds, and the imposing of import duties on television products, have been implemented in many countries.

Aside from legal barriers, there are many other difficulties in selling American programs overseas. Financial problems include costs of shipping, customs, handling, dubbing, and sales and distribution. In the case of live-taped shows, the technical problem of the conversion to the foreign television system usually leads to the necessity of making a kinescope, the first negative of which may cost up to one thousand dollars. Then, too, cultural differences make it extremely difficult to sell many situation comedies overseas. And differences in morals make some programs containing violence, kissing, or drinking impossible to distribute in the Middle East. In short, the market is limited by the country's economic and social characteristics, as well as by the imposition of quotas or other legal restrictions.

These are some of the factors which have inhibited the foreign market. However, American programs continue to be shown all over the world, and have been a significant part of the television fare of a number of countries. Prospects for the future of foreign distribution will be analyzed at the conclusion of this chapter.

Foreign Residuals

The negotiation of supplementary payments for the distribution of programs overseas, payments commonly referred to as foreign residuals, has been an objective of varying significance to AFTRA, SAG, AFM, WGA and DGA, the five unions currently involved in such payments. With the large increase in foreign sales and the appearance of video tape in the late fifties, and the beginning of satellite transmission in the early sixties, the prospects of accelerated foreign distribution have received considerable attention in collective bargaining sessions. The development toward the prevailing systems of foreign residuals is a story of some interest.

Before the introduction of video tape, foreign payments were rarely discussed and, indeed, were never mentioned in most agreements. In fact, with respect to radio, only in the AFRA transcription code was there a specific clause outlining a provision for supplementary payments for the sale, leasing, or otherwise making available of an American-produced program. That clause, drafted in 1941 and still in force as part of AFTRA's 1966–69 transcription code, provides that the industry pay an additional fee equal to the original fee (excluding rehearsal pay) for the use of the recording overseas.[3] This provision has never been of major significance to the industry or to AFTRA, either with respect to money or to negotiations. Occasionally, AFTRA makes a complaint regarding transcriptions made overseas and used in the United States ("runaway transcriptions"), claiming such a procedure undercuts revenues from the residual scheme of the transcription code. But the volume of such transcriptions has never reached the point where the union has felt compelled actively to pursue the issue.

Before the introduction of video tape, there were no specific provisions for supplementary payment for the foreign distribution of kinescopes or television films in television labor agreements. Insofar as film programming was concerned, there were no limitations, express or implied, in the film labor contracts. The live TV agreements presented a myriad of relevant clauses, none of which, however, precluded the networks from making occasional foreign sales without extra payments. The situation was as follows:

(1) The RTDG television network freelance directors agreement provided that "payments of the applicable fee for a program shall entitle the Company to have the program broadcast once in each city either live or by recording."[4] The networks interpreted the clause to mean that a program could be broadcast without extra fees once in each city throughout the world.

(2) The AFTRA network television code allowed supplementary broadcast within sixty days "in any area where the program has not been previously broadcast without additional payment to the performers."[5] Since no territorial restrictions were specified, the networks interpreted the agreements as permitting them to broadcast, without supplementary payments, live-taped or kinescope programs anywhere in the world within sixty days of their production.

(3) The AFM agreement provided for sixty days of supple-

mentary coverage for a kinescope of a live network broadcast, but specified that the program would have to be aired by an "affiliated station."[6] While a network often made some agreements with those stations airing its programs overseas, it is possible that these agreements would not have been considered to constitute bona fide affiliations had the issue been litigated. But it was not.

(4) The 1955 WGA live television freelance minimum basic agreement allowed supplementary coverage within sixty days, but specified that this applied only to network television broadcasts.[7] Moreover, the agreement defined "national television network" to include television stations in the United States, its possessions, dependencies, and territories, the Philippine Islands, and Canada.[8] Of all the agreements, the WGA agreement came closest to placing a territorial restriction upon supplementary coverage and requiring union or individual consent for the distribution of television programs in foreign markets.

However, the number of American television programs distributed overseas before 1957 was quite small, and most of these went to Canada, Mexico, and Cuba. Thus neither the WGA nor any of the other performance unions who already had provisions for domestic residuals applied pressure upon the industry for foreign residuals. Some distributors did consider it advisable, before airing certain programs overseas, to obtain informal permission from the unions, and assurances that no additional compensation would be required. But this was done on an irregular basis, and when such consultation did not take place no major objection was raised by the unions.

In 1957 the networks and others began to negotiate distribution of programs on a regular basis to stations outside the Western Hemisphere. These were mainly programs originally performed live, and taped or kinescoped for subsequent distribution. During that year NBC, the leading network in such transactions, negotiated to distribute programs to Australia, Denmark, England, Italy, Sweden, and Switzerland. The publicity given to these sales, and the expectation that greater use of video tape would accelerate the prospects of continued sales, resulted in direct attempts by certain unions to negotiate provisions for foreign residuals for live-taped-kinescoped programs.

WGA Is First

The Writers Guild, whose existing agreement with the networks suggested the best claim to supplementary payments for the broadcasting of American live or taped programs overseas, became the first union to secure written provisions for additional payments for foreign use of programs. On June 3, 1957, NBC and WGA entered into a letter agreement which provided that NBC could broadcast a program within sixty days of the original broadcast over the "national television network" under the following conditions:

(a) over a network, a recording of such program in any country outside the "national television network," upon agreement with each writer of material for such program, when acquiring his services for such program, or before the original telecast, to pay him a minimum of one dollar for each such country in which such program is broadcast, or

(b) where no network exists, over individual stations a recording of such program in any country outside the "national television network," upon agreement with each writer of material for such program, when acquiring his services for such program, or before the original telecast, to pay him a minimum of one dollar for each station, in each such country over which such program is broadcast.[9]

This arrangement was subsequently applied to live, taped, or kinescoped programs broadcast by the other two national networks, in a letter agreement of April 1, 1958, accompanying the execution of the 1958 WGA live freelance agreement.[10] The WGA documentary film agreement with the networks in 1960 incorporated the payment of one dollar per country.

But while WGA was satisfied to have the principle of foreign supplementary payments recognized in the contracts, and willing to receive only the nominal payment of one dollar for each country airing the program (until such time as WGA could determine the kind of residual it would later demand), the increased volume of American programs overseas and the potential foreign residual payments it promised soon brought a more militant approach from AFTRA.

The AFTRA-NBC Affair

The prevailing AFTRA clause, as we have said, allowed for supplementing the network in any area within sixty days of the original broadcast. In December, 1957, AFTRA officially accused NBC of violating the agreement, contending that the clause did not allow foreign distribution, even within sixty days, and requested that it be consulted before any additional live shows were sold overseas.[11] Since foreign usage had not been discussed at the preceding AFTRA-network negotiation, AFTRA could have sought to bargain with the networks concerning foreign usage, or attempted to enforce its interpretation of the agreement by grievance procedure and arbitration. NBC continued to refuse additional payment for programs aired abroad, and on July 15, 1958, AFTRA filed a demand for arbitration. The following month, NBC filed a petition in court for stay of arbitration.

In its demand for arbitration, AFTRA not only claimed that all performers on the shows in question should be paid a sum equal to their original fee multiplied by the number of countries which had aired the program, but also asked for punitive damages prorated among AFTRA's performers on these shows. The demanded punitive damages included $1,000,000 each for the "Steve Allen Show," the "Dinah Shore Show," *and* the "Perry Como Show," and $250,000 each for the "Festival of Magic Show" and the "General Motor's 50th Anniversary Show," a total of $3,500,000.[12] NBC, in its motion to stay, claimed it had been distributing kinescopes of television programs overseas for many years and that this practice had never been considered to constitute "replay" under the AFTRA agreement, since the programs in question were aired within sixty days on stations where they had not previously been shown.[13] Furthermore, NBC pointed out that it had a clause in its standard individual engagement contract with performers which permitted worldwide use of the performer's product.[14]

After protracted discussions AFTRA and NBC reached an agreement on October 1, and AFTRA's demand for arbitration was withdrawn. Under the terms of this agreement, which was retroactive to September 1, 1958, certain talent covered by the AFTRA network agreement were to receive additional payments for the broadcast of recordings in foreign areas under the following provisions, which reflected the existing foreign sales and pricing patterns:

For broadcasts by one or more stations in area 1, which included the British Isles and Cyprus, 20 percent of the basic minimum appropriate program fees contained in the AFTRA network agreement (the code);

For broadcasts by one or more stations in area 2, which was designated as "Free Europe" and included Scandinavia, Western Europe and Austria, Yugoslavia, Albania, and Greece, 10 percent of the basic minimum appropriate program fee contained in the code;

For broadcasts by one or more stations in area 3, which was designated as "Africa" and included Madagascar, 5 percent of the basic minimum appropriate program fee contained in the code;

For broadcasts by one or more stations in area 4, which was designated as the "Far East" and included Australia, New Zealand, Japan, the East Indies and the adjacent islands, Burma, Malaya, Thailand, and Cambodia, 5 percent of the basic minimum appropriate program fees contained in the code;

For broadcasts by one or more stations in area 5, which was designated as "Latin America" and included Mexico, Central America, and South America, 5 percent of the basic minimum appropriate program fee contained in the code.[15]

Upon payment of 45 percent of the basic minimum appropriate program fee contained in the code, NBC could broadcast recordings in all of the foreign areas.

Several things should be noted about this agreement, which

was later inserted in the 1958 AFTRA television code and applied to all the networks and the entire industry.[16] First, no provisions were made for supplementary payments for any programs distributed in most of the Communist countries. The subject of communism had been a particularly sensitive one for AFTRA in the early fifties, and mention of Communist countries was avoided in the negotiation and, consequently, the agreement. It was only in the 1963 AFTRA code that such provisions were first included, although still in a rather indirect manner.[17]

Second, the percentage payments applied only to scale or slightly above scale performers. For star performers and other high contract players, the new agreement stated that AFTRA would not "influence such talent to obtain additional payments" but went on to state that "nothing in the Agreement precludes such talent from negotiating for such payments."

In practice, it became necessary to negotiate individual agreements with star performers, and this caused some immediate problems for NBC, particularly with respect to the "Perry Como Show." Certain performers refused to have their appearances shown abroad (sometimes because they feared that "overexposure" would reduce the success of their foreign personal appearances). This resulted in shows from which the performances of the nonconsenting artists had been cut. The situation became particularly acute in April, 1959, when four Como shows made available for overseas distribution had to be shortened because at least one major star in each program — Maureen O'Hara, Buddy Hackett, Julie London, or Fernandel — could not reach a satisfactory agreement with NBC.[18]

A third significant aspect of the NBC-AFTRA 1958 agreement was that no restriction was included on the number of times a program could be aired in any of the five areas after the network had made a payment for the first showing. During the negotiations on the agreement, the union strongly objected to the phrase "an unlimited number of times" that had been included in NBC's draft proposal. NBC representatives argued the importance to the networks of having unlimited uses, but agreed to the removal of the phrase on the understanding that AFTRA would not object to NBC's right to show the programs more than once.[19] This understanding is still in force, and there is no limitation in the present AFTRA code on the number of times a program can be aired in a foreign area. In fact, this same type of understanding has long been in force with other performers' unions involved with foreign residuals.

Fourth, there was no provision for additional payment for programs aired in Canada, United States possessions, and a few key affiliates in such places as Mexico City. In general, and uniformly with respect to Canada, this became the rule in the foreign provisions negotiated with other unions.

AFM Developments

In 1959, when its television live and video tape agreement expired, the American Federation of Musicians successfully negotiated the inclusion of provisions for domestic and foreign residuals. The foreign-use provisions were an almost exact replica of the AFTRA formula.[20] However, the federation has not negotiated a domestic or foreign residual structure covering film use. This is largely because the federation's early efforts in film agreements were concentrated upon obtaining 5 percent trust-fund payments for the sale of film programs, to provide free public concert opportunities for unemployed musicians. Later, after a stormy history of lawsuits and the temporary formation of a rival union (the Musicians Guild of America) in protest against the trust fund, the fund payments were scrapped for new programming; but instead of developing a residual system, the federation concentrated on limiting the use of "canned music," increasing the use of "live" musicians for scoring filmed programs, and as will be mentioned later in this chapter, stopping "runaway" film scoring.

The Satellite Influence

Following the negotiation of these agreements there was relative quiet on the subject of foreign use, until the appearance of satellites in 1963 caused renewed interest. In the 1963 AFTRA code, the section on supplementary payments for programs distributed overseas was titled "International Television," and provision was made to include payments, similar to those for recordings, for programs transmitted by satellite.[21] In addition, AFTRA negotiated into its agreement provisions to cover situations in which programs originating in this country would not be seen here but would only be shown by satellite overseas. The industry agreed to pay 75 percent of the applicable minimum network program fee, regardless of where and in how many countries the program was to be played.[22] Again, it was assumed that the payment was for unlimited use. If such programs were subsequently broadcast domestically over a network, the 75 percent would be increased to the full network rate. This concept of a 75 percent payment for programs shown overseas before being shown domestically was adopted by both DGA and AFM in subsequent agreements.

Up to this time, the amounts received by performers or other artists for the broadcast of programs overseas were not tied directly to the revenues that would accrue to the distributor from the sale of these programs. In the AFTRA and AFM network agreements, the geographic area in which the program was aired was the determining factor, and the compensation received by the artist was the applicable percentage of domestic scale. With respect to the dollar per country supplementary coverage provision in the WGA agreement, it was the number of countries buying the program that was to determine the payments to be made to the writer. And whenever a program was shown overseas and not shown domestically, a flat percentage of scale was to be paid under AFTRA, AFM, and DGA, regardless of how many countries or how many foreign stations aired the program and paid the distributor. The unions thus followed in the foreign market essentially the same minimum fee concepts that had been developed domestically: that is, a performer, writer, or director received the same scale for a network of two stations as for a network of two hundred stations.

The Royalty Concept

However, two other varieties of compensation formulas were derived in the 1960s. The pure royalty concept originated in the six-year WGA entertainment film agreement and met with only limited success, in the areas of both domestic and foreign residuals. The agreement provided that union members' compensation be related to a fixed percentage of the distributor's residual gross. Guaranteed minimum payments were thus foresworn in return for a share of the profits. The fixed percentage was set at 4 percent by a fact-finding commission which included representatives from the union, the industry, and an economic-survey firm.[23] "Distributor's residual gross" was defined in the 1960 film agreement to mean:

The absolute gross income (without deductions for commissions or any other items) of the distributors (including any sub-distributors and/or affiliated distributor) of television films from the world-wide television distribution thereof (including, in the case of a foreign territorial sale by any such distributor, the income received from such sale but not the income realized by his licensees).[24]

In subsequent negotiations for live-tape and documentary film programs, WGA negotiated the royalty concept for syndicated domestic and foreign programs while preserving its standard declining-percentage-of-minimum-fee pattern for domestic network repeats. WGA also retained in its live-tape agreement its foreign supplementary coverage concept for nonsyndicated programs, but moved from the dollar per country or per station formula to an AFTRA-like concept of geographic areas, with the world (including the Communist-bloc countries) divided into five areas. Payments of $10 to $25 per area were to be made, for use of the program within a limited period, depending upon where the program was to be shown; a payment of $75 gave the network world-wide rights.[25]

But the pure royalty concept was gradually abandoned by WGA in its subsequent negotiations. Apparently WGA found that the royalty provisions were difficult to administer, and probably brought the writers less money than they had received from the prior minimum-fee formulas. This was mainly because under the royalty formula no residual payment was due for the first repeat of a network program in the same broadcast season, provided this repeat was part of the "initial sale" of the program.

In WGA's most recent agreements for entertainment film television production, the guild negotiated a hybrid of the AFTRA and royalty concepts for foreign broadcasts, and returned to its old type of declining-guaranteed-percentage formula for domestic runs.[26] This hybrid is generally referred to as the SAG formula, since it first appeared in the 1964 SAG television agreement. A substantially similar formula was obtained by WGA in the recent live-tape and documentary film negotiations with the networks.

The SAG Formula

In the 1960 SAG theatrical motion picture agreements, SAG managed (after a major strike) to negotiate provisions for residuals for the sale of post-1960 movies to television. The residuals formula was based on a percentage of world-wide gross receipts received for the sale of these movies to the broadcasting medium.[27] And in the 1960 SAG commercials contract, negotiated jointly with the AFTRA video tape commercial code for the first time, a provision was made for separate payments for the foreign use of commercials.[28] SAG's emphasis upon obtaining residual payments for the showing of motion pictures on television delayed its entry into the marketplace for residuals for foreign distribution of filmed television programs. When it did make foreign residuals a major issue in the 1964 negotiations, it negotiated the principle of percentage of gross which had been included in its

1960 motion picture agreement and added the principle of a guaranteed percentage of scale.

The SAG formula provided that each performer (not just those at or slightly above scale as in the earlier AFTRA agreements) was to be paid a minimum of 15 percent of his total applicable minimum salary payment whenever a program was first shown in any foreign country. In addition, whenever the "distributor's foreign gross" (which was defined in almost identical terms with the "distributor's residual gross" in the WGA agreements) for the television film exceeded $6,000 for a half-hour program, or $12,000 for an hour program, the performer was to receive another 5 percent of his minimum salary payment. If the distributor's foreign gross exceeded $8,000 for a half-hour or $16,000 for an hour, the performer was to receive yet another 5 percent of his minimum salary payment, making a total of at least 25 percent. It was understood, as it had been in the AFTRA agreement, that negotiations for star performers would probably have to take place individually, and therefore it was stated in the agreement that "nothing herein shall preclude any player from bargaining for better terms with respect to such foreign telecasting." [29]

In 1967, SAG succeeded in increasing the supplementary compensation that would accrue to the performer if the distributor's gross reached the specified levels. For example, if an hour program grossed more than $12,000, the performer was to receive a minimum of 10 percent above the base compensation of 15 percent, instead of only 5 percent above that base. Similarly, if the gross exceeded $16,000 for an hour show, an additional 10 percent (instead of 5 percent) was added. Thus the performer could receive up to 35 percent of his minimum salary as foreign residual payments.[30] At the time this change was made, SAG's total yearly revenues for domestic and foreign residuals from television films was approaching $35 million, as opposed to $25 million from post-1960 theatrical films sold to television and $45 million from filmed television commercials. One estimate set the expected increase in foreign residuals that would accrue to SAG contract players from the 1967 increases outlined above, combined with the increases in television minimum salaries that were also negotiated, as high as 68 percent within two years.[31]

Although there undoubtedly will be an increase in the foreign residuals received by SAG performers from the sale of filmed television programs, it should be noted that the amount of money is still quite small when compared with that derived from domestic distribution. Even if the show does well overseas and is replayed several times by stations all over the world, the amount guaranteed to performers is roughly one-third of minimum scale. Anything above that amount must be negotiated on an individual basis, and for other than a star performer, this is rarely done.

On the other hand, it should also be emphasized that the amount of revenue that a distributor receives from the sale of a program overseas is quite small when compared with revenues received from domestic distribution, especially if such distribution takes place over a full national network. The "hottest" half-hour show still will bring in less than $25,000 per episode, even if sold in all the major foreign markets.[32] Therefore, while the total revenues accruing to performers from foreign residuals is small, it is not disproportionate to the payments made in the form of domestic residuals.

DGA

Although DGA had established a domestic residual structure in the middle 1950s comparable to those of the other guilds, it showed a curious lack of interest in the foreign market until its most recent negotiations in 1968 and 1969. In 1968 the DGA negotiated the SAG-type formula into its television film agreement with the Association of Motion Picture & Television Producers. The applicable percentages, however, are different than SAG's: 7.5 percent of minimum scale for the first showing of a program overseas, with the possibility of two additional 5 percent payments if the gross foreign revenue of the film reaches a certain figure, depending on the length of the film.[33] In 1970, these figures will escalate to the full SAG price of 15 percent of scale, with the possibility of two additional 10 percent payments, for a total of 35 percent.[34] In the recent DGA-Network negotiations for the live-tape and documentary film mediums, similar clauses were agreed upon.

These residuals are applicable only to directors. No payments are required for other categories represented by the guild, such as assistant directors, unit managers, and stage managers.

Other Developments

The total export market for filmed television programs increased considerably during the early sixties, but the market for tapes and kinescopes did not. In fact, as a percentage of the total product exported it decreased significantly during those years. At the 1966 AFTRA negotiations, the networks argued that a primary reason the tapes and kinescopes were not being shown abroad, especially those of variety shows, was the talent fees involved. AFTRA countered by saying that other factors were responsible for the decline in tape distribution: the cost of line conversion, duties, quotas, and so forth. There was no question, however, that the labor cost of the major source of tape product for the foreign market, the musical variety show, exceeded the cost of the usual film product, the adventure or comedy series. Musical variety shows require a large number of foreign payments to singers, dancers, and musicians, a burden not borne by the film episodes.

Despite the networks' claim that the reduced volume of tape distributed abroad hurt AFTRA as well as the networks, the new 1966 agreement raised the percentage of scale to be paid for a program aired in the United Kingdom from 20 to 25 percent.[35] This meant that in order to have world-wide distribution, the networks would have to pay every performer eligible for residuals at least 50 percent of scale, instead of the former 45 percent.

Foreign residual payments promise to be a major concern of

the industry in the years to come. AFM claimed residuals payments, but then abandoned the claim, in the recent television film negotiations; the issue could arise again, however, in the future. The Producers Guild, a new organization enjoying bargaining rights in the industry, has recently concluded a ten-year agreement with the theatrical and television film employers; residuals, however, are specifically excluded. Most serious, perhaps, could be any attempt by the craft and technical unions in the industry to extend the concept of residuals to their members. In their January, 1969, film negotiations, IATSE gave up only with reluctance, and at the very end of negotiating, a related demand for a share of gross receipts from the sale of motion picture or television productions. An industry strike would be almost guaranteed if residuals became an important objective of unions other than the five "talent" groups which have traditionally enjoyed the benefits of the residual payment scheme.

Interchange of Union Personnel across National Boundaries

In general, the unions representing performers, writers, and directors have refrained from negotiating provisions requiring that they be taken abroad to work on American-based productions. But while there are no requirements per se that the producers take such personnel abroad, the union agreements indicate that those hired in the United States and sent abroad are fully covered by their U.S. contracts and will be paid no less than the appropriate U.S. union scale. This has long been especially true of regular performers in "travelling shows" — shows which are normally produced and originated in one location in the United States, but which, on special occasions, go to other domestic areas or overseas.

If, when overseas, the producer hires foreign performers or employees who are members of foreign technical and craft unions, the contracts which apply to them are the domestic agreements which exist within their countries. American unions have not yet challenged this jurisdiction, nor has it been made a major issue in any negotiation.

In 1959, a major labor problem did arise over the question of whether a network should be required to take members of the appropriate technicians union (NABET in the case of ABC and NBC, IBEW in the case of CBS) when an American live-tape program travelled overseas. Before this time the question had never been resolved but had not caused much concern. Foreign originations were infrequent and the collective bargaining agreements were imprecise on the point. The potentialities of video tape, also, had not yet been realized.

In April, 1959, NBC decided to send its "Today Show" over to Paris to tape a week's programming. NABET, considering this to be of some consequence and anticipating an increase in pilgrimages abroad, demanded that its entire "Today" crew go to France and refused to accept an NBC offer to take a limited technical crew with it to Paris and to hire the remainder there. Despite a no-strike clause in the labor agreement, NABET called a nationwide strike on April 15 when NBC sought to play the Paris "Today" tapes from New York.

Within a month the strike was over and NABET's claim was lost. Hereafter, its video tape jurisdiction was specifically defined as limited to the continental United States.[36] Thus the network no longer had to be concerned about the matter of whether it would be forced to take any NABET personnel overseas. This limitation of jurisdiction was later incorporated in the NABET-ABC and IBEW-CBS agreements.[37]

The networks do, of course, continue to send members of the appropriate technical and craft unions overseas, either as partial or total crews. When members of IBEW or NABET are involved, the regular network agreements usually apply, including overtime, penalty payments, and so forth, although two or three years ago ABC occasionally worked out other arrangements with NABET for particular crews. The network agreements covering IATSE film cameramen and soundmen working on documentary and news film assignments have been waived, for work abroad, in favor of a flat weekly fee method of payment which does not provide for overtime and penalty payments. The IATSE contracts provide that the cameraman or soundman will be paid a flat weekly rate at roughly a 50 percent higher base than is provided for domestic work. Work on a sixth or seventh day overseas requires an additional one-fifth of the weekly rate for each such day worked.

The flow of American personnel overseas is not only limited by definitions of jurisdiction and considerations of cost, but is, in varying degrees, also limited by the governments and unions of the foreign countries. This is particularly true in the English-speaking countries where the threat of Americans taking jobs is considered to be most acute. The Association of Canadian Radio and Television Artists and the English unions and British Ministry of Labor have been able to make it difficult, especially for scale people, to work on American or other productions in those countries. An American performer with recognized special talent that is not easily duplicated may be more difficult to keep out; often the star is confined to a certain show within a fixed time period, or perhaps a director of photography is permitted on the set to advise but is not allowed to actually direct the shooting of the film.

In many of the non-English-speaking countries, the matter is simpler and more direct. The government can and often does settle the issue by government fiat. Sometimes this occurs after the government has received a petition from one of its unions to settle a specific matter. But sometimes it is done merely as part of a general governmental declaration of policy. On more than one occasion, a government has suddenly proclaimed that hereafter all shows produced in its country will have x number of native performers, x number of domestic union personnel, x percentage of national music, and so forth.

All this is not to suggest that American unions have accepted the foreign performer or technician with open arms. Broadcasting's performers' unions have not, as yet, gone to the extremes of limiting foreign talent that stage unions have (Actors Equity's recent contract provides that it can take to arbitration the case of any non-American who has been offered a role in an American production); that is, they have not attempted to negotiate in their contracts an express provision covering this question. But AFTRA and AFM in particular have frequently tried to "discourage" the United States immigration authorities from granting foreigners a work permit, as opposed to a normal travel visa. These permits are supposed to be granted only to persons of "distinguished merit and ability." In certain cases, as for example those of the English rock 'n' roll groups, the unions question the "distinguished merit" of the performers. Like the overseas unions who attempt to keep Americans off foreign television, American unions have been more successful in excluding scale performers than in excluding recognized stars.

"Runaway" Production

Unions have not been as worried about the "runaway" production of television programs as they have about that of movies, since fewer people have been involved. However, they have at times exerted the same pressures upon television producers as upon motion picture companies. In 1953 the AFL and Hollywood AFL Film Council brought pressure against the producers and sponsors of the programs "Foreign Intrigue" and "China Smith."[38] The pressures were successful and both shows, which had been filmed at overseas locations, soon left the air. At the same time, the council and the AFL launched an attack on the filming of television commercials overseas. All advertisers who had products advertised through films made abroad were contacted by mail. They were sent copies of a resolution against this practice which had been adopted by the American Federation of Labor at its September, 1952, convention and had also been adopted by the

Film Council, the California Theatrical Federation and the California State Federation of Labor.[39]

Of course, television filming overseas did not cease after 1953, and in recent years producers of a number of shows have filmed all or a portion of their series overseas, shows including "Rat Patrol," "Tarzan" and "Maya." This overseas filming is justified by the need for authentic backgrounds and scenes, as well as by salary-cost factors, particularly when large numbers of extras are necessary. Nor has the practice of making television commercials overseas halted; in fact in the early sixties the practice was quite common. But as a July, 1968, issue of *Television Age* points out, the practice of making commercials abroad is not as fashionable as it used to be, and usually if it is done, it is done for "conceptual reasons" rather than to save money.[40] Cost differentials have been reduced, and many ad men now claim that what may first seem "on paper" to be saved in salaries may be lost in time spent shooting. It is likely, therefore, that while SAG has announced that it will again look into the matter of making television commercials overseas and will doubtless pass new resolutions and have more meetings with all parties involved, no great new pressures upon advertisers and agencies will be forthcoming. Instead, attention will be directed toward the runaway production of movies, about which some meeting of the minds between the producers and the unions has already taken place.

One other type of runaway production has been of concern to the American Federation of Musicians. At one time there was an increase in runaway music scoring; AFM union scales were bypassed and AFM union members displaced by foreign musicians hired to score American movies and television programs. As a result, AFM negotiated provisions in its television film agreement and commercial jingles agreement which specify that the producer must have scoring done in the U.S. and Canada.[41] The practical effect of this clause is to guarantee that musical scoring for films and commercials will be done by AFM members.

International Labor Associations and Agreements

The importance of international labor associations in determining conditions and payments for programs produced and distributed, or merely distributed, overseas has been limited by several factors. These include international politics and political ideology, nationalism, self-interest of specific unions which may conflict with interests of other unions (even within the same country), and the fact that even if representatives of labor of different countries can agree on a policy or program, they must still convince their respective employers.

Considerations of politics and ideology affect both the composition of the international bodies that are established and the questions which these bodies will discuss. Most of the American unions severely limit their contact with international associations which they consider to be Communist controlled or influenced. Thus organizations like the International Federation of Musicians, the International Federation of Variety Artists, and the International Federation of Actors, all of whom have negotiated with the European Broadcasting Union a scheme of residual payments for programs broadcast across national boundaries in Europe, have not had firm agreements with American unions. In fact, those international bodies to which most of the American unions do belong limit themselves to non-Communist countries. Many American unions belong to the International Secretariat of Entertainment Trade Unions, which has its headquarters in Brussels and is affiliated with the International Confederation of Free Trade Unions. Many also belong to the Inter-American Federation of Entertainment Workers (FITE), which has its headquarters in Mexico City. American unions not only take an active part in these groups but also pay much of the cost of maintaining them. Neither of these international bodies has affiliates from Communist-bloc countries, although both include affiliates from countries where there are unions thought to have Communist leanings.

Politics, coupled with nationalism, also limits the issues which can be discussed when these organizations hold their meetings. The matter of bringing union scales in all countries up to the level of American scales, for example, might be a goal for which many members strive. While this matter might be discussed informally over drinks after official sessions have ended, it is unlikely that the delegate in open session would suggest that the American situation is best and urge that it be considered the ideal of the organization. Such an action would be considered very unpolitic and has never been done.

What these organizations do, largely, is to collect and circulate data and pass resolutions. For example, at the last FITE meeting it was resolved to send a resolution to the American governments recommending "that transmission through the new satellite (which permits live transmission throughout the hemisphere) does not result in detriment to established employment sources." In this same resolution, considerations of politics and nationalism were reflected by the statement that satellite transmission "should fundamentally involve news of world interest, conferences and sports in the interest of the artistic expression of each country." [42] In an accompanying resolution, all American governmental bodies were asked to provide live programs with actors and musicians for at least 40 percent of the program day in order that "the national cultural and artistic common property of each country" be defended.[43]

Perhaps the most sweeping resolutions on international broadcasting passed at an international labor conference were those passed in Stockholm in May, 1966. These resolutions, adopted by delegates from performers' unions of thirteen countries (including both SAG and AFTRA from the United States and representatives from Poland and Czechoslovakia from Eastern Europe) touch on many of the issues which may concern union performers in the future, as international broadcasting grows in significance. It should be noted that this conference, which resulted in so many agreements on policy, has been one of the few such conferences to include Communist countries. It should also be noted, however, that the delegates represented only performers [44] and that many of the more "delicate" problems regarding performers (for example, the matter of restricting foreign performers) were not discussed in any of the resolutions.

The Stockholm Conference resolutions that are relevant to the interests of this chapter include the following:

(1) If a film made for television is permitted to be exhibited in theatres, domestically or internationally, then the performers should have the right to negotiate additional remuneration, subject to minimum fees, appropriate to the new and separate exploitation of their work.

(2) With respect to instantaneous international transmissions (geotelecommunication) of live television performances transmitted by satellite between two or more countries in different land masses (as defined for world census purposes), received by television stations in such countries and then transmitted to television audiences, an international scale of minimum fees should be established for performers in all countries of origin of such programs. This scale should be based upon the length of the program and the number of television sets throughout the world. (This scale is not intended to apply to relays between countries within the same land mass, nor to existing arrangements for the exchange of programs in limited areas of the world, nor to expected extensions of such arrangements on a small scale.) The international scale of minimum fees should apply to all persons rendering professional services on and off camera in such programs. If an international program is recorded and transmitted later (unless for normal time delay reasons) performers appearing in television films and recorded programs should be paid additional compensation for the foreign use of their performances related to the expanded audience, the economic value of the use of their performances in the foreign country and the fees of performers employed in television programs in that country.

(3) In cases of "runaway productions," when a producer of television motion pictures or recorded programs, by removing his production activities to another country, seeks to evade any minimum rates or conditions, including residuals, which performers are entitled to receive under collective bargaining agreements in the producer's own country, producers will be required to observe the terms and conditions of the collective bargaining agreements sought to be evaded, unless the terms

and conditions in effect in the country of production are more favorable to the performers, in which event such more favorable terms and conditions will apply.

(4) Producers of television motion pictures and recorded programs made in another country should also be required to observe the terms and conditions of the collective bargaining agreements in their own country, unless the terms and conditions in effect in the country where such services are performed are more favorable to the performers, in which event such more favorable terms and conditions will apply.

(5) Producers of television commercials which are intended for exhibition in another country shall be required to observe the terms and conditions of collective bargaining agreements in effect in their own country with respect to the original employment unless the terms and conditions in the intended country of exhibition are more favorable, in which event the more favorable conditions will apply. With respect to residuals payable for the reuse of such commercials, the rate shall be that of the country of exhibition or, if no such rate exists, an appropriate rate shall be established.

(6) The dubbing of theatrical and television motion pictures, recorded programs and commercials, in another language for exhibition in other countries, shall require payment for the original engagement at the rate provided by the collective bargaining agreements of the country of origin, unless the terms and conditions of the country of exhibition are more favorable, in which case the more favorable rate shall apply to the employment. The same principles should apply when dubbing is undertaken in the original language specifically for another country.

(7) With respect to residuals, the rates of the country of exhibition shall apply unless no such rate exists, in which case an appropriate rate shall be fixed by the union in the country of origin.[45]

The Stockholm Conference of 1966 was really the successor to a similar conference of performers' unions held three years earlier. Some of the resolutions of the earlier conference, held at Toronto, were never effectively implemented because of the self-interest of the unions involved. For example, there was a resolution passed in 1963 which supported the right of Canadian performers to work in the United States and of American performers to work in Canada. The attempts to control and sometimes prevent such interchange have not been visibly affected by the resolution.

It is unlikely that the 1966 Stockholm resolutions will ever be completely effective because of an additional limitation on the effectiveness of international labor associations. Any resolutions which these associations pass regarding changes in management practices must, as is true of all such labor resolutions, have the support (reluctant and belated as that support may be) of management, to become meaningful.

The Future

Many American distributors acknowledge that the profit margin from the sale of American television programs in the foreign market is being reduced. Unlike the period in the late fifties and early sixties when sales were increasing by as much as 15 to 20 percent each year, the prices for most programs have stabilized in the most significant markets, including the United Kingdom, Germany, Canada, and to a slightly lesser extent, Australia and Japan.[46] The increases in sales which do occur are largely being offset by higher distribution and selling costs.

The foreign market is now a buyer's market. The number of programs available for import has increased. Meanwhile local production is growing in most countries, sometimes because the government requires it, sometimes because the stations or the audience desire it, and sometimes because the country in question cannot afford the cost of buying overseas productions, particularly American.

Although some American television programs which are extremely popular in this country are difficult if not impossible to sell in certain areas abroad, feature films are in increasing demand. As countries begin to loosen their restrictions on showing such features on television (England, for instance, has recently allowed feature films) and the supply of films is gradually reduced, the demand for the films made will probably continue to grow.

However the distribution of live-taped-kinescoped programs

continues to be an even smaller percentage of the foreign market, both from the point of view of revenue and of program hours. NBC Enterprises, which distributes NBC's live-tape programming to more than eighty countries, estimates that only 10 percent of its non-news programming sold overseas is live-taped material. And if news (which includes sports broadcasts such as "Baseball's Game of the Week," distributed in South America on kinescope) is incorporated in the figures, less than 6 percent of its distribution revenues come from live-taped-kinescoped programming. Indeed, NBC is selling far less taped material today than it sold ten years ago.

There is some expectation that the increased use of satellites may increase the amount of live-taped programming shown in foreign markets. But there is also much caution regarding this prospect. Besides the problems of time differentials, cost, language, and cultural differences (which have been mentioned earlier in this chapter), there are other technical innovations that might reduce the prospect for the regular use of satellites. The supersonic jet, for example, will make it possible to travel "faster than the clock" and actually show a program at an earlier hour in New York than it was originally shown in Paris.

There is also the development of the electronic video recording technique, which might supplement video tape (as well as result in major jurisdictional battles between AFTRA and SAG, and among the craft unions). And finally, home video recorders and video records, although expensive and still in their experimental stages, may be of unimaginable ultimate consequence in affecting the foreign market and the nature of the distribution of programs across boundaries.

In the meantime, satellites are being increasingly used to distribute programs, but the number and variety of programs is still very limited. News, sports, and an occasional political event of world interest have largely been the satellite fare thus far. Yet one problem has already arisen. Many countries are willing to acknowledge distribution rights for such programs as "Meet the Press" and will pay license fees, as well as the fees for the use of the satellite, to carry those programs. Countries are often much less willing to pay license fees for carrying what they consider "hard news," such as the inauguration of the President of the United States. The problem comes in defining what is "hard news."

Various countries showed kinescopes of tapes made by the networks at the time of the assassination of Senator Robert Kennedy. These countries readily paid for the kinescopes which were mailed to them. Had the same tapes been distributed by satellite, these countries might not have been willing to make license payments for them. This type of problem will have to be solved when satellites are used on a more regular basis. Another problem will come from the rebroadcasting of programs by one station simultaneously in many languages. (Who, for instance, would have rerun rights?)

For the present, there are more immediate and more urgent problems that face broadcasting unions. It is likely that no startling change in union policies or union agreements covering the foreign market will be forthcoming in the very near future.

NOTES

1. *Broadcasting*, July 21, 1969, p. 19.
2. The material in this section is based upon the records of the Television Program Export Association, Inc., and upon interviews with executives of NBC's international enterprises department.
3. 1941–43 AFTRA Code of Fair Practice for Transcriptions and Recordings for Radio Broadcasting Purposes, article 5, section 7; 1966–69 National Code of Fair Practice for Transcriptions for Broadcasting Purposes, article 6, section 45.
4. 1952–54 Television Network Freelance Directors Agreement, article 5(e). The RTDG (Radio and Television Directors Guild) merged with the DGA in 1961.
5. 1956–58 AFTRA National Code of Fair Practice for Network Television Broadcasting, article 73(b).

6. 1951–54 AFM National Television Agreement, article 4(b)iii.
7. 1955 WGA Television Freelance Minimum Basic Agreement, article 7(b).
8. *Ibid.*, article 2(e).
9. WGA-NBC Letter Agreement of June 3, 1957.
10. WGA Letter Agreement with ABC, CBS, and NBC, April 1, 1958.
11. Letter from Donald Conaway, AFTRA executive secretary, to NBC, dated December 3, 1957. Earlier publicity had been given to probable complaints; e.g., *Variety*, November 27, 1957.
12. Exhibits B–F of Demand for Arbitration, July 15, 1958.
13. Petition for Stay of Arbitration, August 4, 1958, pp. 3, 6.
14. *Ibid.*, pp. 8–10.
15. AFTRA-NBC Letter Agreement of October 1, 1958.
16. 1958–60 AFTRA National Code of Fair Practice for Network Television Broadcasting, article 73(f).
17. 1963–66 AFTRA Television Code, article 73(f).
18. April 4, O'Hara; April 11, Hackett; April 18, London; and April 25, Fernandel.
19. NBC memo dated September 2, 1958.
20. 1959–64 AFM National Radio and Television Agreement, article 7.
21. 1963–66 AFTRA Television Code, article 73(f)a1.
22. *Ibid.*, article 73(f)a2.
23. 1960 WGA-Networks Television Film Freelance Minimum Basic Agreement, article 20(w).
24. *Ibid.*, article 20(w)2.
25. WGA-Networks Letter Agreement, October 1, 1965.
26. Memorandum Agreement, 1966 WGA Television Film Freelance Negotiations, exhibit f, paragraph 3.
27. Producer–Screen Actors Guild, Inc., Memorandum Agreement of 1960, Theatrical Motion Pictures, article 2.
28. Screen Actors Guild 1960 Commercials Contract, article 18.
29. 1964 SAG Television Agreement, article 14(c)8.
30. 1967 SAG Television Agreement, article 15(c).
31. *Television*, November, 1967, p. 45.
32. E.g., "Get Smart" grossed less than $25,000 during its first year.
33. Summary of 1968 DGA Negotiations by Association of Motion Picture and Television Producers, Inc., September 4, 1968, p. 2.
34. *Ibid.*
35. 1966–69 AFTRA Television Code, article 73(f)b3.
36. Settlement Agreement of May 15, 1959, paragraph 4; now paragraph 16(4) of Stipulation of Agreement, NABET-NBC Master Agreement, 1967–70.

37. 1967 ABC-NABET Agreement, p. 191; 1966 Agreement, CBS, Inc., and IBEW, section 1.04(4).
38. *Daily Variety*, February 4, 11, 1953.
39. Resolution on Foreign Production of Motion Pictures by American Producers adopted at the American Federation of Labor's seventy-first convention, September, 1952.
40. "Who Said It's Cheaper Overseas?" *Television Age*, July 15, 1968, pp. 26–27, 54–55.
41. AFM Basic Television Film Agreement of 1942, article 3. Exceptions to these scoring requirements are provided for news and documentary programs produced by the networks.
42. *Official Publication of the Inter-American Federation of Entertainment Workers*, May–June, 1968, p. 7.
43. *Ibid.*
44. Representatives from WGA, attending a nearby conference, did sit in on some sessions of this conference.
45. Resolutions of the Scandinavian Actors Council Conference on Actors and International Television, Stockholm, May 23–25, 1966.
46. According to *Broadcasting*, July 21, 1969, p. 20, the 1969 price ranges for American one-hour programs are: United Kingdom, $6,000–$7,000; Germany, $5,000–$6,000; Canada, $5,000–$6,000; Australia, $3,200–$4,000; Japan, $5,000.

8 The Creative Artist's Problems

by EVELYN F. BURKEY

The guilds representing creative artists in the broadcasting industry deal, as do other unions, with grievances, disputes, wages, hours, and conditions of work. The basics are the same. The differences are many and varied.[1]

The talent guilds function as collective bargaining representatives in an industry where the talent and professional standing of the individual artist are more determinative of his compensation and working conditions than is the guild's basic agreement establishing minimums. It is usual for his services to be covered by an individual contract between him and his employer as well as by the collective bargaining agreement between his guild and his employer. The individual contract may contain provisions more favorable to the artist than the collective bargaining agreement; it may not contain less favorable terms, nor provisions in conflict with the basic agreement.

A creative artist cannot match his individual bargaining power against corporate might. This is true even of top talent who seem able to dictate their own terms. At key points, usually involving ownership rights and creative control, "company policy" is invoked as a barrier to individual negotiation.

It is necessary for the guilds to set the basic structure of protection: to set minimums in areas in which the artist is presumed to have some individual bargaining power, to set maximums in those areas where the employer would otherwise, through bargaining power or special knowledge, be able to dictate terms to the individual artist.

Basic agreements in the talent fields must provide creative as well as economic protection. Provisions concerning professional prerogatives and standing vary in detail among the agreements, but have in common the elimination of conditions which adversely affect the creativeness of the individual artist or the full expression of his talent. Economic protection involves minimums to be paid, both initially and for subsequent or subsidiary uses, the amount or type of services or time periods within which they may be required, time and method of payment, etc. In the agreements covering the employment of writers, there are also provisions for reversion or termination of exclusivity in the material, reservation of certain rights to the writer, ownership of copyright, warranties, and indemnities. The requirement to give program credit to the artist is found in all the agreements.

All the agreements provide for grievance and arbitration machinery, union recognition and security, notice, necessary technical or legal requirements, and a no-strike, no-lockout clause. At least two of the talent guilds have a special modification of the no-strike clause to protect the individual artist and the guild when the term of the individual contract runs beyond the termination date of the basic agreement and the guild has issued a strike order.

The guilds have various agreements covering employment on a staff basis, but the differences in problems faced by the individual artists and their respective guilds are best illustrated by a look at freelance employment and the freelance agreements. It is also true that in the broadcasting industry the highest percentage of employment of artists is freelance.

Freelance employees constitute an employment pool both industrially and nationally. The freelance agreements are national in scope and negotiated on an industry basis. Freelance employment takes several forms. An artist may be hired by a single employer for a single engagement. He may during a given period have single engagement contracts with several different employers. He may work under a term contract for a single employer or, perhaps simultaneously, under a term contract with one employer and single engagement contracts with others. He may have a contract covering multiple engagements. It is not unusual to have his contract call for the performance of multiple services. Many artists are active across craft lines, as actor-director, actor-writer, director-producer, writer-producer, or other combination.

Given these circumstances of employment, the guilds have negotiated provisions covering exclusivity of services, length of term contracts, exercise of options, and cancellation rights. Where multiple services are to be performed, the agreements have protective clauses to prevent undercutting of minimums by crediting or offsetting of payments.

The problem of exclusivity arises at the time of employment, when the employer seeks the greatest possible protection against other employers who may be in the market for the artist's services. He wants to maintain maximum flexibility in his efforts to attract a sponsor and thus demands protection against potential conflicts. His greatest concern is with term contracts. This type of contract can also present the greatest difficulties for the artist.

On the whole, term contracts are more to the advantage of the employer than the artist. The prospect of a regular income over a fixed period can be an attractive one, but it must be considered in the light of clauses in the artist's contract which provide for options (which may or may not be exercised) and various cancellation rights, most of which refer to factors not within the control of the artist but to a greater or lesser extent within the control of the employer. Meanwhile, exclusivity provisions of the contract have curtailed his freedom to seek other employment.

Special exclusivity problems exist with respect to "pilots." [2] What is the artist to do between the time the pilot is made and the option for his services is exercised? At what point can he be sure that the option will not be exercised — that the pilot has been permanently shelved or abandoned? Obviously the employer's interest is in ensuring continuing availability of the artist's services and avoiding potential sponsor conflicts.

Exclusivity problems continue to exist both for the artist and for the guilds. Although certain restrictions giving some degree of protection have been established in the basic agreements, further steps still have to be taken. In substance, existing provisions require that the period of exclusivity must relate directly to the period of employment, be limited in time as to sponsor conflict, provide for notice to the artist, and be restricted (in most cases) to rendition of services in the broadcasting field. When the artist's name has "marquee value" and the pay is high, the restrictions in the agreement are generally less rigorous.

For many years, the basic agreements negotiated by all the talent guilds have provided for pay for the original use, or performance, and for additional pay for subsequent use, or for use in other media. Artists count on receiving this contingent compensation as part of the total compensation for their services and find such payments especially helpful when they have no current assignments.

In earlier days of live television, recordings were frequently made and the artist did receive some additional compensation, but only rarely would other uses be made of the kinescope. Therefore subsidiary-use pay existed as a source of income generally only for the writers whose material could be licensed for use in other media. With the growth of film television, the use of recordings increased and so did the artist's income from each program. His total income, however, did not necessarily increase. With a better quality of recording, wider distribution, more reruns, he found he was often in competition with himself in terms of reruns versus new engagement possibilities. Payments for subsequent use are lower than those for initial use, and reuses of an old program do not carry with them the possibility of future income that new programs do. The availability of recordings has at times been a concern for the guilds in terms of the effectiveness of a strike, should one become necessary to achieve bargaining objectives. Based on the experience of one of the guilds during a protracted strike in 1960, however, recordings appear to be acceptable to sponsors and audiences during short periods of reuse but not over long periods of time.[3]

The approaches taken by the talent guilds to the problems created by recordings have not been the same. In some instances, specific uses are prohibited, or allowed only with the permission of the appropriate guild and after agreement has been reached on compensation and conditions governing them. Some agreements provide for royalty payments for certain uses, the percentage to be computed on the amount received by the employer from such exploitation (net, or gross, or adjusted gross). Others call for payments of specific percentages of the minimum compensation applicable to the initial use or performance.

As has been pointed out earlier, the artist depends on residual or subsidiary-use payments as a means of earning his livelihood. Neither production nor distribution is guaranteed in the collective bargaining agreement, although there are various requirements involving cancellations or preemptions. In the basic agreements covering writing services, there are provisions for reversion of rights in the event of nonproduction or nonbroadcast, for exclusive rights to become nonexclusive after a set period of time, and for subsidiary rights to be reserved to the writer for his use either immediately, or after a certain period of time or the broadcast, or if the employer does not exercise his options.

Having achieved in their collective bargaining agreements these requirements for additional compensation to the artist, the guilds were faced with an additional problem: the insertion of provisions in the individual contract of employment which allowed the employer to prepay, credit, or reallocate any compensation in excess of the initial-use minimums. The typical minimum set forth in a talent guild agreement is considerably below the "going rate" or "established salary" or "above minimum deal" which the individual artist can obtain, unless he is truly a beginner professionally. Outright prohibition of prepayment is to be found in some agreements, but this is not an appropriate resolution in all cases. Another approach had been to provide that prepayments may be made only with monies in excess of the minimum — double minimum for example, or above a specified amount. Some progress has been made, but the problems are a long way from being solved.

Also a long way from solution is the problem of credits. Credits are important to the artist as recognition of his artistic contribution, and also in economic terms. It is expected that he wants to be identified with his artistic contribution. It is also acknowledged in the broadcasting industry that the artist's professional standing and bargaining power are a reflection of his credits. The actual credit (screen in television, audio in radio) is of value. Its placement relative to other credits has meaning in the industry. It keeps the artist before the eyes of the industry, if not the public eye, where his contribution can be observed by those who are potential employers. The form of the credit and whether it is shared with others may determine the amount which will be paid to the artist for residual uses.

Provisions in the basic guild contracts governing credit requirements, including form and placement, vary considerably. In some agreements the credit provisions are relatively simple; in others, the provisions are complicated, numerous, and lengthy. They have in common, though, that they were achieved in the face of strenuous opposition by the employers. Even today there are employers who are reluctant to give credit or to give it in a meaningful way. Most would like to have complete freedom to negotiate the giving of credit as a part of their bargaining with the individual artist. Having the time available for commercials or promotional announcements also is appealing to them. Some admit to a reluctance to contribute to the enhancement of an artist's reputation and thereby his bargaining power. The manner in which credits are sometimes given poses a continuing problem: with music or a voice-over announcement distracting the viewer; screen credits superimposed on a background which swallows them; crawl credits given at too great a speed for them to be readily identifiable.

Since provisions pertaining to creative aspects must relate to the specific type of artistic contribution covered by the basic agreement, it is not possible to generalize in this area. Further, as will be noted from the following examples, the provisions frequently define the relationship between or among the various production elements.

For the director, it is important that he maintain creative control over the production. From a national network agreement:

It is recognized that the functions and duties of Directors are of a professional creative and responsible character.

The Company shall take all steps which in its opinion are reasonable and are within the framework of the Company policies and methods to support the authority of the Director with respect to the direction of the rehearsal and performance of each commercial or sustaining program for which he is employed.

Within such policies the Company shall recognize that during rehearsal periods, the direction of the component parts of the production shall be the responsibility of the Director, and any changes or suggestions shall be made to the Director; and the Company shall aid the Director by refusing admittance to persons not authorized by them to the studio and control room or the control site at remote location during rehearsal and performance.[4]

From a basic film agreement:

The Director shall be entitled to prepare his cut of the film (hereinafter referred to as the "Director's Cut") for presentation to the individual producer, and, if the individual producer shall not have final cutting authority over the picture, then also to such person or persons as shall have the final cutting authority over the picture; provided, however, that the Director of a television motion picture shall be entitled to prepare such Director's Cut for presentation as set forth above only if so requested by him prior to the close of principal photography. . . .

When the Director's Cut is ready, the Director shall screen such cut for the individual producer or such other person or persons referred to above and shall during such screening be entitled to make such recommendations or suggestions for further changes in the final cut as the results of such screening may indicate.[5]

It is apparent from these excerpts alone, and would be clearly shown by a full reading of the agreements, that the employer has ringed this creative control with various limitations protective of what he regards as his own right to final authority.

With respect to writers, the employer may require them to rewrite under his supervision and control, may assign others to rewrite the material, or may require the writer to collaborate with another writer. This absolute authority over the writer and his material has been somewhat modified in various negotiations. Also now ensured is the writer's right to be present at rehearsals.

The "live" television agreement provides:

> If the Company determines that material written by an Employee requires rewriting, the Company shall give to said Employee the opportunity to do the first rewrite, unless, after reasonable efforts to give reasonable notice, he is not available. The Company may require the Employee to do a total of two rewrites, but not more than two without his consent. Anyone other than the said Employee whom the Company designates to rewrite the material shall have had prior professional writing experience in the entertainment, literary or journalistic fields or editorial experience in any visual entertainment field. In the event of any rewriting the rights of the Company in the material so rewritten shall not be greater than they would have been if all such rewriting had been done by the first Employee. Where any such rewriting is done by a production executive or supervisory employee for a program in connection with which he performs in such capacity, the rights of the first Employee in said material so rewritten shall be the same as they would have been if all such rewriting had been done by the first Employee.[6]

The problems faced by the writer are evident from the specific items of protection. They are similarly clear from the provision for attendance at script conferences and rehearsals, as contained in the television film agreement:

> It is mutually recognized that a writer is a creative and professional employee and that the presence of the writer at script conferences and rehearsals, dealing with material prepared or written by him,

normally will be of mutual benefit to the writer and to the Producer. At the writer's request the Producer shall give the writer reasonable advance notice of such conferences and rehearsals. However, it is understood that the Producer shall have the right, in its sole discretion, in any particular case, to determine who will be present at such conferences and rehearsals. The writer's discussions at conferences and rehearsals attended by him shall be restricted to material prepared or written by him, and he shall not carry on such discussions with anyone other than the Producer or director of the program, or their designees. No compensation shall accrue to the writer by virtue of any such attendance.[7]

These creative and economic problems cannot be expected to disappear completely with the execution of the collective bargaining agreement. There still remains the matter of enforcement. Here again many of the problems and difficulties encountered by artist and guild alike stem from the use of recordings. Take, for example, the matter of payment for residual or subsidiary uses.

At the time of his employment, the artist cannot always be certain of the identity of his actual employer. He may not be able to determine it until he signs the individual contract of employment. Even his agent, who may have taken care of all the business aspects of the assignment, may not be certain. For one thing, it is commonplace in the broadcasting industry for the individual contracts of employment for artists not to be executed until sometime after the assignment has been undertaken, and it is not at all unusual for the delivery of the contract to follow the broadcast of the production. The picture is complicated by coproduction or cofinancing arrangements, as well as by the possibility that the deal between a packager and his coproducer may give initial broadcast rights to one of them and syndication or subsidiary rights to the other. Individual contracts of employment permit the employer to assign the contract. He may also license specific uses without assigning the entire contract. Recordings can be licensed for various separate uses: network, or syndication; domestic or foreign. The licenses may be to the same or to different licensees.

To cope with these problems, the guilds have negotiated various provisions that require payments to be transmitted through the respective guild offices, the keeping of records, and the right of each guild to have the records inspected, or audited where warranted. The volume of payments and the need to police foreign as well as domestic uses have made the use of the computer as essential to the guilds as it is to many of the large corporations with whom they have agreements.

Obtaining agreement from the employers to compensate the artist for foreign uses of the production to which he contributed his services took years of effort. Administering the foreign-use provisions has been neither cheap nor easy, and the artists and their guilds see the need for further improvement in the conditions pertaining to foreign use. Of more vital concern to many of them now, though, is the threat to their employment posed by "runaway" production. The severity of the threat is not equal for all the talent groups. Writers, directors, and actors have frequently gone on location even to a foreign country. It is rare, however, for all those normally associated with a production to go abroad. Where coproduction or cofinancing arrangements have been made in foreign countries which have quotas or subsidies, it may be that no one in these talent groups will find employment.

The efforts of the guilds to meet this challenge to the employment of the artists they represent have been twofold. On the one hand, they have tried to keep production here. Alone or as part of committees of guilds and unions, they have had conferences with the employers, have sought public support through press releases and public appearances, and have sought legislative relief on both the state and federal level. The other avenue of approach followed by some of the guilds has been to participate in the formation of international confederations or committees. Working together with talent guilds of other countries, they have attempted to work out international standards and conditions which would lead to improvements for artists throughout the world. Given such improvement, the "cheap labor" incentive would be removed and the employer presumably would resort to foreign production only when desirable in terms of artistic values.

On an international scale, the talent guilds in many countries are also concerned with developments which could result in a diminution of the protections afforded the artist through copyright laws. Proposed revisions to domestic laws as well as changes in some provisions of international conventions would expand the areas in which the artist's material, or performance, or the recording of the production, could be used without the requirement of payment to the artist or the production company. The proponents of these changes seek to justify them on the basis that cultural achievements should be freely available, since their main purpose is educational rather than profit making. The guilds point out that "fair use" has always permitted use for educational purposes where the circumstances warrant. They further point out that the artist earns a livelihood through the cumulation of earnings from a number of sources, many in relatively small amounts, as evidenced by the collective bargaining agreements.

It is recognized by the artists and their guild representatives that the fight in this arena is of a psychological as well as an economic nature. Without thinking through the problem of how an artist is going to live if he does not receive compensation for his talent and efforts, many people expect him to place little or no monetary value on his services. The publicity given to the pay of some top artists has led many people to believe that all artists receive such pay. In fact, many artists do not average more than a few thousand dollars a year.

The problems arising from satellite transmissions are under study now by copyright experts and by the talent guilds. As greater use is made of satellites and there is further scientific development in transmitting and receiving, problems arising from unauthorized use without payment to the artist can be anticipated. As the use of recordings expanded, the guilds bargained for provisions under which they would be able to follow the recordings and secure payment for their use. Satellite transmission may supplant the use of recordings for most purposes, and new provisions will be necessary, both in copyright laws and in collective bargaining agreements, to ensure payment to the artist of initial compensation as well as compensation for subsequent or subsidiary uses.

Home recording equipment, now mostly in the experimental or early developmental stage, poses another problem. What will be the effect on residual income if reruns decline because the home audience has made its own recordings to be replayed when and as often as desired? Video recordings in the form of cassettes or cartridges, which would be sold directly to the public in much the same manner as phonograph records, also could eliminate or diminish the rerunning of programs. This factor will have to be taken into consideration in determining what compensation the artist should receive for this use of his program.

Neither the individual artist nor his guild can provide all the answers to these anticipated problems. They serve to illustrate, however, the underlying factor which the guilds must consider in all their collective bargaining activities. In the short run, they must find a solution to current problems and grievances. They must, however, keep in mind the long-term goals and make sure that interim solutions follow the same course or at least do not create obstacles along the way. These considerations have guided the guilds in their attempts to improve and protect the artist's pay, both initial and residual, to gain for him sufficient creative control to permit full expression of his talent, to limit exclusivity provisions which might curtail such expression, and to ensure that he be given appropriate credit for his endeavors.

NOTES

1. *Creative artists* is used here to mean actors, directors, and writers, represented for collective bargaining purposes in the broadcasting industry by the American Federation of Television and Radio

Artists and the Screen Actors Guild; the Directors Guild of America, Inc.; and the Writers Guild of America, East, Inc. and the Writers Guild of America, West, Inc. (jointly, WGA). *Broadcasting industry* is used in its widest sense to mean all who employ talent for programs intended for broadcasting; it therefore includes independent producers and motion picture companies.

2. *Pilot* is the term used to identify a program exhibited by the producer to networks, advertising agencies, or other potential buyers for the purpose of selling a series or securing air time. In some instances it is commissioned or cofinanced by the prospective buyer.

3. The strike was that of the Writers Guild of America against independent television producers and motion picture companies, January–June, 1960.

4. 1965–1968 DGA–Network TV Network Free Lance Directors Agreement, p. 34.

5. Directors Guild of America, Inc. Basic Agreement of 1964, pp. 15, 17.

6. 1965 WGA Television Freelance Minimum Basic Agreement, pp. 74–75.

7. Writers Guild of America 1960 Television Film Basic Agreement (ATFP-Independent), pp. 38–39.

9 The Technical Union's Problems

by ROBERT A. LENIHAN
and TIMOTHY J. O'SULLIVAN

The environment in which the broadcast technician-engineer works today is hostile to his chances of successfully continuing to earn his living within it and yet, paradoxically, one that sometimes holds out a promise that he may be able to expand his role as a secure, artistic, and creative employee. Whether or not he plays an expanded role in radio and television, or is reduced to being only a dial twister and button pusher, can be largely determined by the actions of his unions and the course they take in the next decade. This is not to state that the unions are the only factor in the complicated future that lies before the technician-engineer, or even, at this point, a very important factor. However, the unions represent the only completely "sympathetic" ground on which the technician-engineers can stand to view the problems that face them. We will make some brief descriptive comments about these unions, some more critical ones about the industry in which they function, describe the dimensions of the quandary broadcast technician-engineers face, and make some suggestions as to how best they can resolve the problem of remaining productively employed in the radio and television field notwithstanding the impact of automation.

The two main technical unions in broadcasting, the National

Association of Broadcast Employees and Technicians, and the broadcast division of the International Brotherhood of Electrical Workers, although composed in their majority of technicians, represent such diverse occupational groups in the industry as newswriters, radio producers, film editors and cameramen, newswriter-producers, artists, stage managers, continuity overseers, traffic and communication employees, switchboard operators, pages, etc., etc. The third technical union in television, the International Alliance of Theatrical Stage Employes and Moving Picture Operators of the United States and Canada, has only a minor role in broadcasting, and is largely concerned with employees in motion picture production and projection.

NABET was formed in 1933 (under the name of the Association of Technical Employees, which it used until 1940), by engineering employees of the National Broadcasting Company, and remained independent until 1951. Looking then for organizational ties that would strengthen its hand in negotiations and give it support on the flanks from the periodic raids made by competitive unions, the membership voted to affiliate with the Congress of Industrial Organizations. The question of "vertical" as against "horizontal" organization was still at issue between the CIO and the rival American Federation of Labor, and NABET consciously chose verticalism and the structural changes that choice would necessitate in the union.[1] Wanting to keep the shortened form of its name (NABET), and yet anxious to signal its intention to organize outside of the engineering category, the union dropped the word *Engineers* from its title and substituted *Employees*. Shortly thereafter structural forms used in the CIO were adopted. The more genteel *chapter* used to describe a section of the organization gave way to *local*, the title *chapter chairman* was changed to the more aggressive *local president*, etc. More importantly, the union, with its newly adopted vertical policy, moved more deliberately to organize all the unorganized radio and television employees from top to bottom.

The efforts met with some success, and so at this time the union represents varying occupations, some of which we have listed.

The radio and television section of the IBEW had its genesis at about the same time as NABET, and a development that differed somewhat from NABET's because the IBEW was at that time an affiliate of the AFL (the AFL and CIO were still separate and rival) and committed to a horizontal, or craft, type of organization. The strictly craft structure of the IBEW, as well as of the parent AFL, was modified somewhat in the course of the competition between the AFL unions and the rival CIO, so that the Radio and Television Workers (IBEW) does represent some occupational classifications other than engineers.

It has already been pointed out that the American Federation of Television and Radio Artists and NABET are the only two unions of the many that are connected with the broadcasting industry whose origins and growth have been solely in the radio and television field. The IBEW had electrical wiring and manufacturing as its base. The IATSE had the motion picture industry as its starting point and main area of development. Moreover, the others involved in broadcasting — actors, producers, writers, directors, and musicians — came from the movies, the legitimate theatre, vaudeville, and their unions came with them. NABET and AFTRA were created, first in radio and then in television, by the men and women engaged in these industries who realized that new unions were needed to meet the new and unique problems generated by these art forms. And so, we will refer to NABET when it is necessary for the sake of example, but hope that our remarks will apply in general to all technical-engineering workers in the industry.

The transmission of sound and picture signals through the atmosphere in a form that allows them to be reconverted by a home receiver into recognizable music, talk, or images is so complicated that the phenomenon deserves to be termed miraculous. Nonetheless, the state of broadcasting technology is such that the generation, modulation, and transmission of the broadcast signal can be performed with a minimal use of human hands. Because the industry is an electronic one, it lends itself to the elimination of human control by the substitution of automated devices for that control. By the use of these sophisticated devices the broadcasting equipment will more or less faithfully reproduce at the receiver what was put into it at the originating studio, or at points in between, with the use of little or no manpower. Thus it appears that the need for the operating technician-engineer will gradually disappear as electronic devices become more refined. (Because complicated electronic devices are more difficult to keep operating efficiently, and are harder to repair when they fail, the technician-engineer who is skilled in maintenance and repair is less threatened by job insecurity than his colleagues who are engaged in the operations of the broadcasting "machine.") However, the complete elimination of the operating technician-engineers is not yet on the agenda, and the reasons for this are varied and complicated. Among them are the FCC rules, the state of the broadcasting art, the technician-engineers' unions, and the realization by some that the technician-engineer can play an increasingly important role in the creative and artistic aspects of television.

But to visualize some of the serious problems facing technical-engineering workers today it is necessary to take a quick look at radio and television.

Early in the development of radio broadcasting it was recognized that it was necessary to make rules and codify regulations to control the indiscriminate transmission of sound waves. Otherwise, it became apparent, the available ethereal avenues would be jammed with cross-talk and unwanted sound, and the home receivers would be unable to select one program which would be clear of interference from others. Congress created the Federal Communications Commission and charged it with setting up rules to keep the air waves clear, and in general to oversee broadcasting and its development. An important part of its task was to monitor the spectrum so that it would not be used by one broadcaster either to the detriment of other broadcasters or the listening public. Strict engineering criteria were established, as was a rule that broadcasters "log" certain meter readings that reflected the performance of the transmitter. These readings allowed the FCC to police adherence to the criteria. Because of these FCC requirements, and because the broadcast equipment was relatively unsophisticated by present-day standards, it was necessary to man the transmitters during the broadcast hours. Maintenance on the transmitters was performed when the equipment was "off the air." As the broadcasting equipment was refined and improved the broadcasters saw the possibility of reducing costs by substituting automated controls for the transmitter "watches." The technician-engineers and their unions resisted this move and began amassing ammunition for their fight.

The transmitter engineer, they argued, is the stable element in a somewhat unstable system which should be continually monitored by man. He is available to make adjustments and repairs, they reasoned, if the broadcast pattern changes or the transmitter fails. The unions polled their members for information and developed statistics on breakdowns and "outages." These figures, the unions contended, showed a substantial number of emergency situations at transmitters, enough to warrant the retention of the transmitter engineers. These arguments were presented to the FCC and that body took them under advisement, along with the employers' arguments that electrical control devices were so advanced that the transmitter could be "watched" and controlled from the studio. The transmitter operator was superfluous, the employers insisted, and his duties could be performed just as well or better by machine, with a substantial saving in wages to the broadcaster. The argument went on for years, with the FCC finally moving cautiously to a decision to allow the remote control of low-powered, nondirectional radio stations, and then, several years later, expanding the rule to cover the directional stations, and finally to cover all radio stations, even the 50,000-watt facilities. Apparently making some concession to the unions' arguments, the commission rule did make it mandatory that the transmitter be visited daily and meter readings be recorded that would reflect transmitter performance.

The remote-controlled-transmitter rule does not apply to VHF television transmitters, but there seems little reason to doubt that the broadcasters will fight for, and eventually receive, permission from the FCC to operate these facilities with automated equipment.[2]

In post–World War II years, radio stations had degenerated to a point where they could be described as "record players." Their fall was precipitous and was attributable to the rapid development and wide acceptance of television. However, the loss of technician-engineer jobs through the decline of radio was more than offset by the increase in jobs in the growing television field. A decade or so later, when the FCC rule on transmitters struck another blow at the employment of technician-engineers in radio, the expansion in television was still going on, and the ranks of the technicians and the rolls of their unions showed a substantial net increase, notwithstanding the loss of the transmitter jobs.

Unfortunately, however, it is not only at transmitters that the introduction and use of automated equipment threatens the job security of the technician-engineer. The electronic camera and its associated controls in the studio control room are also sophisticated devices and lend themselves to automation, with the resultant displacement of technician-engineers. In addition, the FCC has no jurisdiction over any of the studio control room equipment, with the exception of a link between the studio and the transmitter,[3] so that the technician-engineer who operates this control equipment must look solely to the protection his union can provide, if electronic equipment is manufactured that can do his job as well as he can.

It should be stated here, perhaps belatedly, that when we discuss the displacement of the technician-engineer by the automated machine we are talking of a tendency. Tendencies are subject to qualification and modification. Many factors prevent the prevailing wind from always blowing the same way and at the same speed. The tendency towards complete automation is also subject to some checks and modifications. We have already mentioned two, the unions and the FCC. Moreover, there are station owners who would prefer to have what man can add to the broadcasting operation, rather than see the machine dominate the art. However, it may be sufficient to say that we know of a television station that had one employee assigned to operate a remote control camera from the control booth. While panning and dollying by means of a joy-stick control, opening and closing the iris with a twist of a dial, riding gain on the audio, modulating the video signal, he would on occasion set all controls, and dash into the studio to make announcements before the camera!

The technician-engineer faces yet another threat to his job stability: as the electronic and mechanical equipment he operates becomes easier to understand and use, the employer is tempted to give his duties to another, lower-paid employee, who then may be required to combine his previous duties with his new ones. Moreover, employees engaged in duties at the station that overlap those of the technician-engineer are often tempted to encroach on the technician-engineer's jurisdiction: especially when it is made possible for them to do so as a result of simplification of the control equipment. Rare is the contract negotiation between a technical workers' union and a broadcasting industry employer that does not contain a demand by the employer that the union give up some of its technical jurisdiction and duties to a nontechnical employee. The technical union may be asked to relinquish the operation of tape recorders, the mixing of sound, the operating of cueing devices, electronic switches, cameras, and so on.

A classic example of the turning over of the technician-engineer's duties to nontechnical employees came in radio with the combining of his duties and those of the announcer, who by that time had been reduced to voicing ads and introducing records. When it was possible for the announcer to operate the simplified controls used in mixing sound and controlling gain, it was he who was kept on the job and the engineer who was displaced, for only the exceptional technician-engineer had the voice timbre or voice training required for broadcasting. This "combo" operation became widespread in the nonmetropolitan areas, but has had less impact in the big cities and their environs. The financially successful stations are reluctant to move to combine the announcer's and technician-engineer's jobs, feeling that this might lower the quality of broadcasting, and that it could engender great resistance from the unions representing the technician-engineer.

So, indeed, the technician-engineer in the broadcasting environment does stand on inhospitable terrain. If the equipment which he operates is highly developed and simplified he is no longer needed to make it work; if the simplification is to a lesser degree he may well find his job given to someone else, or combined with other tasks in an area alien to his skills. These ever-present threats to his chances of working in his chosen field, plus in many cases his isolation from the actual production of radio and television shows, lead to alienation from his work and to the creation of difficult problems for the unions which represent him. We suggest that these problems will inevitably be reflected in the attitude of the unions towards the employer and the demands made upon him.

Alienation from the creative and artistic functions of television is a daily reality for many a technician-engineer. Where job assignments place him in a position to avoid this alienation by allowing his participation in the creative production of a broadcast, there his lot is a happier one. Understandably, where his contribution is substantial in the production, a sense of job security will also accompany the feeling of satisfaction that goes with active and meaningful participation. Conversely, when his duties require him merely to relay a fully produced film or video tape from the originating point to the audience, without being able to play any significant role in the production or creation, there his frustration and alienation is intensified.

Of course, alienation can be a by-product of the kinds of productions in which the employee is engaged.[4] The production of "live" studio shows,[5] the taping and broadcasting of great sports spectacles, pageants, and parades, the covering of great news events such as landings on the moon, the funerals of presidents, and the pomp and circumstance that attract the interest of millions upon millions of viewers and listeners; all of these are of great interest to the employees engaged in their production. Creativity and involvement are stimulated. Interest and productivity increase and boredom and insecurity diminish. For instance, at the annual Bing Crosby golf classic at Pebble Beach, California, two television cameramen, at least, can be depended upon to occupy starring roles. One of these men operates his camera from a platform suspended high above the crowds from the boom of a crane. From this perch with his zoom lense he follows the balls from tee to fairway to green, pictures which add immensely to the program. The other technician-engineer covers the game with a unique back-pack camera which can be operated without attached cables. These men, and often their colleagues, stationed with cameras around the course often excite as much interest as the event they are covering.

But to understand the alienation experienced by the technician-engineer in television and radio broadcasting and how that alienation redounds on both the employers and the technical unions, we must take another look, if only briefly, at the broadcasting industry today.

Those who operate a broadcast facility must be licensed to do so by the FCC, and they must abide by a set of rules professedly structured to provide certain protections to the citizens of this country whose air is being used for the transmissions. There are unwritten requirements that the broadcaster provide a wide variety of programs which should be fair and equitable, and which will correspond to the needs, desires and mores of the listening public. He must broadcast a certain number of hours a day, and so on. To abide by these rules and yet profit from his enterprise the commercial broadcaster sells time to advertisers. Over the years, the buying of air time has become a highly developed, sophisticated, and sometimes cynical occupation which counts the price of advertising in radio and television as the "cost per thousand" of viewers. The buyer, usually an advertising agency, buys time on those programs that the ratings tell him are being listened to, or watched, by the majority of listeners or viewers, regardless of the quality or level of the program. (Incidentally, many in the broadcasting industry have no belief in the accuracy of current methods of polling viewers and listeners.) Thus, the broadcaster engaged in selling time for advertising must broadcast that which will be seen or heard by the largest number of people, notwithstanding the possibility that what he broadcasts may have little or no merit. For broadcasters outside the metropolitan areas it is not financially feasible to provide live programming for a relatively small audience. By affiliating with one of the three large networks, or by buying a syndicated video tape or film "package," he can provide programs which have been given lavish promotion and, ostensibly at least, are in demand by millions. He has little or no incentive to provide interesting, unique, and creative programming for an audience that he is convinced will only respond to kitsch.

The radio and television networks in the United States, the National Broadcasting Company, the Columbia Broadcasting System, and the American Broadcasting Company, are uniquely equipped to supply live or video-taped programs of broad interest and high quality, and have on occasion done so.[6] Some of the programs they have produced have been so breathtakingly beautiful and so intensely absorbing that the bountiful promise made by the miracle of television has been almost redeemed. Unfortunately, this is on the rare occasion, and when it occurs it is usually scheduled for showing during prime time, the evening hours between 6:30 and 11:30. The rest of the broadcast day, the "Wasteland," is filled with old movies, soap operas, interview and game shows, cartoons, etc.

This is the environment in which the technician-engineer and his unions work and serve — an industry lying on the very borders of beauty and creativity which occasionally dares to cross that border; an industry created by the magic of man learning to waft pictures and sound through the air from whence they can be plucked by the turn of a dial or the pressing of a button; an industry capable of bringing into the homes of millions the images of man on the football field, the battle field, or the lecture platform; an industry that can bring to millions, in "living" color, skilled and amusing entertainers, beautiful show girls, the songs and dances of the globe, and lovely views of lovely lands and seas; also, an industry where creativity is hampered and sometimes crippled beyond cure by commercialism, conservatism, costs, and the drive for profits. It is our belief that the technician-engineer, more than any other in the broadcasting field, suffers frustration and alienation that is exaggerated by his proximity to the creative milieu but all too infrequent chance to fully participate in the creative process. The promise that he will play an interesting and exciting part in the production of interesting programs is always present, but rarely materializes. The promise is made by the medium itself, which keeps opening the door to more ways in which man can use his magic lantern and get magical response. Then again, the promise is held out to him by the occasional sorties made by the "nets" and by independent producers into the land of live television and radio, where his skills and interest are involved to the utmost. The promise of involvement is always before him, but the demands of the market make its fulfillment rare.

In the mass production industries the phenomenon of alienation, or estrangement, from the process of production has been a subject of study by sociologists for many years, and its pervasive presence is readily apparent to anyone who has worked in the mass production mode, or to anyone who is familiar with others who have worked on the line. The soulless labor involved in the boring, repetitive, seemingly endless jobs necessary to turn out the mass produced "thing" is barely tolerated by those workers trapped in the factories, but to varying degrees the presence and effect of alienation in the factory is at least understood by its victims, and the unions in that environment are continually influenced by its reality. The technician-engineer does not suffer the same degree of alienation; but, unlike the mass production worker who has had to reconcile himself to estrangement from his work, the technician-engineer resists alienation in the broadcasting field, without consciously recognizing or accepting its presence, in such a manner and with such intensity that his protests sometimes reverberate throughout the industry and occasionally shake his unions to their foundations.

These reactions, or overreactions, come from the pressures generated from alienation compounded by job insecurity. The technician-engineer sees more of his work being taken away while his skills at the same time are too infrequently used in the work that remains. The employer is not sympathetic to his plight, and the technician-engineer has not built his union into the kind of organization that is capable of correcting the problems that come with estrangement from work. Often his anger and frustration are directed primarily toward his union, where actually little fault lies, and only secondarily toward the employer who imperils his jurisdictional rights and thus his job. The reasons for this reaction are complicated and contradictory, but if the technical unions are to lead in solving the pressing problems of their members, they must examine these reasons and restructure their organizations to respond to the new challenges.

Broadcast technician-engineers are for the most part conservative in their viewpoint, and thus, most of the time, understanding of the actions of their employers even when those actions hurt them economically. They are, in principle, opposed to featherbedding or make-work projects, and they are in accord, if not always fully in accord, with the aim and ideas of free enterprise as practiced in the broadcasting industry. They look upon their union as a countervailing force and expect this force to help keep the employer enterprising freely but within certain boundaries, so that to some degree the fruits of enterprise accrue to the union member. They are not prepared to allow their unions to challenge the employer's rights in some areas, and yet they often express anger and contempt at what they consider to be the impotence of their unions. This anger sometimes explodes into unreasoned and destructive acts against their own organizations, and in a recent case such acts almost led to the destruction of NABET.[7]

As an organization that is the mirror-image of its members, NABET can serve as an example of the adequacies and inadequacies of broadcasting's technical unions. NABET, by any yardstick used, is for the most part a well-functioning and democratic organization. Its members reserve to themselves the right to run the union, and they jealously guard it against bureaucratic deformations. It can be fairly stated that this union is the creature of the people in the industry who are NABET members, and it moves only at their command. So well do the members guard their control of their union that they do not even welcome their hired representatives and other employees at conventions. All of the officers, both local and international, with the exception of a couple of full-time elected officers in the United States and Canada, work in the radio and television industries, man the negotiating committees and the grievance committees, and do much of the work to keep the union going. Their efforts, and the efforts of their opposites in the IBEW, have resulted in some of the best wages and working conditions provided by labor agreement in the United States. NABET and the IBEW have functioned in their trade union areas and have functioned well. Wages are good, vacations, health plans, pensions, holidays, job conditions, and hours of work all are good, and improving all the time. NABET has done an excellent job as a trade union, as an organization involved in protecting its members' economic interests.

It is in the area of professionalism that NABET, and the other technical unions as well, have not done what they could. This failure is the direct responsibility of the membership of these organizations, who have lacked the interest to make the unions anything more than economic tools. That is not enough. What is broadcast, when it is broadcast, how it is broadcast must concern the unions as professional organizations. Who owns the broadcasting facilities, and why, are legitimate questions for a union of professional workers. What about the public? Is their interest adequately protected from dishonest advertising and shoddy selling? What are the technical practices of the industry that might impinge on the viewers' right to know? What can be done to improve both technical and artistic aspects of broadcasting? The technical unions must change their attitudes and take a broader outlook if they are to successfully continue to represent the workers in the broadcasting industry. They must be prepared to meet swiftly changing times and customs in the field and to move boldly to protect and enhance the professional interests of their members, as well as to fight for job security.

In summary, it is our conviction that if the technician-engineers are going to make their jobs secure and productive, if they are going to ameliorate the effects of alienation and make the environment in which they work more creative and more interesting, they must adopt different attitudes toward their unions and toward the industry in which they work. They will have to understand radio and television in all its facets. They will have to be continually alert to the role of the FCC and other government agencies in the industry. They will have to study the great social impact of the electronic media, and they will have to anticipate its future course. Their unions will have to be alert to the needs and problems of the viewing and listening audience, the aspirations and the conditions of all employees in the industry who are not technicians, and they must try to play an active and constructive role in developing deeper understanding of and sharper insight into the creative and asthetic aspects of broadcasting.

At this point perhaps some disclaimers should be made. When we speak of the technician-engineer moving closer to the artistic and creative aspects of broadcasting we do not mean that he should encroach upon the work of others. Nor are we suggesting anything but the closest fraternal ties with other unions in the industry, and a deep regard for their interests. Neither are we saying that the technician-engineer, in all cases, is removed from the creative aspects of broadcasting as it is today. What we are saying is that television and radio have not fulfilled their early promise, and that it is the technician-engineer's duty to the public and to himself to act as the most responsible and informed of the critics, so that he may play a constructive role in the industry and the public may thereby benefit from his more active participation. If he does not seriously involve himself in the future of broadcasting and if the development of automated controls continues apace, it may be his fate to sit, jobless, watching a still further deterioration of programming while the automated machine — lights blinking and relays clicking — supplies more starkness to the wasteland.

The technician-engineer's job can be, and is at times, as creative and as interesting as any in the broadcasting field. The setting of levels of microphones and the modulation of sound, the lighting of sets and the control of light levels, the development of the techniques of the electronic camera (wipes, fades, dissolves, montage effects, and so on) provide room for his skills, for his abilities, interest, and involvement to make a substantial contribution. No machine, however complicated or infallible, will ever be able to equal the contribution made by the technician-engineer in broadcasting.

The part the technician will take in the future of television and radio broadcasting will be strongly influenced by two groups about which we have said little or nothing, the employers and the nonengineering employees in the industry.

Many nonengineering employees in broadcasting, union-represented or not, may feel challenged by any increase in the scope of the engineer's field. Directors, stage hands, producers, announcers, etc., may well look askance at an expansion of the engineer's role, feeling that such expansion represents a threat to their position in the programming process. It will be necessary to convince these employees that constructive changes in the broadcasting mode, and the retention of the skilled technician-engineer in a secure and creative position in that changing mode, can be of benefit to all. The unions representing these workers must be consulted, cooperated with, and made a part of the planning that will be necessary if the technicians and their unions are to survive and grow with the industry that made them.

As is the case in most industries, management rights and prerogatives are sacred in the broadcasting field. Whatever it is that the broadcasters visualize as their right they will fight ferociously to retain. The response to any union attempt to encroach upon these "prerogatives" can be anticipated. The companies will fight any attempt to broaden the role of the technical unions if they feel that their "right" to broadcast what they want when they want it is being challenged. They have powerful allies in government circles — many members of Congress have business connections with the broadcasting industry — and broadcasters can be expected to call on them for congressional and legislative assistance if they sense a threat to their control emanating from demands for reform and change by the unions.[8] On the other hand, the slowly rising tide of complaint and questioning about the quality and content of broadcasting might make the broadcasters listen to the voice of change, especially if change would not threaten their profits. In any event time, technological developments, and the tempo of life itself will bring change. The technician-engineer and his unions must stand ready to help make these changes, but make them in such a fashion that the public and the quality of broadcasting will benefit at the same time that the status and security of the technician-engineer is enhanced.

NOTES

1. In 1935 a committee was formed within the American Federation of Labor to organize in the mass production industries, i.e., steel, auto, rubber, etc. This committee had marked success in organizing, but departed from the conventional methods by ignoring the difference in skills between classifications in a factory or plant and by placing all the workers in a single establishment in the same local and national union. This method of organization, which placed unskilled, semiskilled, and highly skilled in the same groupings, was called vertical organizing. This violated the traditional method used by the AFL, which organized workers on the basis of their craft skills, plumbers in the plumber's union, electricians in the electrician's union, etc., even if they were employed in the same plant. This was referred to as horizontal organizing.

   In 1936, as a result of internal concerns about the vertical method of organizing, the committee (Committee for Industrial Organization) was ordered by the hierarchy of the AFL to disband. It refused to do so and its members, along with those who wanted the industrial, or vertical, form of organizing were expelled from the AFL. Those expelled continued with vertical organizing and changed their name to the Congress of Industrial Organizations. The CIO continued as an independent organization until February, 1955, when a pact was signed reuniting the two organizations in the AFL-CIO.

2. Ultrahigh frequency transmitters, i.e., those channels above channel 13, need not be manned, under commission rules.

3. This is widely believed but may be in error. The law gives the FCC jurisdiction which "includes both pack transmission and all instrumentalities, facilities, and services incidental to such transmission" (*Communications Act of 1934, as amended*, sec. 318, title 47).

4. One day an employee may be assigned to a simple, boring, and repetitive task in a TV control room. The next day he may well be assigned to a live studio show or outside the studio to some interesting remote broadcast.

5. Most "live" television productions are not seen that way in the home. What is seen is a video tape reproduction of the production people saw live in the studio.
6. Our discussion here does not include the Canadian Broadcasting Corporation, which unlike the U.S. networks is not a great capitalistic venture, but is owned by the Canadian people and operated by a Crown corporation. Neither have we considered the National Educational Television Network, as this network does not handle commercial programming and does not directly hire technicians.
7. In 1967 a series of complaints by locals in NABET against domination by International officers were compounded by internal bickering and "politicking." Moves were made by the large network locals, New York and Hollywood, to leave NABET for the Teamster's Union. When this failed because the Teamsters withdrew, an effort was made to form a new union. The fight to keep the union together succeeded, but the organization was almost destroyed in the process.
8. In 1968 five senators and ten representatives had either a direct or family-related interest in the broadcasting industry (*Broadcasting*, January 15, 1968).

10 ETV Bargaining
Management View

by JAMES L. LOPER
and THOMAS J. McDERMOTT, JR.

The public television station has up until now been little affected by the union movement. Only thirteen of the more than one hundred and fifty stations have any form of contract, and those contracts that do exist primarily cover engineers and technicians. Several stations, in the very largest markets, have multiple contracts which approach in complexity those of large-scale commercial broadcasting.

For the most part unions, guilds, and ETV have signed contracts only in major cities, with community stations which have relatively large budgets and numbers of employees, although the signators include WILL-TV, operated by the University of Illinois, at Urbana. National Educational Television's labor agreements are only with the "above-the-line," or talent, organizations. Thus it would seem that the locally owned and funded noncommercial station has not been an attractive target for unionization.

And well it might not be, for, as the Carnegie Commission on Educational Television reported, the average ETV station in 1966 had a median full-time employment figure of only 23 people. And yet, out of a total employment of 3,910, only 64 people earned over $15,000, according to the study, and most of these in the management categories. Generally, ETV workers are paid less for their services than are their equals in commercial television.

The concept of nonparity has formed the philosophical base for most ETV contracts, and with reason. While it can be argued that employees in similar positions in noncommercial and commercial television perform similar duties and must demonstrate similar capabilities, a basic difference does exist. ETV does not have the advertising revenues which are available to operate a profit-based system of television.

It is true that some commercial stations operate with less than the $258,510 described by the Carnegie report as the median expense of all ETV stations. But the fact remains that commercial television by its very nature is allowed and encouraged by the federal government to develop a steady source of income. ETV stations operating on reserved channels must start from a basis of no advertising income and develop other sources of financing. The very fact that 180 public television stations exist at all is a tribute to the inventiveness of the licensees and management.

This quest for nonadvertising revenue has led many nongovernmentally supported stations, especially community stations, into a number of fund-raising activities some of which are far afield of the concept of educational broadcasting.

It is, incidentally, these very stations in the larger markets — stations dependent upon a variety of recurring and nonrecurring sources of income — that have the largest budgets, produce most of the programming, and have the most labor contracts.

For these stations to negotiate from anything other than a concept that they should pay less than their commercial counterparts would indicate bad management. If the station has developed this approach, not only to salaries and wages but to all services and goods it receives, and consistently applies it, it should not have difficulty presenting a case for less-than-parity contracts with its unions and guilds. But the station must contrive always to preach and sell such a philosophy, not only to the unions, but to the entire community.

This is especially true if the ETV station makes major use of volunteer workers to supplement its regular staff. Volunteers do a remarkable number and variety of jobs in many stations, often working along with salaried employees. If such nonsalaried workers feel that the staff are working for less than they would receive in commercial television, there is likely to be a harmonious relationship. But if the volunteer knows that his salaried coworker is working for a relatively high wage, he is likely to feel abused, disrupt the relationship, and look for activities where his services can better be used.

Thus the ETV station is unable to pay professional staff more because of the absence of advertising revenue, but it also stands to lose valuable volunteer staff if it should choose to pay according to commercial scales.

The following suggestion is the best offered for the settlement of an ETV contract: In lieu of a wage increase, the bargaining unit employees should share in the nonprofit.

This is more than a quip. Within it lies the philosophy for the negotiation of an ETV contract. Simply stated, "We pay less, because we have less to pay." More broadly, educational television is not a commercial broadcasting facility, and concepts adequate for commercial stations have no place in an ETV negotiation.

An ETV station must develop and sustain such a philosophy with its union, or it will find itself in the constant financial peril of the other artistic nonprofit corporations — for example, opera companies, ballet companies, and symphony orchestras — that have attempted to compete with commercial wages, fringe benefits, and work rules. When reliance is placed upon public donors and private foundations for operating expenses, there are no dynamics of the marketplace (such as an increase in advertising rates) to supply the funds to finance high-scale union contracts. Negotiate or perish. Because we are firmly convinced of this, we offer the following guidelines for ETV management in labor negotiation.

An ETV station which faces organization will be dealing with the same unions, and essentially the same techniques of organization, that have faced commercial stations. Only one union may be involved (most likely engineers); WNDT of New York, on the other hand, has twelve separate agreements.[1]

While, in the opinion of the authors, the interests of an ETV station are not served by seeking unionism, it should not be opposed once an organization campaign has commenced, unless there is an excellent chance of avoiding unionization altogether. A picket line may create problems of community goodwill, but a more serious result may be that the union will be less likely to look favorably on special treatment of the ETV station after a prolonged and expensive battle for organization.

And experience indicates that unions in broadcasting are willing to discuss the ETV problem. A union business agent will not accept grossly substandard wages or working conditions for his unit, but he may recognize the educational and cultural nature of the station, its dependency on public contributions, and the superior working conditions at ETV stations. With an appreciation of this fact, the experienced TV management will expound this philosophy at the first bargaining session:

1. ETV is not commercial.
2. ETV depends on public contributions. Contributors will not support the level of wages prevailing in the entertainment industry.
3. ETV provides a cultural and educational service to the community. It deserves union support.
4. Other nonprofit organizations attempting to pay union wages have gone bankrupt, or have gone out of business for one or more years while attempting to negotiate union agreements.
5. Working conditions at ETV stations are more rewarding and interesting in many respects than at commercial stations.

If negotiations are to be successful, extensive preparation is essential. The station should have the advice of a labor lawyer or an experienced labor negotiator, to help them deal intelligently with the union business agent, who will have years of negotiating experience on his side plus ready access to union attorneys. Special care should be given the first contract; once a clause becomes a part of a contract, it becomes almost impossible to pry it out in subsequent negotiations.

An ETV station engaged in bargaining should consult and thoroughly digest source materials. Particularly useful are the "Comparative Analysis, Technicians' Contracts" prepared by the National Association of Educational Broadcasters, which analyzes *all* major clauses of eleven ETV engineering contracts,[2] and "Salary Range of Thirty-Three Educational TV Stations,"[3] which covers more stations but gives salary ranges only. The National Association of Broadcasters has a reservoir of labor information available to its member stations. It is also considering a program of digesting and distributing ETV labor contract information for those of its members who are in the educational field.

A familiarity with local commercial contracts is also very helpful to a negotiating station. In a recent negotiation of the IATSE sound technicians' contract at Station KCET in Los Angeles, the bargaining committee for the station was armed with the NABET-NBC local owned and operated station contract, the IBEW-CBS local O&O contract, and the IATSE contract with a local independent. These covered the range of commercial salaries and working conditions in the area and proved immensely valuable for comparative purposes.

It is obvious that the most desirable contracts to consult are those negotiated with local commercial stations by the union with which you are dealing. There is yet to be discovered an area where it is advisable that an ETV contract be *more* onerous or burdensome for management, than a commercial contract. We urge that they should be less burdensome in all respects. The only way to achieve this is to have the appropriate commercial contracts available during negotiation.

Representatives of commercial stations experienced in dealing with unions can give valuable advice and may be able to warn of undesirable or absolutely unacceptable clauses. A union may try to introduce a new work rule or fringe benefit in an ETV station with the argument that it is innocuous, before presenting it to commercial stations.

In reviewing the contracts which you obtain in preparation for negotiations, note the differences in concept inherent in ETV as opposed to commercial television and attempt to maintain these differences. As an example, everyone is aware of the residual concept and the rerun fees demanded by AFTRA for additional commercial performances. National Educational Television created and successfully inserted in its AFTRA agreements the concept of the "use." Rather than pay for reruns, NET pays for "uses." One use consists of unlimited showings of a particular program for seven consecutive days. This concept conforms to the requirements of ETV and saves considerable money. It has been successfully used, in various avatars, by the authors in contracts with AFTRA, DGA, and IATSE sound technicians.

The nature of educational television makes it ideal for the introduction of an apprentice or student training program. It is the feeling of the authors that such a program should be used when it can be efficiently and economically administered. It has the following advantages:

1. It gives the station an opportunity to perform an additional educational function, particularly in the minority community.
2. It creates a loyal work force to aid in station expansion.
3. If sufficiently funded by outside sources, it cannot help but provide some economic benefit to the station, even though apprentices may not be allowed to perform duties of the union members except on a one-for-one basis. The mere presence of the extra worker makes it easier to get the job done.

Additional concessions which unions are inclined to make for educational television stations take the form of agreeing to:

1. Slightly lower wages than commercial stations.
2. Lower union initiation fees for personnel, or special pay-off arrangements.
3. The use of part-time employees.
4. Longer probationary periods for new employees.
5. Less strict work schedules.
6. The repeated use of amateur performers.
7. The payment of only one premium or penalty pay for any one incident.
8. Allowing supervisory personnel to perform certain duties of the bargaining unit members.

In summary, it can be said that the successful ETV station has had to bargain from the concept that noncommercial television cannot pay as much as commercial television. It has had to rely upon experienced, professional assistance during negotiations, and the staff has done necessary comparative research on other contracts. Labor contracts and negotiation should not be handled by the inexperienced or uninformed.

NOTES

1. The following is a list of unions with which WNDT (Channel 13) has contracts, and the employees covered by the contracts:

> American Federation of Musicians, National (informal agreement), covering musicians.
> American Federation of Musicians, Local 802 (signed contract), covering musicians.
> American Federation of Musicians, Local 16 (New Jersey) (informal agreement), covering musicians.
> American Federation of Television and Radio Artists, National and Local (signed contract), covering actors, performing artists, announcers, and newsmen.
> Directors Guild of America (signed contract), covering directors, associate directors, stage managers.
> International Alliance of Theatrical Stage Employes (signed contract), covering graphic artists.

International Alliance of Theatrical Stage Employes, Local 1 (Manhattan, Bronx, Staten Island) (signed contract), covering stagehands, electricians, carpenters, propmen.

International Alliance of Theatrical Stage Employes, Local 4 (Brooklyn, Queens), covering stagehands, electricians, carpenters, propmen.

International Alliance of Theatrical Stage Employes, Local 21 (New Jersey) (signed contract), covering stagehands, electricians, carpenters, propmen.

International Alliance of Theatrical Stage Employes, Local 771 (signed contract), covering film editors and assistants.

United Scenic Artists, Local 829 (signed contract), covering scenic artists, scenic designers, costume designers.

IBEW Local 1212, covering engineers and technicians.

2. The "Comparative Analysis, Technicians' Contract" may be obtained from the Educational Television Stations Division, National Association of Educational Broadcasters, 1346 Connecticut Avenue, N.W., Washington, D. C.

3. The "Salary Range of Thirty-Three Educational Television Stations," documenting engineering salaries as of September 1967, was compiled by Edna Jean Hershey, Director, Personnel Practices and Procedures, Denver Public Schools. It indicates monthly minimums ranging from $375 to $1,166.66 and monthly maximums ranging from $440 to $1,200.

11 Representation for Television Teachers

by ALLEN E. KOENIG

Television teachers today are a vital part of the communications industry. They teach such subjects as nuclear physics and elementary French over closed-circuit, commercial, and educational television stations to students ranging from graduate scholars to preschoolers. Although these activities are well known to the general public, few are aware of the behind-the-scenes problems of television teachers.

A number of studies indicate that the television teacher is being economically exploited and does not enjoy certain other basic rights. These rights include: reduced teaching loads for the extra effort required by television teaching, i.e., preparation of visuals and supplementary materials as well as rehearsal time; the right to be informed clearly of who owns the television recording and supplementary material; the right of the teacher to edit and update his television lesson; and the right to a firm agreement as to (1) how many times the lesson may be repeated, (2) what type of compensation will accrue from this repetition, and (3) to what extent the television lesson may be distributed on a regional or national basis.

The following organizations have studied the problems of television teachers and have made explicit recommendations as to the rights of these individuals: The American Federation of Television and Radio Artists,[1] The National Education Association,[2]

The American Council on Education,[3] and the American Association of University Professors.[4] In an earlier writing I summarized the results of the research which has been done on the status of the television teacher. It was generally found that the TV teacher's compensation varies widely from one institution to another. Generally he does not receive additional compensation for appearing on educational television. Furthermore, his working conditions vary as widely as compensation practices. Even though a number of schools provide released time for television teaching, there is no consistent way of estimating how much released time the teacher should receive. The TV teacher is not legally protected from having his work improperly used at another time; if a program is out of date he has no legal right to stop distribution of the programming.[5] Later studies further confirm these inequities, with the exception that most teachers and professors now have program revision rights.[6] In 1970, however, I find no reason to depart from my earlier conclusions:

1. The television teacher should receive additional compensation for his unique services.
2. Residual payments should be distributed to the television teacher for *every* replay of his original presentation.
3. Released time should be granted to every television teacher.
4. Subject matter control of any TV program should be retained by either the television teacher himself or a group of academic peers.[7]

While my previous writing was devoted to a review of the research literature on problems faced by television teachers and subsequent recommendations for solving the derived problems, the focus of this chapter will be on the reality of collective bargaining and methods and organizations for *resolving* the economic and professional problems of these individuals.

Collective Bargaining

Loper and McDermott, in a preceding chapter, have presented management's point of view on wages for educational television employees:

The concept of nonparity has formed the philosophical base for most ETV contracts, and with reason. While it can be argued that employees in similar positions in noncommercial and commercial television perform similar duties and must demonstrate similar capabilities, a basic difference does exist. ETV does not have the advertising revenues which are available to operate a profit-based system of television.

Thus, the authors conclude that these employees should be paid less because educational stations receive less financial support than do their commercial counterparts. Today very few teachers or professors are willing to accept their logic, particularly in view of the proposed massive federal aid to become available through the Corporation for Public Broadcasting.

At this time a number of educational associations and unions are actively entering into collective bargaining agreements with both school boards and university trustees. The American Federation of Teachers has been active in these pursuits at both the lower and higher education levels. Recently the National Education Association underwent a complete overhaul of its internal organization with the result that a number of administrators have left that organization. NEA now openly professes collective bargaining and vies with AFT for the right to represent teachers. The over one million members of NEA depend upon it to effectively negotiate minimum wages and fringe benefits for the regular classroom teacher. NEA is now starting to move into college and university bargaining. The American Association of University Professors is a professional organization that has traditionally been concerned primarily with academic freedom and tenure. It too, however, is undergoing change and is moving into collective bargaining with university and college administrations.

A few years ago there was considerable philosophical debate as to whether or not professional educators should bargain with their administrators. This question no longer seems relevant because the practice has become widespread. The arguments, however, persist about collective bargaining and unionism. The most traditional argument is that it is nonprofessional to engage in collective bargaining because the professional does not need to bargain for minimum wages and other fringe benefits. Also, that professionals do not want to be classified into the traditional dichotomy of an employer-employee relationship. Furthermore, it would be distasteful to a professional to be seen striking or participating in a picket line. Above all, a professional would not want to be identified with "blue collar" unionism. Here one could debate the nature and definition of professionalism. I will not broach this controversy, but will assume from my experience that accepted as typically professional are physicians, dentists, teachers, lawyers, and the clergy.

The traditional point of view that union tactics are not appropriate for professionals is becoming blurred as young and militant individuals enter the professions in increasing numbers. Teachers have been participating in strikes in recent years. For example, the National Education Association sponsored a Florida teachers' strike while the American Federation of Teachers struck at San Francisco State College. While the clergy has been affected to a lesser extent, a number of Catholic priests recently formed a union to bargain with their hierarchy. Young militant doctors in 1969 protested, through picketing and speech-making, the American Medical Association's alleged blocking of the appointment of liberal John Knowles as Assistant Secretary of the Department of Health, Education, and Welfare. They also protested the AMA's inaction in the field of health care for the poor.

It is claimed that collective bargaining homogenizes employees; that with the establishment of minimums in both wages and fringe benefits, the special employee who exhibits meritorious service will not be recognized within the system. This argument is known in higher education as the traditional merit versus non-merit syndrome. That is, the professor who produces deserves advancement while the one who does not produce is denied salary increments and promotions. The traditional merit system, however, is not generally found in either secondary or elementary education. Instead, scales usually are predetermined by the number of years of experience and the highest degree or number of credits held by the teacher.

Although the arguments against collective bargaining persist, bargaining is the new reality in the educational marketplace. My own conviction is that television teachers should be protected by contract agreements determined by collective bargaining. These agreements should provide for basic minimum levels of compensation and protection of other rights as mentioned earlier in this chapter. Local, regional, and national contracts would be desirable where appropriate. That is, if a program is to be distributed nationally either over a network or through a national library, such as National Instructional Television, then a national contract would be needed in order to provide for additional levels of compensation and protection.

What must be remembered, however, is that minima achieved through collective bargaining do not necessarily set upper limits; those individuals who possess superior talents should be able to demand more for their services. One precedent has already been set by outstanding artists who belong to the American Federation of Television and Radio Artists, and who have been able to demand more than contract minima because of their public image and demand. Most often they are protected not only by basic minimum contracts, but by individually negotiated ones as well. Thus, although the historical pattern of collective bargaining has been that minima become maxima, this should not become the pattern for the TV teacher.

Towards a New Reality

It is evident from the preceding discussion that some of the primary concerns of the television teacher should be economic self-protection, an equitable salary, generous fringe benefits (such as libel-slander insurance and physical disability protection), and additional compensation for reruns. Equally as important as economic self-protection is the concept of professional protection.

The integrity of the teacher should be protected through agreements that provide, for example, that out-of-date material will not be shown in a local school district, and thus protect the pupils' right to be presented the most recent authoritative statement possible on the topic. The television teacher's professional reputation would be severely damaged if his presentation were less accurate or comprehensive than it should be at the time of the rerun.

In my opinion, three methods should be employed by television teachers to secure their proper rights: collective bargaining, policy statements regarding professional rights, and binding arbitration. I believe that guaranteed minima will ultimately correct the inequities that now persist in our schools, universities, and television stations. Moreover, I also believe that policy statements spelling out the professional rights and responsibilities of television teachers are equally important. Both the National Education Association and the American Association of University Professors have issued significant statements on these matters.[8] Obviously it would be helpful for the television teacher and the administrator to be able to rely upon professional statements delineating such subjects as academic freedom over television, television ownership rights, subject matter control of television teaching materials, and extramural use of television programming.

The collective bargaining process should not include ordinarily, as final weapons, either the strike or lockout. Instead, arbitration should be the court of last resort. Many believe that strikes are costly and unproductive for both labor and management. Also, as mentioned before, there is a feeling on the part of some educators that it is unprofessional for a teacher or professor to participate in a strike. Furthermore, a strike by public employees is illegal in a number of states. My belief is that parties who are unable to resolve their differences should put them before an impartial judge (such as an arbiter from the American Arbitration Association) and allow him to resolve the impasse. In the field of broadcasting, arbitration has traditionally been used primarily for resolving differences regarding the interpretation of collective bargaining agreements. It has not been used, however, to resolve problems involving negotiating these contracts. Thus, if an agreement is not achieved, an individual union goes on strike against the employer, and instances of these strikes appear throughout this volume. In my opinion, even the negotiation process should be subject to arbitration. Although the strike and lockout will be eliminated by guaranteed arbitration, it would be to the advantage of management and labor to resolve their differences without arbitration in order to avoid decisions that may be unsatisfactory to both sides.

Methods are empty devices without an organization or organizations to properly facilitate their implementation and achieve subsequent results. In an earlier publication I suggested that the American Federation of Television and Radio Artists might make a good representative for television teachers. A high official of AFTRA reacted negatively to this idea. The spokesman said that a "grass roots" organizing of TV teachers would not be practical and would exhaust the financial reserves of the union.

As indicated in several chapters of this book, AFTRA in 1967 was engaged in two battles. It conducted its first national strike against the networks and it fined a number of television newsmen for crossing the National Association of Broadcast Employees and Technician picket lines at American Broadcasting Company stations.

The above mentioned reaction of an AFTRA official and these subsequent events caused me to reexamine my opinion as to whether or not AFTRA should represent TV teachers. In a preceding chapter Maloney suggested that unions were victims of an "occupational psychosis" and could not cope with innovation as a social tool for change. It seems to me that the AFTRA position reflects rigidity, since the union is either unwilling or unable to accomplish social change because the pattern does not fit the "known." If AFTRA, for example, had been interested in representing television teachers, to what extent could it have conducted "grass roots" efforts via film or inexpensive video-tape over portable machines — with perhaps an assist from locally concerned teachers?

Furthermore, when a newsman of Chet Huntley's caliber refused to abide by the AFTRA strike against the networks because he felt that the union should not represent newsmen, one must question why. Probably because AFTRA had for too long neglected this segment of its membership, since it did not fit into the regular "performer" category. Later in 1967 the union had to fine its own members for crossing another union's picket lines. The union here had obviously failed to educate the union rank-and-file properly as to the importance of interunion cooperation (as advocated by McCue in his chapter on the subject).

These observations lead me to believe that AFTRA is neither innovative nor interested enough to give television teachers the leadership they need. Also, it is apparent that none of the other unions mentioned in this book are capable of this role.

Most academic men and women belong to professional organizations (like the NEA or AAUP) rather than unions (like AFT). These professional organizations, however, have not taken an active role in collective bargaining for TV teachers. As a consequence I did not recommend in 1967 that these groups represent the teachers. Their positions, however, have changed, as noted earlier, and they are engaging in collective bargaining. Most important of all, however, is that AAUP and NEA have the experience in education and the sympathy for it to represent television teachers effectively. Unfortunately, the two organizations are at odds over who should represent university and college professors. In 1969 the National Education Association discontinued supporting the American Association for Higher Education and set up its own higher education bureau for representing professors. If, however, NEA and AAUP could jointly agree on jurisdictional matters, they could — either separately or jointly — represent television teachers in the elementary, secondary, and higher education fields at the local, regional, and national levels. I strongly recommend that a joint study committee of the two organizations be formed in order to explore these possibilities.

If the 1970s are to be any different from the 1960s, the economic rights of television teachers must be recognized. Today's teacher is not willing to settle for less than his counterpart in industry or any other related field. Parity is a partial answer to the problem, but professional protection is equally important. Let us hope that the new decade will bring adequate protection and representation for the television teacher.

NOTES

The author wishes to thank the following individuals for reviewing this manuscript and offering helpful suggestions for its improvement: Dr. Walter Emery, Ohio State University; Dr. E. Wayne Herron, National Library of Medicine; Mr. Donald Mikes, National Education Association; Dr. Lawrence Poston and Dr. Alfred D. Sumberg, American Association of University Professors.

1. Mortimer Becker, "ETV Performance: Notes on Negotiation," *Television Quarterly* 2 (Winter, 1963), 27–29.
2. *Proceedings of the Conference on Professional Rights and Responsibilities of Teachers in Relation to Newer Educational Media* (Washington: National Education Association, 1962); *Professional Rights and Responsibilities of Television Teachers* (Washington: National Education Association, 1963, 1969); *Practices in Selected Public School Systems Relating to Professional Rights and Responsibilities of Television Teachers* (Washington: National Education Association, 1963); Donald F. Mikes, *Teachers in Television and Other Media: A Survey of Policies and Practices* (Washington: National Education Association, 1969).
3. Fred S. Siebert, *Copyrights, Clearances, and Rights of Teachers in the New Educational Media* (Washington: American Council on Education, 1964).
4. "Report of Committee C: Policy on Educational Television," *AAUP Bulletin* 48 (September, 1962), 290; "Statement on Educational Television," *AAUP Bulletin* 54 (September, 1968), 314–16; "Statement on Instructional Television," *AAUP Bulletin* 55 (March, 1969), 88–90.

5. Allen E. Koenig, "Rights for Television Teachers," in *The Farther Vision: Educational Television Today*, ed. by Allen E. Koenig and Ruane B. Hill (Madison: The University of Wisconsin Press, 1967), p. 255.

6. Mikes, *Teachers in Television and Other Media: A Survey of Policies and Practices*, pp. 28, 44; Fred S. Siebert, *An Analysis of University Policy Statements on Instructional Recordings and Their Re-Use* (Stanford: ERIC Clearinghouse on Educational Media and Technology, 1968).

7. Koenig, *The Farther Vision*, p. 255.

8. "Statement on Instructional Television," *AAUP Bulletin* 55 (March, 1969), 88–90; Mikes, *Teachers in Television and Other Media: A Survey of Policies and Practices*.

12 Blacks and Broadcasting

by RICHARD J. MEYER

> For black and white alike, the air of this nation is perfused
> with the idea of white supremacy and everyone grows to man-
> hood under this influence. Americans find that it is a basic
> part of their nationhood to despise blacks. No man who
> breathes this air can avoid it, and black men are no exception.
> They are taught to hate themselves, and if at some point, they
> are faced with an additional task, nothing less, for the impera-
> tive remains – Negroes are to be despised.
>
> Grier and Cobbs, Black Rage

> Raw, naked truth exchanged between the black man and the
> white man is what a whole lot more of is needed in this coun-
> try – to clear the air of the racial mirages, clichés, and lies
> that this country's very atmosphere has been filled with for
> four hundred years.
>
> The Autobiography of Malcolm X

Have broadcasters unknowingly perpetuated racial mi-
rages? The report of the National Advisory Commission on Civil
Disorders succinctly answered this question: "The news media,
we believe, contributed to the black-white schism in this country."[1] The commission, now widely known as the Kerner Commission, accused the mass media of failing to communicate to the
majority of their audience, which is white, a sense of the degrada-
tion, misery, and helplessness of living in the ghetto. In fact,
when the white press (radio and TV, as well as newspapers)
refers to black problems, according to the commission report, it
frequently does so as if blacks were not part of the audience.

Since the system is organized whereby whites edit and to a large extent write news about attitudes in and of the black community, the Kerner Commission was not surprised about this lack of communication.

Is it any wonder, therefore, that until very recently the majority of Americans were "unaware" of the baseness and inhumanity of black ghettos in the United States? Robert K. Merton offers an explanation of the white American who says, "I didn't know these conditions existed," with his excellent chapter on the self-fulfilling prophecy in *Social Theory and Social Structure*.[2] The American thought he "knew" the black by his stereotype, says Merton, but these social beliefs can be destroyed. According to him, ethnic prejudices may be helped over the threshold of oblivion, not by insisting that it is unreasonable and unworthy of them to survive, but by cutting off the sustenance now provided them by certain institutions of our society. One of the institutions with a disproportionate amount of influence is the broadcasting industry. A self-fulfilling prophecy, Merton believes, only operates in the absence of deliberate institutional controls.

Gordon W. Allport, in his study of the nature of prejudice, found that stereotypes do change in time. In the mass media certain ethnic stereotypes are weakening. Allport claims that with more education these social beliefs might fade out. Although the stereotypes may fade out, however, prejudice may continue, for "stereotypes are not identical with prejudice. They are primarily rationalizers." Attacks against stereotypes in schools, colleges, and in the mass media will not alone eradicate the roots of prejudice.[3] Ethnic and class stereotypes die hard, as they thrive on ignorance. Knowledge that the facts do not support one's stereotype may significantly affect the quantity and quality of intensity with which these stereotypes are held and acted upon.[4] Yet broadcasting has traditionally been the harbinger of mass stereotyping.

It may seem trite to invoke the widely held view that the mass media reflect the values of society. In the case of black America, one may add "trite, but true." Broadcasting's predecessors recall the *Coon Slides* at Illustrated Song Slides which accompanied the nickelodeon, the racist *The Birth of a Nation* and other silent, and later talking, films, the race records among the early recordings, and even the treatment of blacks in the early issues of *Life* magazine.[5] What perhaps is the classic illustration of broadcasting as the reflection and yet pervasive carrier of stereotypes is "Amos 'n' Andy." It was the American humorist and author Irvin S. Cobb who stated:

I claim these two stout fellows won a place in the popular taste and have held it against all comers because they are so natural, so simple, so full of genuine, orthodox, true-to-type, flesh-and-blood, Afro-Americans who, in their naive generosity, have extended to me the pleasant boon of being able to listen in on them while they live their lives and have their successes and their failures, their ups and their downs — but more downs than ups. . . . And, golly, what grand dialect they use! It's perfect, I say — absolutely perfect.[6]

"Amos 'n' Andy" continued in popularity from the radio days of the 1920s until the advent of television, where in this new medium they were played by black actors. The burnt cork syndrome is still deeply imbedded in the American psyche and the mass media. Author Max Wylie reminisced about "Amos 'n' Andy" in *TV Quarterly*: "A lot of humanity has drifted through to us from those fellows."[7] What did Black America think about "Amos 'n' Andy"? Correll and Gosden, their creators, claimed that they had a large following of "colored people" because they treated the "two ignorant, struggling colored boys . . . sympathetically." Correll and Gosden really believed that they had never ridiculed the black race.[8] Eric Barnouw, an historian of the media, does not agree with the originators' conception of themselves. He says: "It was not an accident that Amos 'n' Andy was a national triumph. It was virtually a national self-expression, a vivid amusement park image of its time."[9]

Michael Harrington is convinced that the "Amos 'n' Andy" philosophy is still present in the ghetto. He recalls the story of Adam Clayton Powell being attacked by a political rival: "'But he has an apartment in New York, and a place in Washington, and he's seen in nightclubs, and he travels to Europe all the time, and he's hardly ever in the Congress.' From the crowd, someone yelled, 'Man, that's really living!' The story is funny enough, but at the bottom it is made of the same stuff as 'Amos 'n' Andy': the laughing, childlike, pleasure-loving Negro who must be patronized and taken care of like a child." [10]

W. E. B. DuBois was not taken in by the "Amos 'n' Andy" popularity polls in the twenties:

I see in and through them [Whites]. . . . Not as a foreigner do I come, for I am native, not foreign, borne of their thought and flesh of their language. . . . They deny my right to live and be and call me misbirth! My work is to them mere bitterness and my soul, pessimism. And yet, as they preach and strut and shout and threaten, crouching as they clutch at rags of fact and fancies to hide their nakedness, they go twisting, flying by my tired eyes and I see them stripped, ugly, human. [11]

For DuBois, "Amos 'n' Andy" would never portray the black man:

. . . I believe in the Negro race: in the beauty of its genius, the sweetness of its soul. . . . I believe in Pride of race and lineage and self: in pride of self so deep as to scorn injustice to other selves . . . [12]

If blacks really believed in "the Negro race" as portrayed by DuBois, would they, after listening to "Amos 'n' Andy" portrayed in dialect by whites, want to be part of the broadcasting industry which denied them their "right to live"? Programming and employment have been interlinked since broadcasting's inception. For every laugh guffawed by Andy as he "outwitted" Amos, there might have been an Afro-American listener who realized that this was not *his* medium.

Yet given the latent hostilities between the races and the total lack of communication between them in the United States, there was still a role for blacks in broadcasting. Because of the commercial emphasis of American broadcasting, blacks found their way into the industry purview as performers and sought-after listeners, primarily for economic reasons. Only in very rare instances did owners of broadcast outlets seek to use radio for special pleading or agitation on behalf of the black man. In a study of Afro-American radio by Richard S. Kahlenberg, it was discovered that "far from being a medium for communicating a specifically Negro viewpoint to a white audience, radio has become, because of its commercial nature, a medium by which the white establishment, through advertising, is actually seeking to sell its values to the Negro."[13] His study discovered that by 1947, a generation after radio came into existence, there was only one station, WDIA in Memphis, Tennessee, devoting all of its air time to "Negro radio." Twenty years later, there were over one hundred stations scattered throughout the nation devoting 75 percent of air time to the black man. There were also an additional dozen stations devoting half and four hundred devoting one quarter of their air time to "Negro radio." *Only 1 percent of these stations are owned by blacks.*[14]

These statistics should not surprise those who know that occupational orientations are conditioned by the social structure in which the socialization of the blacks occurs. A conception of what is possible in terms of careers is shaped by blacks' experiences in the community and by advice furnished them by persons they consider competent advisors. Hence, the Afro-American did not try to enter fields where he knew he could not make it.[15] It must be remembered that slavery created the conditions for these occupational orientations. Before the Civil War, black slaves in many cases had developed better craft and artisan skills than poor whites. Animosity built up between the white and black workers, so that after emancipation blacks were excluded from labor unions.[16] As more blacks fought their way into the so-called middle and professional classes after the turn of the century, many of them became teachers. Teaching was to be a step towards another career in the professions. However, large numbers of them were trapped in this profession as it represented the best job opportunity at the time they began to work.[17] The shortage of blacks in broadcasting is related to its high status as a profession. The Afro-American's social mobility was stunted because of the conception of his occupational role.[18]

Yet despite the sociological, economic, and psychological barriers, blacks did participate in the development of radio and television to a limited degree. The first black performer on radio was Jack L. Cooper. Cooper, a vaudeville artist and ventriloquist, began appearing regularly on a musical variety show in 1924 over WCAB in Washington, D.C. He performed a four-character skit playing each character himself. Cooper once remarked that he was "the first four Negroes in radio." Later he developed "The All-Negro Hour" and set the pace and style of black oriented radio for twenty years. His disc jockey programs were sold on a brokerage basis. After the Second World War there were still a handful of black disc jockey time brokers. They succeeded on their personalities alone in the radio of the 1940s and 50s. At first, they did all of their own selling and announcing and often the writing of their own copy. As business became better, salesmen and announcers were hired.[19]

Meanwhile on white radio, black actors remained scarce, except for Eddie "Rochester" Anderson and Hattie McDaniel as "Beulah." Singers had more representation. There were no black announcers, newscasters, or script writers in network radio from its beginning through the fifties. WMCA, New York, was the first station to hire an Afro-American as staff announcer, in 1946.

Television in the fifties employed Negro performers with a little more dignity, according to Langston Hughes. Ed Sullivan, Sid Caesar, and the other variety shows had black performers appear.[20] During the fifties many southern stations did not carry these integrated programs. In 1955, for example, Leontyne Price played the role of Tosca in a production of the NBC Opera Company. Some NBC stations in the South did not carry the opera.[21]

So during the decades prior to the Black Revolution of the 1960s, broadcasting did little or nothing to relate the civil rights struggle to the mainstream of American society. The notable and

noble exceptions such as Edward R. Murrow were scant preparation for the holocaust which was to come. Only black radio, beaming its message to black audiences, built its own images with a
civil rights point of view. Although these stations were white
owned, they realized that "a station has to be community oriented,
aware of what's happening in the community where it draws its
sponsors and listeners." [22] In a sense, the economic consideration
caused the so-called soul stations to focus on civil rights. A top
advertising agency executive was quoted: "It isn't a matter of
idealism, it is just that some people are beginning to get the
idea that there's a whale of a Negro market." [23] As the purchasing
power of blacks increases (for example, from 1940 to 1950 Afro-
Americans increased their buying power fourfold, while their
population increased only slightly) there will be a logical cater-
ing to their programming desires.

Yet in many areas of this nation, logic and reason do not pre-
vail. In the cities, blacks make up substantial percentages of
the population. They possess large numbers in the South. One of
the most extraordinary examples of alleged flagrant violation of the
rights of a community to be represented through its broadcasting
outlet occurred in Jackson, Mississippi. WLBT-TV was accused
by the Office of Communication of the United Church of Christ
and by local black citizens of being a blatant mouthpiece for
segregationist views.[24] Their petition, filed in June, 1964, asked
that the renewal application of WLBT be denied. The group
claimed that the station had a record of ten years of complaints
by Jackson blacks that it systematically excluded them from
access to its facilities and that it had systematically promoted
segregationist views, as well as denied opposing views the opportunity for presentation. Many examples were cited of the station's
racist views: when the local announcement which preceded the
"Today Show" said, "What you are about to see is an example of
biased, managed northern views. Be sure to stay tuned at 7:25
to hear your local newscast"; when a network program featured

news about race relations in Mississippi, or of the work of Thurgood Marshall, etc., a slide appeared stating, "Sorry, cable trouble." [25]

Because of the accusations made by the United Church of Christ *et al.*, the Federal Communications Commission decided to grant a short-term license renewal to WLBT. Robert Lewis Shayon commented that WLBT promised to reform but that its past record was poor. He cited earlier FCC decisions when renewals were not granted even when the offending stations had promised to reform. [26]

In March of 1966, the U.S. Court of Appeals for the District of Columbia held that the FCC had erred in renewing the license of WLBT and directed the commission to hold hearings on the station's renewal application. An important precedent was set in this decision, since the FCC had ruled earlier that the United Church of Christ could not intervene on behalf of the citizens of Jackson, Mississippi. The court held that the general public has a voice in the determining of whether the station has operated in the public interest. Before this, only those having technical or economic interests were eligible to intervene in a license renewal case. [27] The publicity and subsequent ruling in the WLBT case by the U.S. Court of Appeals has encouraged other groups to protest the license renewals of stations. KTYN, Inglewood, California, and WXUR, Media, Pennsylvania, have been challenged in their attempts to renew their licenses. [28] In early 1969, twelve black organizations supported by the United Church of Christ urged the FCC to deny the license renewal application of KTAL-TV, Texarkana, Texas. Before the commission could act, however, an unprecedented agreement between the southern television station and the community organizations, which would insure adequate television programming for the black community and other minority groups, was reached. The agreement also covered fair employment practices. The organizations and the United Church of Christ withdrew their petition requesting that the license not be renewed and joined in requesting that the license be granted. On July 31, 1969, the FCC unanimously renewed the license of KTAL-TV.[29]

After two years of deliberations, as well as public hearings, the FCC voted in June of 1968 to renew the license of television station WLBT for three years. The commission argued that the allegations brought by the United Church of Christ were not proven and that the station had changed its approach to the racial issue and had given the black community representation on the air. Commissioners Cox and Johnson dissented. They were not too impressed with the "minimal improvements" made after the "church's petition put the fear of God into the WLBT's management." They were disappointed that the majority of members of the commission found that WLBT had served the "public interest." [30]

The most important side effect of the WLBT case was the decision by the FCC that, in the future, *if radio and television stations discriminated against Negroes in their employment policies, they would face possible loss of their licenses* (see Appendix 1). In addition, the commission asked station owners to adopt affirmative recruitment and training programs for unqualified blacks for jobs in broadcasting. The FCC announcement merely gave credence to the view that the Civil Rights Act of 1964, which in section 7 bans discrimination by employers of twenty-five or more persons, applied to broadcasters and that refusal to renew licenses would be the penalty for violating it. The commission stated, "Thus, we stress that simply to comply with the requirements of the national policy — to say, 'we can't find qualified Negroes' — is not enough. What is called for is a commitment going beyond the letter of the policy, and attuned to its spirit and the demands of the times." [31]

The United Church of Christ, after fighting the renewal of WLBT's license for four years and going through the litigation and hearings, said the FCC decision to renew "was not unexpected." They added that despite four years of effort and assurances by a majority of the seven-member FCC that marked improvements had been made in WLBT's programming, conditions had not improved sufficiently. Therefore, the United Church of Christ appealed the FCC renewal to the U.S. Circuit Court of Appeals.[32] In his last decision handed down before he joined the United States Supreme Court as the new Chief Justice, Warren Burger ruled in June, 1969, that the license of WLBT "be vacated forthwith" and that the FCC invite applications from other groups to file for the license. The court stated that the FCC had treated the United Church of Christ as an "interloper" and "opponent" and not as an "ally." It further stated that the church had acted with "hostility" and "impatience." Judge Burger wrote that the FCC erred in making the appellants prove that the license of WLBT should not be renewed. The court of appeals stated that the burden of proof that a renewal would be in the public interest should always be upon the licensee.[33] The United Church of Christ Office of Communication has stepped up its campaign against radio and television stations which discriminate both in employment and programming practices. They are organizing groups from the ghettos for this purpose.[34]

The development of groups within the ghetto to pressure the mass media for their rights has far-reaching implications. Although the ghetto is isolated from the mainstream of society, the mass media penetrate and "invade the ghetto in continuous and inevitable communication, largely one way, and project the values and aspirations, the manners and the style of the larger white-dominated society. . . . The Negro lives in part in the world of television and motion pictures, bombarded by the myths of the American middle class . . ."[35]

In a recent study of the New York Afro-American market conducted by Pulse, Inc., it was discovered that 98 percent of the blacks in the audience possessed a television receiver, while 98.5 percent of the audience owned at least one radio set. Over 32 percent possessed two radio sets, while more than 20 percent owned three receivers.[36]

What do these blacks in the ghettos of the United States see on television and hear on radio over one hundred years after the Emancipation Proclamation and after four decades of broadcasting? After much pressure upon broadcasters by national civil rights organizations, investigations by governmental agencies, and research by civic and professional organizations, there was less stereotyping of Negroes in the middle 1960s than in the past. In addition, blacks did appear in a variety of roles in broadcasting, but infrequently. They appeared on news and information programs, while there were very few in daytime serials and children's programs. The National Lawyers Guild summarized the situation by saying that there was still de facto exclusion of Negro performers on television, a failure of the medium to show Negro community activities, and a distorted image of the Negro on the television screen.[37] In a recent NAACP study of television commercials, conducted by Lawrence Plotkin, it was found "that Negroes are so rarely presented in significant ways in commercials that they learn that the products of middle class prosperity are not meant for them."[38] The Plotkin study clearly discovered that there is underrepresentation of the black in television. The researchers selected sports programs to view because of the high incidence of Negro athletes. Although they discovered an increase in the number of blacks in television commercials since 1962, they concluded that this improvement did not reflect the black's increased purchasing power nor his incidence in the population. "When one speaks of an improvement in a patient whose temperature has dropped from 105° to 102°, one does not conclude that the patient is well."[39] According to the Plotkin study, historical injustice was being perpetuated by many advertising corporations when they did not use blacks in their commercials.

Robert Lewis Shayon believes that "The Negro male . . . is simply no part of the picture of middle class life which the television commercials paint." He agrees with the conclusion of the Plotkin study that very few blacks are used in commercials, and where they are employed, it is merely tokenism.[40]

If blacks have not fared well in their appearances in commercials, how have they been represented in the body of regular programming? In 1968 only eight regular commercial series included blacks, and only two of the entire season's series let Afro-Americans share top billing: NBC's "I Spy," with Bill Cosby, and ABC's "N.Y.P.D.," with Robert Hooks. In 1969, ABC offered three more series, while NBC produced "Julia" for the second year.[41] "Julia" is a half-hour situation comedy series starring the Afro-American actress Diahann Caroll. It tells the story of Julia Baker, widow of a Vietnam war hero and mother of a six-year-old boy, Corey. Julia works as a nurse in the office of a white doctor, while her son looks for a potential father.[42] Robert Lewis Shayon has attacked the concept of "Julia" on the grounds that the program gives middle class viewers a glimpse of the middle class, not the reality of the poor. "What curious irony that this well-meaning television program should contribute to the castration theme in the history of the American Negro male."[43]

Apart from these exceptions, and the big-name singers and comics, the black on most television shows exists in a limbo. In the words of Dr. Kenneth Clark, "Television perpetuates in the Negro youngster's mind that he is a non-being."[44] Harry Belafonte believes that "For the shuffling, simpleminded Amos 'n' Andy type of Negro, television has substituted a new, one-dimensional Negro without reality." According to Belafonte, the black character in the average television drama represents a "super-Negro" or a "button-down Brooks Brothers eunuch."[45] Belafonte was involved in the infamous "touch incident" in an April, 1968, television special on NBC with Petula Clark, the "British songbird." Miss Clark touched Belafonte as they sang "On the Path of Glory." The sponsor's advertising manager asked for a retake of the tape. Belafonte refused: "This was the most outrageous case of racism I have ever seen in the business." Doyle Lott, the Chrysler-Plymouth official, apologized and recanted, but Belafonte said the apology came "one hundred years too late."[46]

The reader may be distressed by the "touch incident," but may rationalize that since this program was being produced for national consumption, southern stations might be offended. However, when the motion picture *A Taste of Honey* was shown over television in New York City (the northern "hotbed" of liberalism) the love scene between the white girl and the Negro sailor was cut.[47] Al Peters, writing in *TV Guide*, claimed that "the Negroes on TV are gaining acceptance as *Negroes*," but not as human beings. The image of the black is reinforced on television because the medium, by excluding him from most of its programs, helps to reinforce his image of rejection.[48]

Noncommercial radio and television have made miniscule attempts to provide more programming by and for the black audience. According to Robert Lewis Shayon, "Noncommercial television is endeavoring to let the inner core communicate to the suburbs in many 'tell it like it is' programs. Commercial television perpetuates the happy consciousness — the belief that the real is rational and that the system delivers the goods." [49] A recent study of educational television stations concluded that they have programmed either nothing or have applied a tokenism philosophy to their offerings for the black audience.[50]

Will the improvement in the image of the black man on television and radio continue at a snail's pace? When one compares the programming and employment policies of the commercial and noncommercial networks as well as the various craft unions with actual accomplishments, he must conclude that the snail's pace will continue. RCA serves as an example — a company that has had a policy of nondiscrimination in employment "because of race, color, age, creed or national origin" since 1919. In addition, the corporation has held equal employment opportunity seminars for all members of management — some five thousand in all.[51] The NBC network is also trying to create additional employment opportunities for performers. Mort Werner, vice-president, believes that NBC has made considerable progress "in making the Negro a part of the television scene." [52]

CBS has had a policy of nondiscrimination in hiring. Immediately following World War II, the network "determined to search actively for nonwhite employees." One of the problems encountered by CBS was the comparatively few job openings because of small turnover, except for the "white collar area."[53] Mike Dann, senior vice-president of CBS television network programs, has urged network producers and executives to seek more employment for blacks, both on camera and behind the scenes. The programming executive claimed that he had 100 percent backing of the advertisers.[54]

The American Broadcasting Company places in the hands of every department head in the company "and in fact in the hands of everyone else who has any responsibility for employing, upgrading, or discharging personnel" the following statement: "All applicants and employees will be given equal opportunity for employment and advancement, regardless of race, creed, color, national origin, age or sex."[55] According to the director of personnel at the network, the increase of minority employment from March, 1966, to March, 1967, was 13.5 percent.[56] ABC's programming policies took into account that the overwhelming majority of their entertainment programs were produced by independent companies. The network "won't accept a program that contains racial misrepresentation, ridicule or attack."[57] The network also plans to develop programs with blacks in the permanent cast. It believes that "the Negroes who appear on our game shows are ordinary, everyday people — young married couples, housewives, professional men, and white- and blue-collar workers — who are just being themselves, and having fun in the bargain."[58] As far back as 1962, for example, "three Negro ladies" were crowned "Queen for a Day" in one year.[59]

The noncommercial television network, NET, "has no specific written policies concerning practices in employing persons from minority groups."[60] NET has had members of minority groups on its staff for several years, but not as a result of any particular campaign to obtain them nor to discriminate against them. The noncommercial network's programming policy has often treated the problems of minorities and, with one recent exception, has sought people for production positions and on-the-air talent on the basis of their ability and specialization. A series, "Black Journal," employed an approximately 50 percent black production staff and "virtually all of the regular on camera talent" were Afro-American.[61]

Broadcasting labor unions have also had nondiscriminatory policies. Since 1963, the American Federation of Television and Radio Artists has had its policy against discrimination in the employment of talent included in all of its collective bargaining agreements. In addition, the delegates to AFTRA's 1968 annual convention resolved that the union was to arrange a program for the production and broadcast of public service announcements "designed to develop a public attitude in favor of equality of opportunity in employment, education and housing for all segments of our society." AFTRA members pledged their talent without compensation to this public service.[62] AFTRA also established a training program for nonprofessionals, with emphasis on nonwhites, to increase the percentage of black performers appearing on radio and television.[63] The union also resolved to pressure employers to hire more minority group members.[64]

The International Brotherhood of Electrical Workers has exercised a nondiscriminatory policy with respect to membership in the union ever since its involvement in the broadcasting industry in 1926. Since the union does not keep a record of religious affiliation, national origin, or color of any member, it is impossible to discover how many blacks belong to IBEW. As the broadcasting industry is subject to the National Labor Relations Act, and "federal law prohibits the so-called closed shop, broadcasting employers have complete and sole control of hiring their employees." IBEW, therefore, is not a hiring agent and hence, according to its officials, cannot discriminate in employment.[65] It appears that if blacks receive employment with broadcasting networks and stations, they have no problem joining the requisite unions.

A plan for increasing the number of blacks in broadcasting

was established at the national conference of the Urban League in August, 1964. This Broadcast Skills Bank, involving ABC, CBS, NBC, and the Westinghouse Broadcasting Company, makes a joint effort to recruit, train, and employ minority group manpower on a national basis. The bank, which operates as a branch of the Urban League's National Skills Bank, operates a national clearinghouse, with local branches in the seventy-two cities where the league has offices.[66] According to the vice-president of personnel at NBC, the Broadcast Skills Bank has not accomplished its objectives, even though a substantial degree of effort, imagination, and money was expended on the part of the broadcasting industry in attempting to make it a successful venture.[67] Local urban broadcasting workshops to recruit minority group members have been undertaken by various radio and television stations around the country. The National Association of Broadcasters, in its radio and television codes, specifically prohibits the portrayal of racial or national types which ridicule race or nationality.[68] Noncommercial broadcasters have also taken steps to foster the participation of blacks in educational radio and television. The National Association of Educational Broadcasters has established employment and programming practices committees concerned with minority groups.[69]

It would be naive to believe that if only blacks were trained in the skills of broadcasting and taught the essentials of production, doors would open for them immediately in the media. Michael Harrington has noted that "the more education a Negro has, the more economic discrimination he faces." The author of *The Other America* reminds his readers that the black doctor or lawyer finds it extremely difficult to set up a practice in a white neighborhood, while "the Negro academic often finds himself trapped in a segregated educational system in which Negro colleges are short on salaries, equipment, libraries, and so on."[70] The nature of the broadcasting industry is such that the majority of the hundreds of radio and television stations are relatively small companies. Only the networks are massive bureaucracies. Glazer and Moynihan, writing in *Beyond the Melting Pot,* pointed out that it is much easier to change employment patterns in huge, bureaucratically organized, strongly led organizations than in small ones. The authors noted that a small business "finds it easier to be tricky and evasive than the big one. For the big organization has personnel directors, formal application forms, formal tests, formal rating arrangements, formal rules" which various commissions against discrimination are empowered to observe or study.[71]

There seems to be a dichotomy between broadcasting practices on the transmission side of radio and television and black habits of reception in the ghettos. When one compares the employment and programming record of broadcasting vis-à-vis the black segment of the population with the pervasiveness and ubiquity of the media among that segment, a dilemma is created. Even though the black, by and large, is excluded from the mainstream of broadcasting, he is nevertheless surfeited with its products. As a matter of fact, according to Dr. Kenneth Clark, "the starvation for serious attention and respect, which characterizes so many of the forgotten people of the ghetto, made the microphone a symbol of respect and status."[72]

What then is the future of the black in broadcasting in the United States? Will radio and television continue to reflect the divided races of this nation? Will there emerge still more black radio stations and perhaps black television stations owned by whites?

Several years ago, an editorial in the *Nation* stated that integrated broadcasting is preferable to electronic segregation. The editors of the liberal periodical suggested that "an all-Negro television station" would talk only to blacks. They believed that "Negro-oriented television" would tend to perpetuate a feeling of separateness.[73] Yet, the so-called soul stations have been performing a real service to their communities. In New York City, for example, WLIB, "The Voice of Harlem," used its radio facilities to enable local residents to "let off steam" using the telephone talk-in format, especially in periods of tension. Leon Lewis's

"Community Opinion" program brought latent hostilities to the surface. The station planned to establish an on-the-air telephone dialogue between whites and blacks.[74] In April, 1968, WNEW-TV, a commercial television station in New York, began a sponsored series entitled "Inside Bedford-Stuyvesant" which was produced in the Bedford-Stuyvesant ghetto and featured local inhabitants. The program was aired at 7 A.M. and repeated after midnight.[75] Several educational television stations have attempted to set up satellite ghetto studios, but only two have obtained the necessary funds. WHA-TV in Madison, Wisconsin, received a grant from the Ford Foundation for fifty one-half hour broadcasts from a store front studio located in the poor section of that city. KCET received another grant to produce a daily magazine *Ahora* from a studio in the East Los Angeles barrio.[76]

Jack Gould of the *New York Times* has suggested the use of WYNC-TV, the UHF channel owned by the City of New York, as a ghetto television station. He believes that opportunities do not exist in the normal television system for an expression of ghetto views: "The white establishment retains the ultimate power of decision over what shall or shall not be seen, both in commercial and noncommercial video, and in prime evening hours the resources, talents and interests of the Negro culture continue to face substantial electronic disenfranchment."[77]

There are those who believe that blacks should participate in the mainstream of American broadcasting. This participation, however, is fraught with problems. Robert Lewis Shayon explored one of these problems: "How can he keep working and yet avoid a neo-Uncle Tomism that would vitiate his artistry and impoverish the media? . . . Negro performers do have something special to contribute — a flavor, tone, passion — the sum of their experience in a dominant white culture. Shall all this be ignored as they merely add more of the same to the present television scene, or shall they try to enrich the general culture by their special experience?"[78] The broadcasting critic of the *Saturday Review* believes that there should be black television workshops to seek out and train Afro-American youths for the broadcasting establishment.[79] Ed Dowling of the *New Republic* believes that television must be integrated so that blacks can communicate not only with fellow blacks but also with whites, in order to inform them of the realities of black America. Unfortunately, says Dowling, "commercial television is unwilling to make room for Negroes" and has "paid no attention to the counsels of the Kerner Commission." Dowling feels that public television is trying to do a good job but has no money, while commercial broadcasting's role has been mere "tokenism." [80]

If what has been stated is true, then television addiction in the ghetto is far more expensive than "booze or heroin or cocaine." [81] Television, as the black's chosen instrument of revolution, can widen or heal the black-white schism in the United States.[82]

Will broadcasting, and especially television, widen the racial gap, or is the medium proceeding with integration? Militant blacks argue that nothing new is really happening. They feel that because of pressures the networks are sprinkling a few Afro-Americans around the screen. The 1969 television season had about thirty blacks in continuing roles on the three networks. They were cast in a variety of roles. Michael L. Vallon, who conducted the hearings into the use of black actors on television for the New York City Human Rights Commission said: "On paper, there seems to be a considerable increase in the use of the black man on television. We are hopeful that blacks will be three-dimensional characters instead of ebony furniture." [83] Robert Dallos, writing in the *New York Times*, asks, "Can television move fast enough to catch up with the onrushing events of the world it pretends to represent?" [84]

In a sense, however, broadcasting cannot be expected to do for the black man what it has not done for the white man. The emergence of the black revolution has tested the very fabric of society's values and goals. Black pressure on radio and television

may improve the media for all races. In the meantime, one pleads
that the Institute of Urban Communications, recommended by the
National Advisory Commission on Civil Disorders, be organized
immediately. This institute could make a broad study of blacks
in broadcasting and recommend a course for future action.[85]

But even if an Institute of Urban Communications is formed,
the solutions cannot be found in the broadcasting media alone.
The causes of broadcasting's failure to come to grips with the
black revolution is a reflection of the racist nature of American
society. Perhaps, as some believe, the media can heal the black-
white schism, but this will only occur when the white establishment truly desires to bind the wounds of racial separation.

Although the FCC threatens possible loss of licenses to those
radio and television stations which discriminate, it must be
remembered that the commission in the past has only revoked
licenses from stations advocating "goat-gland transplants" and the
triumph of Adolf Hitler. While the soul radio stations remain in
the hands of white owners, and no black television outlets exist,
blacks for the most part will be unable to contribute on an equal
basis to the establishment's outlets. Ghetto television and radio
stations must become realities. Blacks must first "make it on their
own" in broadcasting. Only then may they come as equals to the
white world of broadcasting.

It may be argued that the networks and labor unions have been
"brave" by advocating nondiscrimination policies. NBC has had
a nondiscrimination policy since it began broadcasting in the
1920s. CBS and ABC have also had these nondiscriminatory procedures for decades. CBS, for example, sought out non-whites
after World War II, but found that there were few job openings.
The broadcasting labor unions for many years have had antidiscrimination policies.

The commercial broadcasting industry did establish a Skills
Bank in 1964, although it has failed, while the NAEB in 1967
decided to talk about the problems of programming and employment practices. The National Educational Television Network,

while mounting no campaign for black employment, did produce "Black Journal."

With all the antidiscrimination policies in programming and employment of commercial and noncommercial broadcasting, labor unions, and interested parties, where are the blacks in broadcasting? If the white establishment has been working so diligently these past years to insure equal opportunities for minority groups in their industry, where are the invisible men? The Kerner Commission answers the question.

Broadcasters are reflecting three hundred years of racial prejudice. Social scientists believe that these ethnic prejudices may be destroyed by institutions of society. The broadcasting industry is one which can play a very substantial role in the eradication of racism.

There is still time and hope for broadcasting. The media of radio and television must be in the vanguard of the black revolution. They must not only stimulate and communicate the urgency of the struggle, but must be a part of the contest. Only if the leaders of the broadcasting industry take affirmative steps to close the ever-widening gap between white and black can there be any hope for the United States.

James Baldwin, talking in 1960 about mass media and culture in America, said:

I feel very strongly, though, that this amorphous people are in desperate search for something which will help them to re-establish their connection with themselves, and with one another. This can only begin to happen as the truth begins to be told. We are in the middle of an immense metamorphosis here, a metamorphosis which will, it is devoutly to be hoped, rob us of our myths and give us our history, which will destroy our attitudes and give us back our personalities. The mass culture, in the meantime, can only reflect our chaos: and perhaps we had better remember that this chaos contains life — and a great transforming energy.[86]

Would Mr. Baldwin be as optimistic today about blacks and broadcasting? The truth is beginning to be told. Whether it is too late remains to be seen.

NOTES

The passages opening the chapter can be found in William H. Grier and Price M. Cobbs, *Black Rage* (New York: Basic Books, 1968), p. 198, and *The Autobiography of Malcolm X* (New York: Grove Press, 1966), p. 273.

1. *Report of the National Advisory Commission on Civil Disorders* (New York: Bantam Books, 1968), p. 383.
2. New York: The Free Press, 1967, pp. 421–36.
3. *The Nature of Prejudice* (Garden City, New York: Doubleday and Co., 1958), pp. 198–99.
4. Wilbert E. Moore and Melvin M. Tumin, "Some Social Functions of Ignorance," *American Sociological Review* 14 (Dec. 1949), 787–95.
5. Thomas F. Pettigrew, "Complexity and Change," *Daedalus*, Fall, 1965; Erik Barnouw, *A Tower in Babel* (New York: Oxford University Press, 1966), pp. 128–31.
6. Quoted in Charles J. Correll and Freeman F. Gosden, *Here They Are — Amos 'n' Andy* (New York: Ray Long and Richard R. Smith, 1931), pp. v–vi.
7. Max Wylie, "Amos 'n' Andy — Loving Remembrance," *TV Quarterly*, Summer, 1963, pp. 17–24.
8. Charles J. Correll and Freeman F. Gosden, *All About Amos 'n' Andy* (New York: Rand McNally & Co., 1929), p. 9.
9. Barnouw, *Tower in Babel*, pp. 224–31.
10. Michael Harrington, *The Other America* (Baltimore: Penguin Books, 1963), pp. 71–72.
11. W. E. Burghardt DuBois, *Dark Water* (New York: Harcourt, Brace & Howe, 1920), p. 29.
12. *Ibid.*, p. 3.
13. Richard S. Kahlenberg, "Negro Radio," *Negro History Bulletin*, March, 1966, pp. 127–128 ff.
14. *Ibid.*
15. G. Franklin Edwards, *The Negro Professional Class* (Glencoe, Illinois: The Free Press of Glencoe, 1959), p. 120.
16. Sterling D. Spero and Abram L. Harris, *The Black Worker* (Port Washington, New York: Kennikat Press, 1966).
17. Edwards, *Negro Professional Class*, p. 168.
18. *Ibid.*, p. 172.
19. Kahlenberg, "Negro Radio."
20. Langston Hughes and Milton Meltzer, *Black Magic* (Englewood Cliffs, New Jersey: Prentice Hall, 1967), pp. 323–35.

21. Testimony of Mort Werner, vice-president in charge of programs and talent, NBC Television Network, before the New York City Commission on Human Rights, March 15, 1968.
22. Kahlenberg, "Negro Radio."
23. Hughes and Meltzer, *Black Magic.*
24. FCC, *Application of Lamar Life Broadcasting Company for Renewal of License of Television Station WLBT*, docket number 16663, BRCT–326, FCC 68-689, 18285, June 27, 1968.
25. Walter Pincus, "Discrimination in TV in Jackson, Mississippi," *New Republic*, June 5, 1965.
26. Robert Lewis Shayon, "FCC Investigation of WLBT," *Saturday Review*, June 26, 1965.
27. Robert Lewis Shayon, "FCC Aired in Renewing WLBT," *Saturday Review*, May 7, 1966.
28. *Newsweek*, May 29, 1967.
29. *Broadcasting*, August 4, 1969.
30. FCC, *Application of Lamar Life Broadcasting Company.*
31. FCC, *Petition for Rulemaking to Require Broadcast Licensees to Show Non-discrimination in Their Employment Practices*, docket number 18244, RM–1144, FCC 68–702, 18337, July 3, 1968.
32. *New York Times*, July 6, 1968.
33. United States Court of Appeals for the District of Columbia Circuit, No. 19,409, *Office of Communication of the United Church of Christ, et al.*, vs. *FCC*, appellee, *Lamar Life Broadcasting Company*, intervenor, decided June 20, 1969.
34. *How To Protect Citizen Rights in Television and Radio* (New York: Office of Communication, United Church of Christ, 1968).
35. Kenneth B. Clark, *Dark Ghetto* (New York: Harper & Row, 1965), p. 12.
36. "Demographic Study of the New York Negro Market," survey conducted for WLIB by Pulse, Inc., January 2, 1968.
37. Lawrence Plotkin, *Report on the Frequency of Appearance of Negroes on Televised Commercials* (New York: NAACP Legal Defense and Educational Fund, April, 1967), pp. 1–3.
38. *Ibid.*, p. 10.
39. *Ibid.*, pp. 8–10.
40. Robert Lewis Shayon, "Negroes in Commercials," *Saturday Review*, November 4, 1967.
41. *Newsweek*, March 18, 1968.
42. Judy Stone, "Black is the Color of Diahann's 'Julia,'" *The New York Times*, August 18, 1968.

43. Robert Lewis Shayon, "'Julia': Breakthrough or Letdown?" *Saturday Review*, April 20, 1968, May 25, 1968.
44. Bruce Porter, "The Negro Stereotype," *Newsweek*, April 3, 1967.
45. "Black on Channels," *Time*, May 24, 1968.
46. *Newsweek*, March 18, 1968.
47. Porter, "The Negro Stereotype," pp. 59–60.
48. Al Peters, "What the Negro Wants from TV," *TV Guide*, January 20, 1968, pp. 6–10.
49. Shayon, "'Julia': Breakthrough or Letdown?"
50. Richard J. Meyer, "ETV and the Ghetto," *Educational Broadcasting Review*, August, 1968, pp. 19–24.
51. Testimony of George H. Fuchs, vice-president in charge of personnel, NBC Television Network, before the New York City Commission on Human Rights, March 14, 1968.
52. Testimony of Mort Werner before New York City Commission on Human Rights.
53. Testimony of William C. Fitts, Jr., vice-president, CBS Television Network, before the New York City Commission on Human Rights, March 14, 1968; before the Equal Employment Opportunity Commission, January 17, 1968.
54. *Hollywood Daily Variety*, April 29, 1968.
55. Testimony of Miss Marie McWilliams, director of personnel, ABC, before the Equal Employment Opportunity Commission, January 17, 1968.
56. *Ibid.*
57. Testimony of Leonard Goldberg, vice-president of TV network programming, ABC, before the New York City Commission on Human Rights, March 15, 1968.
58. *Ibid.*
59. Testimony of Theodore Fetter, vice-president and director of programs, ABC Television Network, before congressional subcommittee chaired by Rep. Adam Clayton Powell, October, 1962.
60. Gerard L. Appy, vice-president of network affairs, NET, to Richard J. Meyer, August 12, 1968.
61. *Ibid.*
62. "Resolution CVR-8A regarding equal employment opportunities," adopted by AFTRA National Convention, 1968.
63. "Resolution CVR-15 on the job training program," adopted by AFTRA National Convention, 1968.
64. Sanford I. Wolff, national executive secretary, AFTRA, to Richard J. Meyer, July 29, 1968.

65. Letter and policy statement from Albert O. Hardy, director, Radio, Television and Recording Division, IBEW, to Richard J. Meyer, August 14, 1968.
66. *Broadcast Skills Bank: Career Opportunities in Broadcasting* (New York: National Urban League, n.d.).
67. Testimony of George H. Fuchs before New York City Commission on Human Rights.
68. NAB, *The Radio Code* (Washington, D.C., September, 1967); NAB, *The Television Code* (Washington, D.C., October, 1967).
69. *NAEB Newsletter*, June, 1968.
70. Harrington, *The Other America*, p. 77.
71. Nathan Glazer and Daniel Patrick Moynihan, *Beyond the Melting Pot* (Cambridge: The M.I.T. Press, 1963), pp. 40–41.
72. Clark, *Dark Ghetto*, pp. xviii–xix.
73. "Negro on TV," *Nation*, November 22, 1965.
74. "WLIB Community Opinion," *Newsweek*, May 8, 1967.
75. "Inside Bedford-Stuyvesant," *Newsweek*, April 29, 1968.
76. Ford Foundation news release, April 9, 1969, p. 6.
77. Jack Gould, "A New Gateway for the Ghetto?" *New York Times*, August 4, 1968.
78. Robert Lewis Shayon, "Negro Performers," *Saturday Review*, March 26, 1966.
79. Shayon, " 'Julia': Breakthrough or Letdown?"
80. Ed Dowling, "Color Us Black," *New Republic*, June 8, 1968.
81. *Ibid.*
82. "TV and Race," *America*, April 6, 1968.
83. Robert E. Dallos, "Will the Black Say Too Little Too Late?" *New York Times*, September 1, 1968.
84. *Ibid.*
85. *Report of the National Advisory Commission on Civil Disorders*, pp. 386–89.
86. James Baldwin, "Mass Culture and the Creative Artist: Some Personal Notes," *Daedalus*, Spring, 1960, p. 376.

13 Blacklisting

by GARY GUMPERT

The phenomenon of blacklisting made its appearance in the entertainment world shortly after World War II, and the story of its effect upon the radio and television industry has been narrated by a number of authors. As early as 1952 Merle Miller's *The Judges and the Judged*, based upon an investigation sponsored by the American Civil Liberties Union, appeared, with a foreword by Robert E. Sherwood expressing the growing public concern over the effects of blacklisting on American life:

> Our American culture is based not on our natural resources, our mountains and prairies and rivers, our farms, factories and mines: it is based on freedom — and when freedom is abrogated, then we must become tongue-tied, impotent, doomed.[1]

In 1956 the Fund for the Republic published a major two-volume *Report on Blacklisting*, by John Cogley, dealing with the motion picture industry (volume 1) and the radio and television industries (volume 2). In the foreword to the second volume Paul G. Hoffman presented the Fund for the Republic's reasons for sponsoring the study:

> Most Americans are convinced that loyalty-security investigations of people working for the government in sensitive positions or seeking key federal jobs are necessary to protect the government from the infiltration of persons who might try to destroy it. But when loyalty

tests are applied by private groups to people in private industries — and people are barred from jobs because they are "controversial" — many citizens become alarmed.[2]

Another significant study, a long personal account of the effects of such exclusion on the life of one man, appeared in 1964: *Fear on Trial*, written by John Henry Faulk,[3] a successful radio and television performer who fought a six-year legal battle to clear himself of accusations seriously damaging to his career.

While much has been written, however, there is still much to be weighed, to be determined about the relation of blacklisting to the structure of American life and of American broadcasting. This chapter can only suggest this in the process of reviewing the meaning of blacklisting, the political climate in which it developed, and what transpired during its most flagrant and uninhibited use.

The term *blacklisting* is a familiar one in the history of labor and unionism, defined as a "procedure whereby employers or employers' associations circulated the name or names of 'undesirable' employees, mostly those who were active union men, 'disrupters' or 'outside agitators.'"[4] In somewhat more general terms, a blacklist has been defined as "a listing of persons who are felt to deserve public censure,"[5] or as "a list of persons considered objectionable by a given organization."[6] The expression *to blacklist* has been used in many ways, but its most general meaning in recent times has been "to single out a person for some kind of discriminatory treatment, such as vigilance, exclusion, censure, or punishment,"[7] and it is in this sense that it is used here.

In his study of contemporary American life Max Lerner has described what he calls the "cultural vigilantism" or "security syndrome" that developed after World War II. It began with the fear that the United States was threatened by a Communist conspiracy, and led to "congressional investigations, destructive publicity, purges, blacklists, and indirect pressure,"[8] in the course of which the civil liberties of Americans were diminished, disregarded, and distorted in the name of patriotism. If, as Lerner says, freedom is always relative, never absolute, and "may be seen partly as a function of the way power is distributed, separated, and diffused in a society," [9] the fact that an alarming degree of power rested within the grasp of relatively few in broadcasting must be considered significant in the transformation of this general fear into an acceptance of the practice of blacklisting in the industry.

This problem of relative freedom was involved in a situation that arose in 1947. When can an employer refuse employment to someone for reasons other than job capability? When is refusal to hire illegal? The answers were not simple and clear. Morality and legality were not necessarily coterminous, or, as it turned out, the right to say something did not necessarily guarantee the sponsorship that would enable one to say it. The case of William L. Shirer presents some of the intricacies of the problem.

The Shirer Case

In 1947 William L. Shirer was a news commentator for the Columbia Broadcasting System, and was considered to represent a liberal point of view. On March 23, 1947, he announced during his broadcast that the network had notified him that his sponsor, the J. B. Williams Company, was dropping him from the program the following Sunday. Shirer felt that he was being "gagged" because of his liberal views. Edward R. Murrow, CBS vice-president, stated that the commentator was merely being replaced and that the decision was not connected with Shirer's political views. "The decision to replace Mr. Shirer on the air was the decision of CBS. Mr. Shirer will have a new spot but what it will be is not yet known." [10] A number of other newscasters and commentators were faced with a similar predicament at this time, and the *New York Times*, a week after the Shirer announcement, referred to the "large-scale departure of so called 'liberal' newscasters and commentators from the networks. Their sympathizers call it expulsion."[11] This was not strictly a case of blacklisting, although it is related, for the power and rights of the sponsor as an employer were germane both to this case and to the larger problem of blacklisting. A *New York Times* editorial analyzed the departure of the commentators in this way:

> We may deplore the fact that a sponsor has it in his power to evict a news commentator who has built up a public of five million listeners, but this does not enter into the problem we are here discussing. If the sponsor is sincere in saying that he wants an audience of fifteen million to listen to his wares instead of only five million, then the question of freedom of utterance is not involved.
>
> But if it should turn out that the sponsor is actuated by ideological considerations in dispensing with this former "liberal" program, then we come back to our former contention. It was not really the sponsor who "determined" the change; it was the voice of the people last November, or what the sponsor sincerely regards as the voice of the people. A man with something to sell does not quarrel with his potential customers.[12]

In other words, in this editorial view, if the sponsor recognizes a shift in the political climate of the nation, he is within his rights to modify his programming in order to reach a larger audience. The ethics and morality of the decision might be argued, but the rights of the sponsor should be recognized in this case.

The Shirer case and such analyses as the *Times'* provide some insight into the political climate of the day and into the structure and inherently economic motivation of the American broadcasting system. The sponsor wishes to reach the greatest number of people for the smallest advertising cost. At the same time, he wishes to remain within the good graces of the buying public. Should that public become unhappy with the program or should the advertising cost of reaching that public rise because of a dwindling audience, the sponsor takes action rather quickly. He is a nervous individual who could be easily managed by outside pressure of any who might object to the content, performers, or production personnel of a particular program.

Counterattack

In the year of the Shirer case, 1947, a new publication "designed 'to obtain, file and index factual information on Communists, Communist fronts and other subversive organizations'" was founded under the name of *Counterattack*.[13] The three founding editors were Ken Bierly, Ted Kirkpatrick, and John Keenan. All three were ex-FBI men. (Of the original editors, only John Keenan remains with the publication today.) The three men had collaborated earlier as the John Quincy Adams Associates and published another anti-Communist newsletter called *Plain Talk*. When the John Quincy Adams Associates dissolved after their failure to secure tax-exempt status, Bierly, Kirkpatrick, and Keenan formed the American Business Consultants in April, 1947.[14] This organization became the basic organization publishing *Counterattack*. A yearly subscription cost twenty-four dollars and included a number of irregularly published special reports (one of them to be *Red Channels*, published in 1950). By 1952 the circulation of the newsletter was slightly less than 4000 copies per issue. The yearly income from the newsletter was approximately $96,000.[15] This figure does not include the investigative and research services conducted by the group for various individuals and organizations. Ken Bierly, one of the editors, stated that for those special services, " 'The minimum fee is five dollars, where we charge a fee. The maximum fee runs into several thousands of dollars.' " [16]

Counterattack did not limit itself to praise and condemnation of individuals within the broadcasting field. Its interests were wide and far ranging.

Among the targets of the newsletter have been Trygve Lie ("Stalin's choice"); the U.N. itself ("its officials deny it is a shelter or cover for Communists and pro-Communists"); a judge of the New York State Supreme Court who used the words "witch hunt" in one of his decisions; William L. Green and Philip Murray; the Blatz Beer Company, for using a "fellow-traveling" actress from Milwaukee in one of its ads (the newsletter asked its readers to write directly to the brewery and complain); the book-review sections of both the *New York Times* and the *Herald Tribune* (sometimes for damning a book like "Seeds of Treason" of which *Counterattack* approved, again for praising a volume the newsletter disliked); the Yale Law School, for having "Reds" on its staff; the Associated Press, for distributing an article "misleading" the public on communism in Hollywood; the "slick, sophisticated *New Yorker* magazine . . . read in all parts of the United States . . . for what the C.P. calls its 'upper-middle-class' type of humor and culture"; *Life, Look, Time,* the *Atlantic, Fortune,* Standard Oil of New Jersey, U.S. Steel, all the major radio and television networks, and scores of producers, directors, actors, singers, and dancers, and, of course, *The Nation.*[17]

The editors asserted that " 'proof is available for every statement made in *Counterattack.*' "[18] Some of this proof was provided by congressional investigations.

Trial by Committee

In August of 1947 the House Committee on Un-American Activities began its investigation of Communist infiltration and influence in the motion picture industry, using procedures which, like those of the Senate Subcommittee on Internal Security, came to be questioned by a number of critics. A group of individuals known as the Hollywood Ten emerged from the hearings of the committee. They had taken the witness stand, invoked the First Amendment to the Constitution, and refused to reveal whether they were, or ever had been, members of the Communist Party.

In November they were cited for contempt of Congress, a misdemeanor. In December they were blacklisted by the producers in a public statement known as the Waldorf Agreement. The following year saw them indicted, arraigned, tried, convicted, sentenced and released on bail pending appeal.[19]

The Hollywood Ten did not work in their professions for a number of years — at least not under their real names — and those who supported them or who fought the procedures of the committee were in turn attacked.

Among the individuals and organizations who questioned the conduct of the House and Senate investigations was the American

Civil Liberties Union. On April 3, 1950, the union warned the Motion Picture Association of America against reprisal toward witnesses who refused to answer the questions of the House committee. Patrick Murphy Malin, ACLU executive director, in a letter to Joyce O'Hara, vice-president of the Motion Picture Association, pointed out that a person has the right not to incriminate himself, if only to protect himself from the fear of prosecution, and that this right should not be interpreted as any admission of guilt or the commission of a crime:

Nobody has a constitutional right to employment in the motion picture industry, or any other. But the maintenance of our free society requires that employers should observe the *spirit* of our constitutional civil liberties — including among other things, equality of treatment with regard to employment in positions where risk to national security is not involved.[20]

In reality, however, if an individual was named by either a witness testifying before the committee or by a member of the committee itself, that utterance became public record, and the fact that the accused might be innocent of any charges or that he would not be confronted by his accuser was not important to those groups seeking evidence. *Counterattack* and the other participants in blacklisting used any public record which suited their purposes in an interlocking fashion. For example, the following citation appeared in *Red Channels* under the name Irwin Shaw:

Committee for the First Amendment	Signer. Advertisement, *Hollywood Reporter*, 10/24/47, protesting the conduct of the Washington hearings. *Un-Am. Act in California, 1947*, p. 211.[21]

Mr. Shaw's exercising of his right to protest the conduct of the committee was used as proof of some activity which the editors of *Red Channels* frowned upon. There were numerous other sources available to the publishers of *Counterattack*, such as the proceedings of the California Un-American Activities Committee (the Tenney Committee), the Attorney General's list of subversive organizations, the content of the *Daily Worker*, and the letterheads of a variety of national organizations. The interlocking citation system operated by using any one source as evidence for further citation. Therefore, praise by the *Daily Worker* placed an individual in danger, since *Counterattack* might then also mention the fact that the *Daily Worker* had praised a certain individual. Later, when the American Business Consultants published *Red Channels*, *Counterattack* sometimes provided the citation necessary for inclusion in *Red Channels*. Sometimes the procedure was reversed. Citation in one source provided the evidence for citation by any other source.

Red Channels

On June 22, 1950, *Counterattack* published *Red Channels: The Report of Communist Influence in Radio and Television*. *Red Channels* included the names of 151 persons who were allegedly sympathetic to Communism. The impact of this publication was increased by the start of the Korean conflict several days later. The introduction to the volume was written by Vincent Hartnett, a former television supervisor at an advertising agency and subsequently, as Hartnett described himself, "a professional consultant on the Communist and/or Communist-front records of persons working in the entertainment industry; particularly radio and television." [22] (He later joined Aware, Inc.) There is some confusion over Hartnett's role in *Red Channels*. According to Ted Kirkpatrick, Hartnett was not officially an employee of American Business Consultants, although he became known as the author of *Red Channels*. Hartnett did write the introduction to the volume and was paid a percentage of royalties on the sale of the book. [23]

The introduction to *Red Channels* gives its rationale for blacklisting:

Basically, the Cominform (previously known as the Comintern) seeks to exploit American Radio and TV to gain the following:

(1) Channels (known to the Communist Party as "transmission belts") for the pro-Soviet, pro-Communist, anti-American, anti-democratic propaganda.

(2) Financial support.

(3) The great prestige and crowd-gathering power that derives from having glamorous personalities of radio and TV as sponsors of Communist fronts and as performers or speakers at front meetings and rallies (which incidentally adds to the performers' prestige).

(4) Increasing domination of American broadcasting and telecasting, preparatory to the day when — the Cominform believes — the Communist Party will assume control of this nation as the result of a final upheaval and civil war.[24]

With such broad aims of the Cominform in mind, the nature of an individual's involvement with a radio or television program was unimportant to pressure groups of the Right. The program did not have to have a left-of-center message in order to aid the cause of communism. As long as the accused person gained his livelihood through employment in the radio and television field, he could, it was assumed, be aiding the causes of communism. Nor were guilt or awareness prerequisite to condemnation. The unaware, the dupes, the cases of mistaken identity — all had to eventually prove their innocence and loyalty through the machinery of blacklisting and clearance. The process of citation, pressure, and for some, rehabilitation and clearance, became part of institutionalized blacklisting.

While *Red Channels* outlined the aims of the Cominform, it also claimed the existence of a blacklist of anti-Communists:

The "Boost" and the "Blacklist"

If the Communist Party USA exacts a heavy financial toll of its members and dupes, it has been no less energetic in seeing to it that they get ahead in show business, while articulate anti-Communists are blacklisted and smeared with that venomous intensity which is characteristic of Red Fascists alone.

The Communist-operated "escalator system" in show business has been in force for at least 12 years — since the Spanish Civil War. Those who are "right" are "boosted" from one job to another, from humble beginnings in Communist-dominated night clubs or on small programs which have been "colonized," to more important programs and finally to stardom. Literally scores of our most prominent producers, directors, writers, actors and musicians owe their present success largely to the Party "boost" system, a system which involves not only "reliable" producers and directors, but also ad agency executives, network and station executives, writers, fellow-actors and critics and reviewers. In turn, the Party member or "reliable" who has "arrived" gives the "boost" to others who, the Red grapevine whispers, are to be helped.

A prominent entertainer has recently confided that whenever a certain critic on one of our great American newspapers asks him to entertain for or sponsor a Communist front meeting, he always complies. Understandably so! Without favorable reviews from this important critic, his career could be jeopardized.

Contrary-wise, those who know radio and TV can recite dozens of examples of anti-Communists who, for mysterious reasons, are *persona non grata* on numerous programs, and who are slandered unmercifully in certain "progressive" circles.

That this system should be so prevalent is a matter for utmost consideration by those who employ radio and TV talent.[25]

Red Channels retaliated with its own list, actually two lists. The first named individuals and their affiliations. The second was a list of organizations and their citations as Communist fronts.

The Muir Incident

Let the record also show that Miss Muir has volunteered, to the chairman, to come before the committee and give facts pertinent to the investigations being conducted by the committee into the infiltration of communism and other subversion in the entertainment field.

. . . . .

MR. KUNSIG: Miss Muir I want you to state, also for the record, your reasons for voluntarily coming here today.

MISS MUIR: Yes. When the Aldrich Family incident took place, and I was thrown off the show, people called both my husband and myself asking permission to create committees of protest, or Jean Muir committees. We turned down all these requests and offers in an effort to keep it out of the hands of any committees which might later become fronts, or be supported by Communists, and also to try and prevent me from being turned into a martyr by people with whom I did not wish to become associated. We didn't want it to become a cause celebre. Unfortunately, it did become that. When they learned we would not join them, they began a violent and organized protest on my behalf anyhow, which caused me to become confident that the Communist Party fronts are actually trying to harm me, the results of this being that in so doing they hurt this committee. As you know, they have tried many times. I, therefore, wanted to come here. What has happened to me in the last 3 years is not, I feel, the responsibility of this committee. I wanted to come because I felt this committee is not for the purpose of persecution, but for the purpose of finding out just who is causing this kind of thing.

. . . . .

That following August, in 1950, I was signed to play the part of Mrs. Aldrich, in the Aldrich Family show. It was to be a half-hour TV show. I was very excited about this, and went to dress rehearsal the Sunday evening before the time to start, and we were all told the show would not go on. The reason for this was not told to us at the time. Nobody seemed to know the reason, but a newspaperman on the New York Times called and found out about it, and it was on the front page of the New York Times the following day, all about me. Consequently it spread all over the country.

MR. VELDE: Then you actually never did appear on the Henry Aldrich TV show?

MISS MUIR: No.

MR. CLARDY: What date was that?

MISS MUIR: August 25, 1950. Since then I have not worked.

MR. SCHERER: What appeared in the New York Times?

MISS MUIR: The fact that the reason for the cancelling of the show was because NBC had received, I believe, 10 telephone calls and 2 telegrams — I believe that was the number, wasn't it? [26]

Blacklisting became an industry reality with the Jean Muir incident described in this excerpt from 1953 testimony before the House Un-American Activities Committee. When Miss Muir's contract to appear as the mother in the Aldrich Family television series was cancelled by the General Foods Corporation, and the sponsor entered the arena, it was the stimulus for panic on Madison Avenue. While the sponsor could act out of political conviction, he could also be manipulated by outside pressures which might threaten his income. In turn, the sponsor could threaten the advertising agencies, stations, and networks by depriving them of income. With sponsor pressure the broadcasting establishment became concerned not with guilt as an issue, but only controversy. Television producer Mark Goodson testified on this point during the libel suit of John Henry Faulk against Aware, Inc., Vincent W. Hartnett, and Laurence A. Johnson:

GOODSON: A sponsor is in business to sell his goods. He has no interest in being involved in causes. He does not want controversy.

NIZER: [Louis Nizer was Faulk's lawyer.] He does not want what?
GOODSON: Controversy. The favorite slogan along Madison Avenue is
"Why buy yourself a headache?" The advertising agency's job is to see
to it that the products are sold but that the sponsor keeps out of trouble, and the advertising agency can lose a great deal, it can lose the
account. The sponsor can lose a little bit of business, but he still can
recoup it. The agency can lose the account and I would say that a
great portion of an agency's job is concerned with the pleasing and
taking care and serving a client.[27]

Goodson also stated that an advertising agency did not really
take a political position, but rather an apolitical one which was
merely "anti-controversial."[28]

Blacklisting did not immediately become institutionalized in
the sense that it became an integral, systematic part of the broadcasting world. There were some members of the broadcasting
profession who refused to be intimidated by the growing pressure. Their number, however, dwindled rapidly, particularly as
the figure of Senator Joseph R. McCarthy loomed larger on the
political scene. It is tempting to equate McCarthyism with blacklisting or to suggest a causal relationship, but both can be considered symptoms of a climate of insecurity and fear which per-
vaded the nation during the 1950s. One of those individuals who
refused to be intimidated, at least in 1950, was Robert E. Kintner,
president of the American Broadcasting Company. Gypsy Rose
Lee had been scheduled to appear on an ABC network radio
show, but Miss Lee was listed in *Red Channels*, and the American Business Consultants and the Illinois American Legion
applied pressure for Miss Lee's dismissal from the program. Kintner refused to heed the warnings of the pressure groups and
challenged them by refusing to interfere with the scheduled
broadcast.[29]

The Clearance Officer

Interference in another instance caused Elmer Rice, Pulitzer
Prize playwright, to dissociate himself from television's Celanese
Theater. A. Walter Socolaw, attorney for Ellington and Company,
representatives of the sponsor, refused to clear actor John Gar-

field for a production of Rice's *Counselor-at-Law*. Rice's contract stipulated that he had a voice in casting, but the advertising agency felt that "when you get somebody who may cause a lot of bad publicity for your program, you do have to be a little careful. It's an ordinary business safeguard."[30] In this case one more addition to the mechanism of blacklisting, clearance officers, appeared: individuals within networks and advertising agencies who became responsible for the stamp of approval or disapproval of potential cast members on the basis of noncontroversiality. The investigative and research services of the American Business Consultants were available to the clearance officers. The development of clearance officers, security officers, and loyalty oaths gave rise to a number of lists running along a monochromatic spectrum from black to white. There were also "gray" lists of persons who could be hired for specific programs under special conditions.

While blacklisting became institutionalized, the practice was not acknowledged and it was referred to indirectly. This conversation between a producer and an agent was reported:

Who . . . have you got like John Garfield?

What do you mean who've I got like Garfield? I've got the boy himself. Why don't you use him?

We just can't do it. I'm sorry but we just can't, and you know why we can't.

You're damn right I know why.[31]

The FCC

On April 9, 1952, the issue of blacklisting in radio and television broadcasting was placed before the Federal Communications Commission by the American Civil Liberties Union. The complaint prepared by James Lawrence Fly, former FCC chairman, and the ACLU board of directors asked for a general investigation of the blacklisting practice and for FCC regulations to end it.[32] The following were named as defendants in the complaint: the National Broadcasting Company, the American Broadcasting Company, the Dumont Television Network, the Columbia Broadcasting System, WPIX (the New York *Daily News* television station), and radio station KOWL of Santa Monica, California. WPIX was cited because it cancelled some old silent Charlie Chaplin films when a New Jersey war veterans post protested. The Weavers, a folk-singing quartet, were dropped from an NBC show, apparently because of their political associations. The Jean Muir case involved the National Broadcasting Company. Paul Draper, a dancer, was dropped from the CBS Ed Sullivan "Toast of the Town" show. Dumont cancelled the appearance of pianist Hazel Scott after she was listed in *Red Channels*.

The ACLU complaint asserted that blacklisting was against the public interest "because it denied the public 'the right to see or hear artists or their work-products because of irrelevant considerations.'" [33] The ACLU asked the FCC to deny the renewal of licenses to the defendants

unless they pledge under oath not to "discriminate in employment upon the basis of alleged or real associations and beliefs, whether past, present, or future" or to permit such discrimination by any advertiser, advertising agency, or others responsible for programming.[34]

The Federal Communications Commission's reaction to the complaint was a vote to grant only temporary renewal of licenses to the stations involved. (The FCC cannot take action against the networks themselves, since only the stations are licensed.) However, the commission reversed its action on June 11, 1953, after *Counterattack*, other pressure groups, and news commentator Fulton Lewis, Jr., attacked the commission on the general questions raised by the ACLU complaint.[35] The final disposition of the case is not clear. The ACLU did subsequently petition the FCC for a rehearing of the June 11th order, "asserting that the Commission had acted before the Union filed its brief in reply to the networks' and stations' answers to the ACLU's charges — a brief the Commission itself had requested." [36]

Aware, Inc.

The forces of blacklisting were strengthened when another organization dedicated to anti-Communism, Aware, Inc., was formed in 1953. Its president was Godfrey Schmidt, a professor at Fordham University and an associate member of the American Federation of Television and Radio Artists. Vincent Hartnett, earlier associated with *Red Channels*, was one of the organization's directors, along with seven other members of AFTRA. Aware, Inc., stated that its aim was to fight Communist influence in the entertainment and communication fields. Schmidt said that his group was

concerned with Communist influence as insinuated by a) Communists; or b) persons (no matter what their conscious loyalty) with extensive but never disavowed Communist-front affiliations; or c) "innocents" who, whatever their loyalty, permit their names, talents or prestige to be used (often and continuously, without the slightest protest) to aid Communist fronts.[37]

Aware, Inc., did not publish blacklists, although its bulletins were instrumental in the process of blacklisting, and one of them became the center of controversy involving the American Federation of Television and Radio Artists and that union's relationship to blacklisting. One of Aware's unique contributions to the system was to formalize the process of self-clearance and rehabilitation for those individuals who had been linked with communism in the manner articulated by Schmidt. This rehabilitation process was specified in *The Road Back: Self Clearance*. Among the twelve steps in that process were the following:

1. Questions to ask oneself: Do I love my country: Do I believe in my country in danger? Can I do anything to relieve that danger? Will I tell the full, relevant and unflattering truth?

. . . . .

7. The subject should make public his new position on communism by all other means available: statements in trade publications, "Letters to the Editor," personal correspondence to all who might be interested; such as anti-Communist journalists and organizations, employers, friends, and fellow professionals.

. . . . .

9. Support anti-Communist persons, groups, and organizations.[38]

Other steps in the process involved cooperation with the Federal Bureau of Investigation, a written offer to cooperate with investigations of such committees as the Committee on Un-American Activities of the House of Representatives and the Subcommittee on Internal Security of the Senate Judiciary Committee, and the active support of anti-Communist legislation.

AFTRA

The relationship between Aware, Inc., and the American Federation of Television and Radio Artists was both an intimate and a controversial one. The 1954 AFTRA handbook included one section dealing with the union's opposition to communism.

> Our National Constitution provides: "No person shall remain a member of, or be eligible in AFTRA, who maintains membership in, knowingly promotes the special interests of, makes financial contribution to, or renders aid and assistance by lending his name or talents to the Communist Party or any organization known to him to be a portion, branch, or subdivision thereof, or any organization established by due Federal process, legal or judicial, to be subversive. [39]

AFTRA also asserted in the handbook its willingness to cooperate with the government in "an affirmative program" as part of a crusade against subversion. Although the language of the union constitution is clear, a number of union members threatened by blacklisting and a violation of civil liberties turned to their union for help. The New York chapter of AFTRA set up a committee to deal with blacklisting, headed by the chapter president, Vinton Hayworth.[40] Hayworth was also an officer of Aware, Inc.[41] This committee did not take any positive action in regard to blacklisting, and opposition to the Aware-dominated board of directors grew. The dissenters attempted to elect a new board, but lost the December 9, 1954, election. After that election Aware, Inc., issued "Aware Publication Number 12" in which the losing opposition candidates were listed along with their past "associations."[42] Members of the opposition found that jobs for them became rather scarce thereafter.

But the tactics of Aware, Inc., tended to unify the opposition rather than weaken or destroy it. In March, 1955, a majority of the local membership, at a general membership meeting, adopted a resolution which condemned the blacklisting activities of Aware, Inc. The resolution was not, however, acceptable to the AFTRA board of directors, who "insisted that this resolution be not effective until it was submitted by referendum to the entire membership."[43] Even though Aware warned the union of the dangerous consequences of such an action, the resolution was passed by the membership by a two-to-one vote. Administrative supporters still demonstrated strength on the national level of the organization, particularly on the national executive board. The board reacted by initiating a ballot on a referendum proposition mailed to all members "that any member who refuses to tell a Congressional committee whether or not he was then or had ever been a Communist was subject to punishment by his local, including possible fine, suspension, or expulsion." Without warning of this action, opposition to the referendum never really crystallized, and the proposal was approved by a vote of four to one.[44]

Nevertheless, the antiblacklisting faction of the union campaigned for the election of a new board of directors. A "Middle of the Road" slate was headed by Charles Collingwood, Garry Moore, Orson Bean, and John Henry Faulk.

This new slate issued a "Declaration of Independents," . . . affirming that it was "unalterably opposed to Communism and all other totalitarian ideologies," even before and more prominently than it was opposed to "denial of employment by discriminatory and intimidating practices, especially by outside organizations."[45]

The Middle of the Road slate won twenty-seven of the thirty-five board places in the December 15, 1955, election. Aware, Inc., responded with *Bulletin 16*, made public at the January 1956 membership meeting of that organization. The bulletin was distributed to the members and to a mailing list of two thousand names. Among the names were those of every newspaper in New York, of law enforcement agencies, and of leading columnists. (A number of columnists were effective spokesmen for the anti-Com-

munist groups and were used in the condemnation and rehabilitation process.) *Bulletin 16* questioned whether the Middle of the
Road slate would enforce the AFTRA constitution in respect to
fighting communism, and attacked the new leadership by listing
past associations and links in the *Red Channel* style. One of the
main authors of the bulletin was Vincent Hartnett.

The Role of Laurence A. Johnson

Bulletin 16 later became "Exhibit 41" in the libel case of John
Henry Faulk, plaintiff, against Aware, Inc., and Vincent W.
Hartnett, defendants, and Laurence A. Johnson, defendant. Johnson was a Syracuse businessman, owner of a chain of supermarkets. He established a connection between himself and American
Legion Post no. 41 in Syracuse, through which to disseminate his
demands and convictions. In September of 1951 the Syracuse
American Legion Post had established an un-American activities
committee and several months later began the publication of a
newsletter which became known as *Spotlight*. Johnson used his
American Legion connection to add to the force of his demands.
The Veterans Action Committee of Syracuse Super Markets was
another pressure group which issued a publication backing up
the claims of Johnson. The group was led by Francis W. Neuser,
an employee of Johnson.[46] The chain of relationships between
Laurence Johnson, Aware, Inc., Vincent Hartnett, and AFTRA
was proven in the John Henry Faulk case.

Johnson used a number of techniques to accomplish his purposes. One method was to post a questionnaire ballot in his
stores asking the customers "to choose between the product of
a company . . . that supports 'Stalin's little creatures' and the
product of 'a good American company.'"[47] In addition, direct
letters were sent and sometimes visits were made to the sponsors
of programs which used questionable, from Johnson's point of
view, personnel.

Tom Murray was an account executive at the Gray advertising

agency when he met with Laurence Johnson. Murray handled a number of accounts which advertised on John Henry Faulk's program. Murray testified to the following conversation he had with Johnson:

First Mr. Johnson identified himself as Larry Johnson of Syracuse. He said that he owned several supermarkets and had influence over a number of others in central New York State. He gave me an indication of the total gross volume of food business that was done in the area and it was most impressive. It ran into the millions. I believe the figure was eighteen to twenty million dollars annually.

He then said, Mr. Johnson then said that he felt that it was a disgrace that our company was using a Communist, John Henry Faulk, to advertise its products.

I replied that I had no such knowledge about Mr. Faulk. And he said, "Well you had better get in line because a lot of people along Madison Avenue are getting in line and the display space which the Pabst Brewing Company has in the stores that I either own or control" is what he called "hard-won space."

. . . . .

Then he (Johnson) said, "How would you like it if your client were to receive a letter from an American Legion Post up here?" [48]

John Henry Faulk won his case and the jury awarded him compensatory damages in the sum of one million dollars against Aware, Inc., Vincent Hartnett, and the estate of Laurence Johnson (Johnson died shortly before the conclusion of the court case). Faulk also was awarded punitive damages in the sum of $1,250,000 against Aware, Inc., and the same sum against Hartnett.[49] The case was appealed to the Appellate Division of the New York Supreme Court on October 1, 1963, and although the damages were somewhat reduced, the court ruled in favor of John Henry Faulk.[50]

While Faulk won his long-fought case and while collusion was proven between Aware, Inc., Hartnett, and Johnson, the illegality of blacklisting was never proven. Blacklisting may have been the central issue, but the case was decided on a question of libel. "Exhibit 41" (Aware *Bulletin 16*) was proven to be a lie.

On May 8, 1964, *Counterattack* published an issue responding

to the Faulk decision under the title "The Great Blacklist Hoax."
In its characteristic style it associated a number of individuals
and productions with the plaintiff in the trial: a well-known television performer who served as a witness for Faulk; the producers
of his program; another television program from the same producers; an actor who had been a guest on that program; the
producer-writer-director of a film in which the actor had starred
(referring to testimony before the House Committee on Un-
American Activities); this man's attorney; the film which he had
produced; a popular singer who performed in the film; and so
forth.[51]

The Morality of Blacklisting

Blacklisting involved every facet of the broadcasting world
during its epidemic stages. There were black lists, white lists,
and gray lists. There were also charges that anti-Communist lists
existed. There is no doubt that there were lists which deprived
men and women of work in their professions. The lists existed in
a physical sense, but also within the consciousness of the industry.
They were part of the institutionalized process of blacklisting
in which the procedures and operations of the phenomenon were
recognized, kept secret, and followed.

While most people kept quiet, a few proponents of blacklisting did articulate that belief in print. Father John R. Connery
came to the following conclusion:

Within the proper limits . . . blacklisting cannot be shown to be a
violation of anyone's rights. But the morality of blacklisting cannot be
reduced merely to a question of right. Ultimately it must rest on a pru-
dential decision which judges it to be the only effective means of
protecting the community against serious harm and does not prejudice
in any way its greater good.[52]

John Cogley articulated the argument made against blacklisting
when he answered Father Connery:

If actors, writers, directors, and producers had final responsibility
for what was seen and heard on the screen and over the airwaves;

If there were some foolproof way to avoid hurting the innocent, in the absence of legal safeguards and due process;

If the fabric of democratic law and government were not torn when private groups assume the rights (but not the duties) of government;

If the constitutional guarantees and the spirit, as well as the letter of American democracy, could be reasonably set aside whenever a private group declares an emergency;

If the judgment of the self-appointed watchdogs were only half as balanced as they think it is;

If all these conditions were fulfilled, and then some, the case for blacklisting might stand up, though there would still be the problem of reconciling the constitutional rights of individual Americans with drastic security measures taken, not by the government, but by private citizens.

I don't think these conditions have been fullfilled.[53]

Can the "ifs" ever be fulfilled and yet a democratic society be maintained? It is highly improbable.

Death of the List?

What happened to blacklisting? Did it simply cease? Did the practice fade with the demise of McCarthyism? As blacklisting received notoriety its effectiveness diminished, because as an institution it thrived on public unawareness and secrecy. In the early 1960s the practice had decreased to a degree, but there were still some incidents. In 1962 the folk-singing Weavers, with Pete Seeger, were dropped from an appearance on the "Jack Paar Show" because they refused to sign a loyalty oath.

Once again the American Civil Liberties Union protested to the Federal Communications Commission on the basis that such affidavits were not in the public interest and that such procedures should be taken into account when the stations concerned came up for their license renewals. John de J. Pemberton, Jr., Executive Director of the ACLU, wrote a letter of appeal to Newton Minow, Chairman of the Federal Communications Commission at that time, in which he explained the ACLU's position:

It has come to our attention that some broadcast licensees, as a result of network requirements, are denying the use of television and radio facilities to those who refuse to sign affidavits as to their political beliefs or memberships. We believe that such procedures are not in the public interest and therefore fall within the FCC's jurisdiction over broadcast practices. We urge that the Commission take immediate action to insure the elimination of such affidavit requirements.

A good example of such "blacklisting" was the banning of the Weavers from appearing on Jack Paar's NBC television show last January 2nd. The Weavers had been specifically asked to appear on the show, which had been publicly announced. However, just prior to the performance, they were asked to sign an affidavit that they are not and never were members of the Communist Party. Upon their refusal to sign, their appearance was cancelled. The Commission subsequently rejected their protest on the grounds that it had no power to direct stations to carry or not to carry particular programs, and that to attempt to do so would be illegal censorship.

In our opinion, the issue is *not* whether or not a station licensee should carry the Weavers or any other particular program. Rather, it is whether it is in the public interest for a station or network to apply a *political test or qualification* to determine who will or will not be allowed to perform. For the FCC to declare such a criterion improper would no more be censorship than is the FCC policy of considering "balanced programming" in its license renewal proceedings. In each case, the policy is aimed at a general defect and does not require or preclude specific presentations.

· · · · ·

Public entertainment is not equivalent to "sensitive" positions in government or defense work. It is inconceivable that a performer could threaten national security by earning his living in full hearing and view of the public on radio and television. The net result of political affidavit requirements is to deny the public talented entertainment and, in many cases, important information and to inhibit the freedom of thought, belief and association of all those in the entertainment field, without countervailing gain to the society.

· · · · ·

The Weavers case is one aspect of blacklisting, which the Union has vigorously opposed over the years as violative of the First Amendment's right of free expression and association. The fact that blacklisting no longer receives the public attention it did in the early 50's is no proof that the practice has ceased. It is no secret that the abuse has been institutionalized and made part of the administrative machinery of program casting. If the FCC were to act in the Weavers case, in the manner we have indicated, it would serve to point up the generic blacklisting problem which so seriously intrudes on vital First Amendment guarantees.

The ACLU's argument was not accepted by the FCC, which declared that "it would be 'illegal censorship' on its part to direct stations to carry or not to carry particular programs."[54]

In 1963 the Weavers and Pete Seeger still could not gain admittance to the world of network television. They did not appear on the folk-singing series "Hootenanny." The producer of that series, Richard Lewine, said that the group had not been invited because he was seeking better folk singers. Harold Leventhal, business manager of the Weavers and Seeger, maintained that the American Broadcasting Company was "passing off a 'dirty job' of blacklisting to their producer, Lewine."

What he's saying is a fraud and the highest form of hypocrisy conceivable. How can he say that Pete, who originated the term "hootenanny" in concerts 15 years ago, and the Weavers, with 6,000,000 records sold, are not as good as other groups.[55]

Pete Seeger did appear on programs of the National Educational Television Network, but commercial television doors were closed to him for seventeen years. On September 10, 1967, Seeger appeared on "The Smothers Brothers Comedy Hour," broadcast over the facilities of the Columbia Broadcasting System. A *New York Times* editorial noted Mr. Seeger's appearance and stated that "it is time to nail the lid on the blacklist coffin."[56] Another *New York Times* article announcing Seeger's "new chance" on television quoted an industry source *who refused to be identified*:

This change came about because the network feels this man is entitled to perform for the American public," the source said. "He is a great artist despite his earlier political affiliations and beliefs. This move will reflect throughout the industry.[57]

It is significant that the economic structure of sponsorship had changed and that by 1967, because of the rising costs of programming, participating sponsorship had displaced single sponsorship of major shows. Therefore, no single sponsor had control over the program. Seeger's appearance was not without con-

troversy. Columbia Broadcasting System's network-practice office
objected to part of one of Seeger's songs, "Waist Deep in the
Big Muddy." The twenty-minute taped appearance was cut to
ten minutes and fifteen seconds when the song was edited out.
In a subsequent Smothers Brothers show Seeger was, however,
allowed to sing the entire song. The demands of public opinion
were heard and artists were becoming more independent.

Fifteen years after Jean Muir had encountered blacklisting,
she was invited to recount her experiences on the WABC-TV
show "Girl Talk." In that ten-minute interview, a number of
Miss Muir's comments were "blooped out" or, in other words, the
video tape was edited. The title of the show from which she was
dismissed, "The Aldrich Family"; the network which concurred
in the action, the National Broadcasting Company; the identity
of the sponsor, the General Foods Corporation — these and several other facts were deleted. The attorneys for ABC Films
justified their action on the basis of possible libel and damage to
those individuals and companies mentioned. ABC had alternatives open to them other than censorship, according to critic
Jack Gould, who reported these facts. He suggested that Miss
Muir could have been asked to document her case "within the
everyday standards of fair comment."[58] The *Nation* interpreted
the incident to mean that "fifteen years later, we are still living
psychologically in the blacklist era. The taboos that must not be
violated are the taboos that ruled then, the interests that were
sacred then are sacred still."[59]

The effects of blacklisting do not vanish. While McCarthyism
may be a thing of the past, those people who were labeled controversial are not today uncontroversial. In 1968 John Henry
Faulk pointed out that there is still a negative reaction to his
name on the network level of broadcasting.[60] Faulk may have
won a libel suit, but his career was damaged.

The ingredients which made blacklisting a reality have not
disappeared. The causes and commitments may change but the
fear of controversy still exists among those who control the in-

stitution called broadcasting. Even today there is a reticence among the broadcasting establishment to discuss the issues of blacklisting.

Contemporary commitments are made without a crystal ball. A question does, however, remain unanswered. Will the civil liberties of a minority be abrogated sometime in the future because of an anti-establishment activity by that minority today? As long as people dedicate themselves to principles and issues they will become involved. We must guard against the condemnation of involvement if the democratic process is to thrive. The airwaves are not an exception to that process, and blacklisting is antithetical to broadcasting in the public welfare. The causes of today might become the sins of tomorrow. It could happen again. Russell Baker has offered the prospect to our imaginations in his own style:

> Look, you're before the committee. It's 1970. The whole country is angry at the idea that in 1968 people wore long hair. In 1970, long hair is un-American. You're put in the witness chair before 200 reporters, and the Congressman says, 'Did you, on or about Sept. 25, 1968, wear hair that was shoulder length?' If you say yes, there will be headlines screaming, 'Admits to Hair.' If you say no, they'll charge you with perjury. Either way you're ruined.[61]

NOTES

1. Merle Miller, *The Judges and the Judged* (New York: Doubleday & Company, 1952), p. 13.
2. John Cogley, *Report on Blacklisting*, vol. 2, *Radio–Television* (New York: The Fund for the Republic, 1956), p. vii.
3. Published by Simon and Schuster, New York.
4. Harold S. Roberts, *Roberts Dictionary of Industrial Relations* (Washington, D.C.: BNA, 1966), p. 40.
5. Hans Sperber and Travis Trittschuh, *American Political Terms: An Historical Dictionary* (Detroit: Wayne State University, 1962), p. 42.
6. John T. Zadrozny, *Dictionary of Social Science* (Washington, D.C.: Public Affairs Press, 1959), p. 29.

7. John R. Connery, "The Morality of Blacklisting," *America* 96 (Feb. 16, 1957): 550.
8. Max Lerner, *America as a Civilization: Life and Thought in the United States Today* (New York: Simon and Schuster, 1957), p. 456.
9. *Ibid.*, p. 454.
10. *New York Times*, March 24, 1947, p. 19.
11. *New York Times*, March 30, 1947, sec. 4, p. 8.
12. *Ibid.*
13. Cogley, *Blacklisting*, p. 3.
14. *Ibid.*
15. Miller, *The Judges*, p. 85.
16. *Ibid.*
17. Merle Miller, "Trouble on Madison Avenue, N.Y.," *Nation* 174 (June 28, 1952): 633.
18. Cogley, *Blacklisting*, p. 5.
19. Dalton Trumbo, "Honor Bright and All That Jazz," *Nation* 201 (September 20, 1965): 184.
20. American Civil Liberties Union news release, New York, April 2, 1951.
21. *Red Channels: The Report of Communist Influence in Radio and Television* (New York: Counterattack, 1950), p. 134.
22. Faulk, *Fear on Trial*, p. 292.
23. Miller, *The Judges*, p. 117.
24. *Red Channels*, p. 1.
25. *Ibid.*, pp. 4–5.
26. U.S. Congress, House, Committee on Un-American Activities, *Investigation of Communist Activities New York Area — Part I*, 84th Cong., 1st Session, June 15, 1963, p. 1.
27. Faulk, *Fear on Trial*, p. 239.
28. *Ibid.*
29. "Fighting the Blacklist, Red Channels," *New Republic* 123 (October 2, 1950): 8.
30. "Elmer Rice Against McCarthyism in Radio," *Nation* 173 (November 24, 1951): 434.
31. Miller, "Trouble on Madison Avenue," p. 631.
32. American Civil Liberties Union news release, New York, April 4, 1952, p. 1.
33. *Ibid.*
34. *Ibid.*, p. 2.

35. American Civil Liberties Union, "Report on Civil Liberties: January 1951–June 1953," (New York, 1953), p. 31.
36. *Ibid.*
37. Godfrey P. Schmidt, in "Blacklisting Revisited: A Symposium," *America* 96 (March 30, 1957): 730–31.
38. Cogley, *Blacklisting*, pp. 135–36.
39. American Federation of Television and Radio Artists, *AFTRA: A Handbook of Information for all Radio and Television Artists* (New York, 1954), p. 22.
40. Jay Nelson Tuck, "Unholy Alliance: AFTRA and the Blacklist," *Nation* 181 (September 3, 1955): 188.
41. Faulk, *Fear on Trial*, p. 11.
42. Cogley, *Blacklisting*, p. 155.
43. John Henry Faulk against Aware Inc. and Vincent W. Hartnett, and Lois Johnson Wangerman, Marilyn Johnson, Giancola and Mary Coyne, as Executrices of the Last Will and Testament of Laurence A. Johnson, Deceased, *Respondent's Brief*. New York Supreme Court, Appellate Division, pp. 4–5.
44. Tuck, "Unholy Alliance," p. 189.
45. *Respondent's Brief*, p. 6.
46. Cogley, *Blacklisting*, p. 106.
47. *Respondent's Brief*, p. 40.
48. Faulk, *Fear on Trial*, pp. 216–17.
49. *Ibid.*, p. 390.
50. *Ibid.*, p. 395.
51. *Counterattack*, May 8, 1964.
52. Connery, "Morality of Blacklisting," p. 554.
53. Cogley, in "Blacklisting Revisited," p. 732.
54. American Civil Liberties Union news release, New York, December 5, 1962.
55. "Denies Weavers' Ban Was Political," *Newsday*, March 22, 1963.
56. "Breaking the TV Blacklist," *The New York Times*, September 4, 1967, p. 20.
57. "Pete Seeger Gets New Chance on TV," *The New York Times*, August 25, 1967, p. 72.
58. Jack Gould, "TV: Blacklisting's Effect," *The New York Times*, January 15, 1966, p. 55.
59. *The Nation* 202 (January 10, 1966): 50.
60. Personal Interview, March 15, 1968.
61. Russell Baker, "Observer: Dialogue About the Coming Repression," *The New York Times*, September 26, 1968, p. 46.

Part IV

THE FUTURE OF BROADCASTING
LABOR RELATIONS

14 Interunion Cooperation

by CLAUDE L. McCUE

Most labor leaders in the broadcasting industry would admit there is room for vast improvement in cooperation between unions. The trade union movement was founded on cooperation — by the individual with other fellow workers, his local unit with the local union, that local with the national union, nationals with internationals, and between internationals through the top parent (the AFL, the CIO, or the merged AFL-CIO).

Obviously, cooperation on this ladder of organization will vary in degree, even between individuals in the same working unit. Self-interest is often a stronger motivation than the "good of the whole." When it becomes the prevailing motive for workers in the trade unions, the unions become, from the point of view of the trade union movement, tools of the greater economic power (the employer).

Some of the union leaders in the broadcasting industry have in the past contributed toward this imbalance of economic strength by discouraging cooperation with other unions. Desire for Autonomy is one of the principle factors leading to various degrees of noncooperation between those in the pyramid of the union orga-

The views presented in this chapter are the author's, and do not necessarily represent those of the American Federation of Television and Radio Artists.

nizational structure. Related to this, of course, are the selfish mo-
tives of individuals.

Mutual Aid in Strikes

Full cooperation between unions (and the members thereof)
is the ideal that unions have striven for. Unselfishness, conditioned by an objective attitude toward achieving the immediate
goal of the unit for the betterment of the whole, has been the
characteristic most essential to the success of a strike. In each
strike, however, there have been varying degrees of selfishness
manifested — related, without doubt, to the personal ambitions of
some labor leaders, and to the concern of some rank and file union
members with "What do I get out of this?" or "Why should I
suffer to help those guys? I've got a family to feed." Too often, the
examination of the merit of a strike by the individual through his
organized unit and up through the organizational ladder of his
union is completely subjective, and results in a rationalization of
self-interest.

To argue against the justification for "self-determination" in
deciding whether one union will support another is to argue
against democracy, but until such time as more universal recognition of the need for solidarity is achieved, it is quite apparent
that the union movement will need to rely on mutual strike assistance rarely limited by self-determinative choice. There will have
to be more reliance on the judgment of the members and leaders
immediately involved in a strike, and recognition of a basic fact
that strike action is normally a reluctant action taken only when
vital issues cannot be resolved through the give and take of collective bargaining, although it is true that there are unions,
spurred by an extremely militant membership or leadership,
which resort to precipitous strike action — often because of internal political situations which propel unrealistic demands.

Many times when a union refuses support to another striking
union, the crutch or guise used to avoid an admission of selfish

motivation is the charge that the striking union is "unreasonable." In the absence of a contractual prohibition, however, the union withholding aid probably has one of the following undisclosed reasons: 1) it has made a "deal" with the employer to withhold support (of less frequency during the past several years); 2) it fears that its own members may defy an order to respect the picket line; 3) it anticipates that reciprocal aid will be of no significance to its own strong bargaining position; or 4) it believes that an "entangling alliance" is to be avoided at almost any cost. Obviously, too, whenever a threat to jurisdiction is involved, support is a rarity. Members of many unions, however, have voluntarily supported other colleagues without their own union's sanction, even in contractually prohibited cases, relying on the striking union to protect them for return to their jobs.

The No-Strike Clause

With some exceptions, the no-strike clause was originally imposed on unions by the networks in the late thirties and early forties, setting the pattern for other employers in the industry. This contract restriction in some cases went so far as to require the union to *order* its members to fulfill their contracts with the employer (AFTRA Codes of Fair Practice). Other major employers who succeeded in obtaining no-strike clauses were local stations and, for talent and the creative professions, the advertising agencies.

As the broadcast unions became organized throughout the country, the contractual limitation on the right to support other unions was accepted by unions in the majority of cases. The local exceptions were in those communities of overall labor strength and tradition. Even in such cities the same restrictive clauses were carried, on the local level, in contracts with the network-owned stations. Other local employers often prevailed by following this precedent.

It must be acknowledged that some unions may have welcomed, or at least did not resist, the company's insistence on the industry's no-strike clause. In this way the union hoped to avoid the embarrassment of non-support to other striking unions by hiding behind the collective bargaining agreement.

There was more manifestation of mutual aid among the broadcasting unions on a local level. Many factors explain this inconsistency, but perhaps the most important was the obviously closer relationship between the two work forces, and between the local labor leaders. Many of the latter were accustomed to working together in local labor councils. There was a closer personal relationship in labor's local community than between the national or international union heads, who may have met only once every year or two at the AFL, CIO, or AFL-CIO Conventions — even then on a very cursory basis. These conventions afford practically no opportunity (or at least, no opportunity has been created) for caucus or conference of international representatives of the broadcasting unions.

Thus, the formative years of broadcasting (1938–42), the peak of the radio business (1948–50) and the phenomenal growth of television (since 1950) witnessed only limited cooperation among broadcast unions on a national level.

Major Unions in the Industry

The National Association of Broadcast Engineers and Technicians was generally considered a company union at NBC in the early forties, created to combat organizing efforts of the International Brotherhood of Electrical Workers, which had become the entrenched technicians' union at CBS. At this time, NBC owned two radio networks, known as the Red and Blue. It was forced by the FCC to sell one transcontinental chain, which then became the American Broadcasting Company. NABET continued as the union representing the technicians and engineers at these two major networks. Soon the natural progress of collectivism expressed itself and the baby created by NBC became a somewhat unruly and militant CIO union. It obviously could not go into the AFL where the IBEW, as one of the larger international unions in that organization, held jurisdiction.

Thus there sprang up two competing unions for the technician-engineers in the industry. As the CIO vertical union, NABET had no jurisdictional limitations. On a network basis, jurisdiction of the creative groups had been established, but NABET soon organized, where possible, the clerical workers and other unorganized groups. In many cities where AFL unions had not organized the writers, directors, and announcers, they were taken in by this CIO union. The American Federation of Radio Artists was organized in most of the major cities, but the directors and writers had limited their organizing activities to the networks and some network owned and operated stations in the major cities.

The IBEW became well established at CBS nationally and at its locally owned stations, and with the strength of its large and influential international expanded into many cities. In spite of the AFL craft jurisdictional structure, the IBEW, often using international representatives, also organized announcers and others where no organization existed.

Upon the advent of television, several new unions became involved in the broadcasting industry. These were principally the several groups within the International Alliance of Theatrical Stage Employes who had moved over from the motion picture business into the television production facilities of the networks. IBEW at CBS and NABET at NBC and ABC outnumber the IATSE-covered employees. Lack of cooperation between them reflects a history of jurisdictional disputes, charges of raiding, and general competition for the same bargaining units. The main IATSE groups at the networks are sound technicians, news film cameramen, publicists, make-up and hair stylists, scenic and title artists, film editors, motion picture costumers, and stage employees. The Teamsters Union has assumed a greater role in the industry. Although not a part of the AFL-CIO, members of this union, ironically, are often the first to respect picket lines of the other unions.

Strikes in the Industry

The broadcasting industry has had a history, generally, of peaceful labor relations. In spite of the fact that in most cases each union has relied on its own strength, comparatively high standards have been created for the union members in the industry. Strife has grown, however, and the number of strikes has increased in recent years. The year 1967 saw two major national walkouts. Before that year, both technician-engineer unions had struck their respective networks, but with several years intervening. NABET struck the Red and Blue (NBC) networks in 1942, and IBEW struck the CBS network in 1958. NABET was out for twenty-two days at NBC in 1959, and its members conducted a wild-cat walkout against ABC in 1958.

In these pre-1967 engineer-technicians' strikes, both IBEW and NABET were "on their own," except for isolated help from local unions or individual employees. There had been some effort toward mutual-aid pacts, but in the final test each union was motivated by its own self-interest, blinded to the constant weakening of the bargaining power of all unions in this increasingly automated industry.

The talent union in radio (American Federation of Radio Artists) was led by militant leadership, but because of its jurisdictional monopoly in radio, attained high degrees of success without exercising its ultimate economic weapon, the strike. It could, therefore, afford an isolationist position. Many members were high earners (including the stars), and the individual loss of income in the event of a strike would have been very great (far greater than for the crews). This also was true to some degree of the writers and directors. In 1952 a *T* was added to AFRA, representing the absorption of jurisdictional areas in television, and the organization became known as the American Federation of Television and Radio Artists, and covered workers in live or recorded performances on network broadcasts as well as in local production in most major markets. It was not until 1967 that AFTRA's first national strike occurred.

Networks vs. Motion Picture Producers for Control Over Television

Commencing about 1948, a bitter struggle developed for power and control over the budding new medium of television, soon to become the predominant vehicle for advertising and home entertainment. The three networks had the initial advantage as owners of the broadcasting facilities and possessors of a "know-how" in advertising. The motion picture producers of Hollywood had the experience and the studios for production of film. In the short-sighted desire of some unions to protect the sanctity of their traditional jurisdictions, they separated television into the two fields, film and live production. The motion picture producers and the networks quickly realized that a joining together of experience and financial resources would pay bigger dividends than continuing as bitter adversaries. It soon became the practice for the networks to join with the major motion picture studios or independent producers in the financing of film programs. The unions in the fields of live and film production in television have largely failed to respond with similar cooperation among themselves.

Union Involvement

The tug of war in this struggle for control of television was exemplified by the several years of jurisdictional dispute between the Screen Actors Guild and AFTRA. The latter claimed jurisdiction because it represented performers in broadcasting. TV was a method of broadcasting, and AFTRA was the union with background and experience in dealing with the networks and advertising agencies. Therefore, familiar with the procedures of those who would finance television with the advertising dollar, AFTRA claimed that the method of production (live or film) had no bearing on jurisdiction; television was a single industry using the product in a single manner. SAG insisted that technique of producing TV films was basically the same as that of producing films for theatrical exhibition — "film is film," "anything in the can is ours" were familiar slogans coming from the actors' union based in Hollywood, whose star-studded board of directors personified the motion picture industry. The great bulk of SAG membership was in Hollywood, with only one branch office in New York.

AFTRA was a national organization, with its principal office in New York, the home of the top network and ad agency officials, and with about thirty locals throughout the country. Two-thirds of its membership was divided equally between New York and Hollywood.

AFTRA proposed to SAG the principle later adopted by the networks — "If you can't beat 'em, join 'em." Television was the springboard for the proposal by AFTRA for a merger with SAG; there had long been a grass-roots membership agitation for a one-card talent union. The slogan "Don't split television" was often used by the AFTRA actor.

SAG, led by Ronald Reagan as its president, rejected all efforts by AFTRA to merge. The Four A's International, under threat by SAG to withdraw from that International if AFTRA were awarded TV film jurisdiction, was unable to settle the dispute. NLRB elections were held, and SAG successfully maintained its position as a single unit for TV and theatrical film productions. Consequently, jurisdiction of actors and other performers in television was split, with SAG covering all film productions and AFTRA covering live and tape. (An unresolved or "gray" area remained in the coverage of tape productions in motion picture studios.) Leaders of both unions realized it would be foolhardy and disastrous (and the actor would have revolted if they hadn't so realized) to compete with each other by undercutting the other's standards for the performer. Thus, soon after the clouds of jurisdictional strife were dissipated, joint SAG-AFTRA committees were formed to develop plans toward standardizing minimum contract terms for performers in both types of production. This crystalized in the unprecedented joint bargaining in 1958 by SAG and AFTRA for television commercials. The great bulk of these were on film made under the SAG contract, but video tape commercials were beginning to take a share of this advertising. True cooperation was born between the two talent unions.

Since that time, joint SAG-AFTRA committees prepare the TV commercial contract demands for both unions, and bargaining is conducted jointly by their negotiators with a committee from the major advertising agencies and the sponsors' organization, the networks playing the role of observer in the talks.

In most situations in broadcasting, however, joint negotiations would not be practical, and even a common expiration date for all union contracts (as suggested by several union executives) would place an almost impossible physical burden on the negotiators for all parties. Several months are often required by AFTRA and some of the other unions to negotiate their own packages of agreements. Were these attempted concurrently, the time required would stretch the patience of the membership of any of these unions beyond the breaking point.

Balance of Power

It seems a reasonable conclusion to draw from the increased number of strikes in broadcasting that there is a change in the relative bargaining power of the networks and the unions. Technological changes have progressed to the point of high automation in the many phases of television and, of course, radio broadcasting. ABC recently claimed that the fifty-two day NABET strike in the fall of 1967 proved that they could operate with about two-thirds of the staff that they had had before the strike.

There is also ample evidence that during the last decade a greater balance of economic power has developed between the networks and other producers, bringing a tougher line of resistance to the union demands. Major growth in the film production of TV programs has split the unions into two competing factions. The motion picture unions act as unwilling strike-breakers against their counterparts in the broadcasting business. During a network strike, the IATSE crafts, the AFM, the Writers Guild and the Directors Guild are "scabbing" on their own members by continuing to furnish film productions to the networks, and thus maintaining a high level of regular original first-run programming. Talent from the Screen Actors Guild supplies the actors on these shows to replace AFTRA's striking performers, most of whom also are members of their sister union, SAG.

Not only is there a general lack of unified bargaining in the production and broadcasting facilities of television, but a form of automation is used to transport the AFTRA actor across his own picket line. Video tape has so improved that practically all "live" shows are pretaped without loss of picture quality. The entire work force on that taped production are acting as strikebreakers of their own strike through this automated device of replay used during the strike.

Use of old movies, filmed TV shows, and reruns of taped shows during a strike in the broadcasting industry have made it the height of folly for a single union to rely on its own bargaining strength.

The cannibalism among unions in this schizophrenic industry has created a jungle of competition between workers trying to supplant each other. Even if the companies had developed a plan with a blueprint to computerized perfection, they would not have reaped greater benefits than they do from this voluntary indulgence by the unions of their own appetites.

Recent Developments in Mutual Aid

In view of the thirteen-day strike by AFTRA against all three networks and the subsequent fifty-two day NABET strike against ABC, it appears unrealistic to expect short strikes. The replacement of supervisors for the well-known news personalities during the AFTRA strike was accepted by the public for a brief period. Continuation of regular film programming was an important factor for sponsors and ad agencies in financing the networks in their economic combat with these unions. Top live or pretaped shows were replaced by reruns. It was evident, however, that the longer the strike, the more the scales were tipping to the union's advantage.

AFTRA, probably considered the most powerful of these unions until the time of the strike, was not prepared for a long strike. The AFTRA strike was successful from the standpoint of displaying the national unity within the talent groups, and strategically as proof that the union was willing to go all-out in maintaining a bargaining position. Performers withstood heavy loss of income for that period, with all of the prominent personalities as well as rank and file performers respecting the AFTRA picket line. Four network newsmen on NBC were the only defectors among the thousands of performers involved.

In seeking strike support, the leadership of AFTRA hastened to pledge reciprocity to all other unions, and the first to respond was the AFM, by ordering its members to respect the AFTRA picket lines in New York and Los Angeles. Many members of the Writers Guild and NABET quickly responded as individuals, but there was no concerted action by a union other than the AFM, partly because of restrictions in contracts.

AFTRA received announced support from the NABET and IBEW leaders, and during the last few days of the strike the networks were operating without musicians, most of their technician-engineers, and some writers, but still had at their command the IATSE cameramen, stage hands, film editors, set designers, make-up artists, etc. Continued use of "IA" news cameramen was an important contribution to the networks, for it made possible the maintenance of fairly high standards of news coverage. It was reported that the rank and file of the IATSE wished to support AFTRA but were forbidden by their International leadership.

NABET struck ABC in September of the same year, and that network had its second experience within five months of operating without AFTRA talent and all of its NABET employees. AFTRA had not concluded its contracts, so that for the first time it was free of the no-strike contractual prohibition and it ordered its members to respect the NABET picket lines, an order in effect for nineteen days. The order was withdrawn following the return to work of over fifty AFTRA newsmen on network and local news programs in New York, Washington, Chicago, Los Angeles, and San Francisco. (It should be noted that the great majority of AFTRA performers respected the NABET lines during the entire period of the AFTRA order.) This first joint action by two major unions at one network proved far more effective than the previous AFTRA strike of April, 1967, had been with only sporadic support.

The sudden reversal by AFTRA of its past go-it-alone policy by its pledge and delivery of support to NABET inspired the other unions, creating an atmosphere of cooperation which many have described as a new era in relations among these unions.

Other Methods of Cooperation

Full cooperation has been referred to here only in relation to the union's ultimate weapon, the strike. There are many other areas of cooperation which have been available and utilized in varying degrees, depending on the locals and, too often, on the compatibility of the personalities involved.

A fact-finding committee, consisting of union representatives from the Broadway stage and the broadcasting industry, has long existed in New York. It has served as a sounding board and avenue for the exchange of information. Assurances of cooperation have sprung out of this committee, but have been ineffective in some instances because of lack of support by the national organization of the various unions.

A Committee of Broadcast Unions (CBU) was formed in

Hollywood in the fall of 1967 as an outgrowth of the AFTRA strike. Whether the leadership, including those within the national and international unions, develop reciprocal support pacts among all unions in the broadcasting industry remains to be seen. AFTRA has declared by resolution of its 1967 convention that it will strike in 1969, if necessary, to remove the prohibition contained in the traditional no-strike clause. Some union executives have declared that there is no other recourse available to meet the increased bargaining strength of the networks. The employers recognized many years ago the added strength that joint bargaining with a singleness of purpose gives to combat the strength of the unions. The analogy is too obvious for unions to fail to join forces if they wish to survive.

Local Cooperation

The foregoing has been a review and analysis of the cooperation of unions within the national network and major productions of television. There are many instances of full cooperation and mutual support on local levels — at individual stations. For example, in New York there have been many instances of mutual AFTRA-IBEW support. This is traditional in San Francisco and several other cities where there is a large union work force.

Before 1965 the IBEW and AFTRA had separate strikes at local stations in Los Angeles, each unsupported by the other. Perhaps as a forerunner of the future cooperation of broadcasting unions, AFTRA and the IBEW conducted a joint strike in 1965 against KLAC, a local radio station in Los Angeles. Engineers and announcers marched the picket lines together carrying their own identifying signs. The same scene occurred later in the year at another Los Angeles radio station, KPOL.

In the broadcasting industry the networks have worked closely together not only in joint bargaining where desirable but also in the exchange of information. Large labor relations departments are headed by skilled experts with almost unlimited clerical and machine help. They have available appropriate statistics to support their positions from the vast resources of the advertising industry.

The unions have limited resources, some operating under a severe shortage. It is apparent that the unions must now follow the way of the employers by a greater use of their combined resources, exchanging contract information and economic studies. These unions should join in obtaining statistics and other information of mutual interest.

The special local union groups within the industry, the New York fact-finding committee and the Hollywood committee, are developing techniques to develop closer liaison, exchange of information, and generally greater cooperation. Similar councils or committees could be formed on a national level, with more personal contact between the top national administrators of the several unions. This would be essential to greater cooperation. Here, again, the national unions could take a leaf from the employers' manual by pooling information on the economics of the industry, with an emphasis on its increasingly high profits. An economist-statistician might be retained. With their combined strength, unions could better match the almost unlimited resources of the networks, the advertising agencies, and the sponsors. Among the latter, of course, are the giants of our economic and business world. It is more than coincidental that the resistance of the networks grew in direct proportion to the interest and participation by these buyers of time in the negotiations with the talent unions.

So long as the industry can "take on" each union by itself, there will be increased strife and strikes. Strikes will be avoided by close and maximum cooperation among the unions.

To permit reciprocal support, all broadcast unions will need to eliminate the contract limitation on the right to respect other unions' picket lines. Most have pledged to do so, and there are signs that the IATSE locals may challenge any efforts by their

International to prevent this development. No doubt the industry will resist these efforts with a determination which may lead to more national strikes, but from the long range view, peace will be restored through an equalizing of the bargaining strengths of both parties.

If the unions acquire the contractual freedom to respect the picket lines of other unions, education of the membership on the need to make this sacrifice for the good of the whole will be a necessary follow-up. In the absence of such an understanding by the rank and file, any efforts to support could boomerang and undermine the strength of that union in its own bargaining. AFTRA experienced this to a degree when some of the newsmen refused to abide by the order to respect the NABET picket lines at ABC in September, 1967. These men had long been members of AFTRA but were new to the processes of collective bargaining and to the need for unified strength within the trade union movement.

If the individual worker does not respond to the need, the full cycle of cooperation in the pyramid of the union structure will not have been completed — without cooperation among the individual members of the unit, the foundation will have washed away. The networks and other employers should not anticipate such an occurrence within the ranks of labor.

Cooperation on an International Level

In 1963, the first conference of talent union representatives from English-speaking countries was held in Toronto, Canada, at the instigation of AFTRA. In 1966, there was held in Stockholm a three-day conference of union representatives from European, British, Canadian, and United States talent unions, many of which included other classifications of employees in their coverage. The Stockholm conference, for which the Scandinavian Actors' Council served as hosts in historic Hasselby Slott, resulted in a proclamation by performers' unions from thirteen countries of the establishment of fair competitive-talent and use-fee standards for television programs and commercials produced in one country and broadcast in another. Satellite transmission and relay has brought into full international scope another plateau of cooperation among unions in the broadcasting fields.

Signs point to a continuing improvement in cooperation among the broadcast unions. Many of the barriers of traditional isolationism in unions are being dissipated in the face of the greater bargaining strength of the employers and the apparent desire of some to undermine the union movement. The pendulum in labor relations has often swung away from an abuse of power toward aid of the abused — whether the abuse has been that of labor or of management. There is some evidence that there are major employers in the broadcasting industry tending toward such abuse. Maximum cooperation between the broadcasting unions could be the consequence.

15 Higher Education's Role

by CHARLES F. HUNTER

In discussing the role of higher education in broadcasting labor relations one treads on uneven ground. Within the traditional broadcasting curriculum, the attention given broadcasting unionism is assuredly low on academic priority lists. One reason, of course, is the unavailability of competent instructors. Where, indeed, does one learn all the intricacies of such a subject except through experiences on the front line of union-management negotiations? A problem is that the front lines vary with each battle, and those who return, somewhat battle-scarred, have lost much of their objectivity.

Further, locating an individual among these veterans who has either the time or inclination for college instruction is no simple task, although the assignment may be only on a part-time basis. The instruction, reportedly, is limited by its emphasis on "this is the way I did it."

It bears emphasizing, however, that unionism is a significant aspect of work in broadcasting, at least in the larger markets, and it rightfully deserves a place in the professional education of future employees. As a case in point, one television station in Chicago has twenty-one operating unions in its shop. Those of us who are involved in professional education are therefore remiss in our responsibilities if we in any way denigrate the importance of labor activities in broadcasting. One would insist, further, that any instruction in broadcasting labor relations should be anchored in materials considerably above those found in some courses on college campuses which incorporate the word "appreciation" in their title or description. Such courses may well serve a purpose for the student who has peripheral interest in music, art, or what have you, but their value in professional education is dubious.

On the other hand, we cannot see the university's role in the training for professional union administration, which would seem to be beyond our legitimate scope. These positions are normally acquired only after considerable experience in labor activities, and there is nothing in the college graduate's background which can substitute for this.

Where, then, are our responsibilities, and what is the judicious role of the university in this regard? We can begin to answer the first by observing that our responsibilities in the future are going to be greater than they have been in the past. No one would presume to forecast the demise of labor unions in broadcasting or elsewhere, and one can easily make a strong case for their continued growth and extension.

The broadcasting student of the future, therefore, should know the development and history of the labor union movement in this country as it relates to broadcasting. Unless he wishes to be condemned to repeat the mistakes of the past, he should know both the problems and results of this development. He should also know the legitimate goals of unionism, and the principal areas of conflict with management in times past. Assuredly, he should know the names of the broadcasting unions and something of their current contracts. Union organization, membership requirements, grievance procedures, and matters of tenure also deserve his attention. Further, the responsibility of the union member both toward the union and toward management must not be overlooked. There is such a thing as dual loyalty, and it must be emphasized. Our first formal course would then be one in the history of unionism itself.

Since collective bargaining is protected by statute, knowledge of these statutes and of the employer-employee contractual relationships should be within the professional student's frame of reference. The importance of communication, or dialogue, within the organization ought not to be overlooked. Attention should also be given to non-wage benefits as they relate to union contracts, to station policy, and to legislation. A course in labor-management law could be a second formal offering.

It is not inconceivable that a third formal course could be devoted to methods of negotiation. This specialized subject would have to be team-taught and probably cross-credited with schools of business or commerce. Semantics, small-group discussion theory, management attitudes, and union techniques could be among the areas explored.

The assumption, rightly, or wrongly, behind these suggestions is that other departments within the university are offering courses on the broader aspects of unionism, including labor theory, the development of unions in Europe, union public relations, and the protection of minority groups. Where such courses are available, they should be incorporated in the broadcast student's education.

The difficulty of locating university faculty with both the background and interest in broadcast labor relations has already been noted. Some part-time instruction is a possibility and should be explored. However, another problem for the instruction of the future will be the difficulty in locating accurate information about industry-union relations. Of all areas of broadcasting it seems to be the one most protected by secrecy. Union administrators, members themselves, and management, with few exceptions in each case, seem reluctant to discuss the subject with any degree of candor. Whether as a result of natural distrust or of painful lessons from the past, or from a desire to protect the status quo, inquiries directed to matters of labor relations in broadcasting receive guarded, even suspicious, and certainly minimal replies. A perusal of the list of titles of all dissertations in the broadcast field reveals a significantly small number devoted to unions. This observation must bear some relationship to the difficulty of research in the area.

By nature, the role of the university is identified with probing and meaningful research. As all teachers in some measure are teachers of English, all broadcasting instructional personnel, are, or should be, research minded. The direct involvement of graduate students in the entire field of broadcasting labor research is a responsibility of the university and an integral part of its role. While research difficulties may have been a deterrent in the past, ways must be found to minimize resistance where it is met in the future. Enlightened management and cooperative labor administration must become the *sine qua non* of the future. One does not need to dwell on the value of personal contacts between broadcasting faculty and responsible persons in union and management or the role of professional organizations in encouraging such contacts.

If the goals, then, for our university-trained professional of the future include both an orientation to and a considerable knowledge of broadcasting's union-management relations, what better way to augment these than by seminars, institutes, or programs sponsored by the university on the campus? Not every such institute will leave its mark (we are no better or worse in planning such activities than are our colleagues), but a sufficient number over a period of time could not fail to open the dialogue and extend the value of the participants' experiences. If more heat than light ensues on occasion, what matter?

Such programs, for best results, should be cooperative efforts between the university, the unions, and management. The university's goal would be the wider dissemination of information and its value to its students. We leave to the unions and to management what their goals will be.

It will be noted that the presentation of seminar or institute programs rests on the assumption that they will be concerned with the interests of both unions and management. We suggest that the sponsoring institution should determine whether this is the best organization. It is not inconceivable that wholly separate programs might be instigated or that they might operate as parallel activities with occasional points of contact. Until an institution has had some experience in the sponsorship of such institutes, open mindedness about participants and organization would seem to be the best directive.

It is our feeling that in addition to presentation of formal classroom instruction in broadcast labor relations, the encouragement of research, and the joint presentation of institutes or seminars on the college campus, the university has an added role to play in the development of instructional materials. The production of audio tapes, videotapes, films and film-strips, and slides could well be within the province of the university. These instructional materials would be only an extension of a department's current library. Their development would provide a valuable supplement to instruction.

Again, the unions and managements themselves have a responsibility in assisting in the preparation of these materials. Recorded interviews, panels, and discussions would seem to pose no great problems in either cost or production. Documentary films on the other hand would obviously need some form of subsidy. These kinds of materials, however, are used in many areas of instruction, and their use in this field would seem to be warranted. In any event the possibility merits further exploration.

Although some of the larger unions have had special education or training programs for their own members, one questions the value of such a procedure for universities. If, as departments, our goal is the development of broadcast professionals in the best sense of that term, the extension of training to all broadcast employees would seem to spread our resources very thin. Further, one suspects that the specialized nature of this type of training would make it more appropriate for the unions themselves to handle. University personnel, where called upon and needed, should of course participate, but the role of the university itself should be that of consultant rather than organizer.

In summary, we view the role of higher education in relation to broadcasting unions as encompassing the need:

1. To recognize that knowledge of unionism is a valid part of the training of the future broadcast employee;
2. To locate competent faculty, whether on full or part-time basis, to conduct formalized instruction in the area;
3. To provide formal instruction in the history of unionism, in labor-management law, and in methods of negotiation;
4. To incorporate other courses available at the institution which deal with unionism in the broadcasting major's program of study;
5. To encourage responsible research into the subject of broadcasting unions on the part of its graduate students;
6. To conduct seminars or institutes on its campus in cooperation with the unions and management;
7. To take the initiative in the preparation of meaningful teaching tools for student and professional use.

We question any roles which involve responsibility for training efficient union administrators or for educating workers, although conceivably some institutions might wish to assume these.

In the event that we achieve our goals we will have more enlightened broadcasting employees in the future, and perhaps more satisfied ones, and through the research and institute programs we will have provided unions and management with stimuli and insights not readily available to them. These are legitimate goals worthy of a university.

16 Researching the Problems

by A. EDWARD FOOTE
and ROBERT R. MONAGHAN

In earlier chapters various questions are suggested by authors of this book. We have attempted to summarize and synthesize some of these and relate them to at least a portion of research findings which might offer additional enlightenment. We also take the liberty of hinting at some research strategies for certain of these areas which we feel could be profitably pursued further. There is no pretense here that we have related all of the significant research to all of the important questions. Nor do we assume that our way of categorizing the questions is the most practical. For a time we considered a theoretical model, for we felt this might place the various questions into some logical relation to one another. However, our later thinking suggested that such a model at this point might make these question categories appear static or stable, when in fact they are not. It now seems to us that a premature model could do more to hinder theory-building than help it. When we focus attention on those communication and process-of-change variables which are particularly related to broadcast labor relations, we seem more at the begin-

We wish to gratefully express special appreciation to Ralph M. Stogdill, Professor of Business Research at Ohio State University, for his criticisms and suggestions on the manuscript for this chapter.

ning of a search than far enough along for fancy iconographic summaries of "truth." Paul Lazarsfeld, Leo Bogart, Malcolm S. MacLean, Jr., and others have indicated a need to *begin* studies of the professional broadcaster himself. Insights into broadcast labor relations — such as those provided in this book — may help contribute to the total picture of the broadcaster within his social-professional orbit, but such a picture is not yet in sufficiently clear relief for seemingly absolute statements.

It follows from this that one of the jobs of this chapter is to focus attention on what is *not* known, to point out the gap in our state of knowledge. As one scans the available literature for understanding of the mass communication processes the categories "broadcast management" and "broadcast labor organizations" seem to contend with each other for the *least* amount of research attention. There are only a few theses and dissertations, for example, on the broadcast unions; and there are even fewer behavioral science studies on the operations, influence, and consequences of broadcast labor organizations. Perhaps communication researchers have neglected the communication processes at the message dissemination centers. It is also possible that rigorous scientific investigation conducted by competent behavioral scientists would threaten vested interests — especially in such a situation, where parties on both sides of the relationship may see each other as "opposition." In any case, bibliographies reflect very little systematic inquiry in this area.

It seems odd that so much attention has been devoted to audience studies while the other half of the mass communication process has been virtually ignored. Certainly the social role of broadcasters and broadcast union members is greatly magnified by the public service they provide — or do not provide. As the number of audience-consumers increases in proportion to the number of media practitioners the more important it becomes to understand the communication processes at the "sending" side of mass communication systems. The more trust and understanding these media persons can build among themselves the more we may expect them to work in harmony toward communicating with their audiences.

It would be misleading to create the impression that nothing has been done, for Paul J. Deutschmann, Malcolm S. MacLean, Jr., John T. McNelly, Walter Gieber, William Stephenson, Robert L. Jones, and others have each contributed in his own way along these lines, and the *Journalism Quarterly* has especially responded to the need. However, in the main it is necessary to search for understanding in the social and behavioral sciences more generally, and then apply this insight to questions more central to our concern. Books such as *The Planning of Change*,[1] for example, supply insights into interpersonal, group, and intra-organizational communication, as well as understanding of interconflict situations and the like which may be related to problems such as those summarized here. There is further research in other disciplines and industries that can help us ask questions, formulate hypotheses, and get some enlightening clues. One illustration is Miller's article in *Personnel Psychology* which reports a study of national union officials. Miller found that the union organizational structure is a major determinant of how officials see the psychological demands of their jobs, and that generally, union officials feel that the "organization man," the one who is cooperative, adaptable, cautious, agreeable, and tactful, is more necessary for success at low levels than high levels of the union administrative hierarchy.[2]

Miller believes that future research will show several conditions bearing on the types of behavior seen necessary for success in union leadership, and these include the extent to which management openly accepts unions, the degree of success of union-organizing attempts, and how much the union leaders feel their jobs are personal property. Studies of this type provide insight into union leadership's thinking and offer guidelines for predicting future broadcast labor-management relations. Such findings as we have mentioned here will be used throughout the remainder of the chapter, whenever the results seem to promote the understanding of labor-management relations in broadcasting. They are in no way considered exhaustive.

Can We Improve Broadcast Management?

In researching broadcast labor relations it is not enough just to study the employee-union portion of the interaction continuum, for the actions of broadcast management are obviously vital to the manner in which relationships develop. To properly evaluate the variables and hypothesize about management and formal leadership, descriptive studies of the type performed and reported by Winick are useful. He analyzed data from 287 television station general managers and found that they were relatively young, in their early forties on the average. Most were born in small towns, served in World War II, performing hazardous duty in many instances, and as station managers were involved in many local community activities. The typical station manager liked his job responsibility and its special demands, and found enjoyment in opportunity, challenge, decision, and policy-making.[3]

Social psychologists have been studying leadership empirically since the earliest days of research in social psychology; therefore, much data is available for analysis, but it often results in conflicting conclusions. Nevertheless, Collins and Guetzkow have summarized some interesting findings about leadership traits which show that the best leader in a group is probably not the best liked member of the group. In fact, over time the idea man will slip lower in the group rankings of the best liked. The idea man is the highest in giving suggestions and opinions, and the best liked man is higher in giving and receiving solidarity and tension release. There is a tendency for the group members with the greatest interaction with others not to be the best liked.[4] Sociometric analysis is one way such studies may be conducted. (See J. L. Moreno, *Who Shall Survive?*, Beacon, N.Y., 1953.)

Another method for assessing the communicative styles of task-oriented group members in terms of productivity vs. a concern for people and the quality of interpersonal relationship is the "managerial grid."[5] Blake's managerial training design allows persons to change their ways of dealing with each other in a way that produces maximum concern for productivity and also maximum concern for people. The managerial grid is appropriate beyond this question category. It is a more general method which can be applied for research and for increased communicative effectiveness within almost any social organization.

Is Nonmonetary Job Satisfaction in Broadcasting Unusually High?

Broadcasting is always top-heavy with job applicants. Obviously, there are many attractive reasons for working in the media. These are satisfactions unique to broadcasting that employees find appealing. Are these significant enough to cause the unions to demand less in monetary reward for their employees? Related to these research questions are investigations into the psychological and educational makeup of a person who seeks employment in the broadcasting industry. We would probably expect that differences exist between the before-camera performer and the behind-the-camera worker, but empirical evidence could be obtained of real help to an industry plagued with rising costs.

Probably the most effective way to gain insight into this — as well as many other questions — would be through Stephenson's "Q-technique," Kelly's "repertory grid," or a combination of the two.[6] Those persons having particular aspirations and career goals might be identified by Q analysis in such a way as to provide essentially a theory of personality. Those persons who share similar orientations toward idealized goal aspirations could subsequently respond to the repertory grid in order to provide a full-blown picture of individual personality. Such data could also be compared with long-range career success, general communicative effectiveness, and other closely related questions. Such a study might help educators make predictions about students' success and enjoyment in various jobs, and would likely aid in student counseling and perhaps in station hiring practices.

How do Attitudes of Nontechnical and Technical Employees toward Unionization Differ?

Burkey's and Lenihan and O'Sullivan's descriptions of the difficult problems of the artistic and nonartistic broadcast unions imply that the interests of the groups vary greatly. Matters of importance to a technical union may be insignificant to a nontechnical union and vice-versa. Experimental methodology can seek out and isolate the mediating variables affecting beliefs, values, and attitude formation. For example, Klein and Maher compared educational level and satisfaction with pay, having noted that other research showed that satisfactions in any industry depend to some extent upon the reference groups of the individual. They found that higher education was directly associated with relative dissatisfaction with pay. Major predicators for satisfaction appeared to be the expectation of what salary an individual feels he could or will get internally or could get externally. The college educated manager was not as optimistic about changes in wages internally as were non-college educated managers, but the college educated person was more optimistic about external opportunities.[7] Knowing more about what each type of employee expects from his employment and union membership could form the basis for comprehensive descriptive studies. Other related researchable questions are: What do different types of employees think should be the role of the broadcast unions? Is there an optimum span of influence for a typical technical and nontechnical union? What are the effects of technical unions representing nontechnical employees? What form does the decision-making process take in a broadcast union?

Much insight into the broadcast union's decision-making processes could be gained by systematic case studies of union organizations. They could add to our understanding of how the union functions and why conflicts of interest develop and interunion cooperation breaks down.[8] Such attitude variables as those mentioned here could be assessed by the "semantic differential," since the "content" of the instrument is open and flexible enough to adapt to specific attitude problems.

Can We Predict Effective Contract Negotiation and Strikes?

Union-management relations are affected by every contact that is made between the representatives of each and with third parties, which in broadcasting includes the radio or television audience. Because of the special relationship of the third party audience to the opposing interests, the audience becomes an important variable to consider whenever research in the area is planned.

Because of the restricted nature of the contact in the formal bargaining situation, it is relatively easy to investigate. The literature is filled with studies related directly and indirectly to interpersonal bargaining. Several will be surveyed here. Deutsch and Kraus found that the availability of threat made it more difficult for bargainers to reach a mutually profitable agreement. When bilateral threat was present, no amount of communication could overcome the negative effects. They also found that the greater the competition situation the less likely that available communication channels would be used.[10] Swirth discovered that five times as many people responded to the initiative to establish trust by another as attempted the initiative of trust themselves.[11] Douglas drew some quasi-experimental observations based upon an intensive study of a sample of labor-management negotiations. She found that institutional groups usually make moves clumsily, but once the steps are taken they tend to be almost irreversible. The outcome of bargaining, Douglas observed, bears some direct relationship to the willingness of the parties involved to begin negotiations in a state of flexibility so that they are not firmly committed to only one contract agreement early in the negotiations.[12] Kraus and Deutsch reported results showing that bargaining participants who were tutored in communicating fair proposals achieved significantly higher joint payoffs. In another experiment conducted on the same subjects they found that communication initiated during the first half of the bargaining session and limited to that part of the bargaining was less successful in gaining higher joint payoffs than communication initiated and limited to the latter half of the negotiations.[13] Johnson studied the use of role reversal in negotiation and discovered that role reversal results in more understanding of the opponent's position than does self-presentation. He found that this greater understanding increases competition when positions are incompatible and decreases it when they are compatible.[14] Hornstein reported that mediators who intervene between groups in conflict can use techniques of process analysis, such as survey feedback, to increase the negotiator's positive evaluation of the negotiation and its outcome. He also noted experimentally that high commitment to one's own group tends to interfere with cooperation, and high satisfaction with one's role in the home group will tend to enhance negotiations.[15]

As these findings attest, although the literature furnishes many valuable studies about conflict and negotiations, it can only form the theoretical framework for specialized studies in broadcasting labor relations. The authors in this book have raised researchable questions regarding contract negotiation and strikes. There may be a variety of ways of predicting strikes or of predicting the "lines" drawn by management. Since data for such predictions must be taken in such a way that the respondent is unable to "cheat," the repertory grid would have special utility here — although the method is highly flexible and has a very wide range of applications.

Does Managerial Behavior in a Nonorganized Station Differ from Managerial Behavior in an Organized Station?

That the mere existence of a union would change the goals of management in employee related actions seems to be a reasonable assumption gathered from Warnock's chapter. How does the union affect the day-to-day direction of the station's business? Must management adapt to altered employee demands brought about by unionization? How does the leadership pattern in an organized station differ from the leadership pattern in a nonorganized station? This last question, raised by reading Loper and McDermott, of course is closely related to a preceding one on managerial behavior, but leadership may develop which includes not only formal management but also unionized employees. What is the role of the shop steward in a broadcasting station? Are old patterns of informal leadership disrupted when the station is unionized? All of these questions require creative investigation beyond the traditional boundaries of broadcasting research, whether experimental or descriptive. They call for research designs such as those suggested by Stephenson, Moreno, Cattell,[16] and others, and the integration of two or more of these in some cases.

How Do the Attitudes toward Labor Unions of the Nonowning Manager Differ from Those of the Owner-Manager?

To gain a general insight into the union-employee-employer relationship, researchers should look into the questions of how both see each other. Certain mediating variables obviously influence these attitudes, as suggested by the chapters of McDermott and Loper and of Coe and Holt. Descriptive comparisons between stations with varying philosophies toward unions and labor relations could help isolate the critical variables. Blake and Mouton found that training by seminar is a useful way to change the attitudes of both management and labor about supervisory practices.[17] Adapting this technique to the investigation of opinions toward each other might provide interesting data on changing attitudes. When properly tested in meaningful research, such methods may prove efficient in creating the right bargaining atmosphere by neutralizing the negative feeling of middle and upper broadcasting management toward unionization, where it exists. Similar research questions have been effectively answered in other areas by direct correlation between two or more rankings taken from the respective persons involved in the communication situation. There are various examples of this basic design, such as may be found in Rogers and Dymond's *Psychotherapy and Personality Change.*[18]

What are the Patterns in Union Contracts?

Cole and Goldstein's observations regarding the problems facing broadcast unions point up the need for investigation in this area. Content analysis[19] of contracts in the various above- and below-the-line unions would be valuable, especially to the practicing negotiator. McCue's discussion of the no-strike clause raises the question, How did the no-strike clause originate and remain as a regular part of the contracts of various unions? The content analysis technique would also be useful in answering the question raised by Cole and Goldstein, What are the trends in international labor agreements?

How do Decisions of Arbitrators Familiar with Broadcasting Compare with Arbitrators not Familiar with the Industry?

From Coulson's discussion questions immediately arise about the mediating variables affecting the awarding of favorable decisions to broadcasting unions and management. Does the arbitrator's own background sway his final judgment, and in whose favor? An experimental approach would be beneficial here, for it would allow direct comparison of decisions from both types of arbitrators in a laboratory controlled situation, allowing the exclusion, to a great extent, of error-causing influences. Case studies of arbitrators, and of specific case histories, would also be enlightening.[20]

What is the History of the Broadcasting Labor Movement?

Several of the preceding chapters have given an interesting glimpse of union history, failure and achievement. Schubert and Lynch provide an overview of broadcast union history, but as with any attempt to cover so much information in one chapter, little expansion was possible. Maloney in particular helps us to gain a historical perspective of the union's place in broadcasting, and he raises a related, historically researchable question of social significance: What has been the effect of unions on the nature of the medium? To what extent have they been responsible for it's becoming predominately a commercial enterprise? Have the unions historically given direction and form to program content? Coe and Holt provide the basis for another interesting historical study of the union's effect on broadcasting wages and working conditions over the years. While libraries can often furnish complete and lengthy histories of the major labor movements and unions in other industries, this is not true in broadcasting.

Can the Working Environment Be Changed?

Working conditions among broadcast station employees vary greatly between sections of the country, between small, medium, and large market stations, and between the major production centers and the rest of the nation. For example, Harwood reported that payrolls were very unequally distributed, with the five states of New York, California, Illinois, Pennsylvania, and Ohio reporting more than 50 percent of the total payroll. He also found payroll value per employee in the three major production centers was greater than the national average, with Chicago reporting a 36 percent greater than average share, New York 30 percent greater, and Los Angeles 8 percent.[21]

Lawton analyzed data from 696 radio stations and 276 television stations on the discharge of employees. He discovered that small stations were less likely to discharge employees than large stations, but that at least a fourth of the small stations discharge at such a high rate that they appeared to be places of unstable employment. The reasons most given for discharge were in descending order: (1) employees behavior, personal application; (2) ability and training; (3) management factors (automation, economy, etc.). Lawson noted that four people at one station were discharged because of union activities.[22]

In an article in the *Journal of Broadcasting*, Starlin reported employee attitudes taken from an employment study made by the Association for Professional Broadcasting Education and the National Association of Broadcasters. About 30 percent of radio and television employees were concerned with what they considered unfair methods of wage increase and promotion. Roughly the same percentage said that management should improve its leadership in general, draw better lines of authority and responsibility in jobs, provide better physical equipment, have fairer compensation practices, more cooperation between workers, and better on-the-job training for new employees. Starlin in another article in the same publication, and again taken from the same APBE-NAB study, reported that over 90 percent of radio and television employees felt that a decision to enter broadcasting was a good one, and over 80 percent planned to continue working in the broadcast media. About 50 percent were looking for advancement from their present jobs while about 30 percent were satisfied with their positions. Roughly 40 percent expressed hopes for management-level jobs or station ownership. At the time data for the study was collected 50 percent of the television employees and 25 percent of the radio employees had earned college degrees.[23]

What Are the Hiring and Discharge Practices of Small, Medium, and Large Market Stations?

This question, related to the problems which Coulson discusses, has been partially answered by Lawton's study. But a new descriptive study should be designed to determine what trends have taken place in the industry in recent years. It should be expanded to include not only discharge practices but hiring practices as well, since hiring and discharge practices are closely related to the problems of upward mobility. Often in the smaller markets, employees move from station to station on a horizontal plane but are unable to achieve significant upward, or vertical, movement in the system. This horizontal movement is closely related to the turnover and the hiring and discharge practices of the industry. Of course, of prime importance is a comparison of these practices between union and nonunion stations of all sizes.

What Types of Conflicts are Sources of Frustration for Production, Sales, and Technical Personnel?

McCue points up the need for cooperation between unions. Of course, union cooperation can exist only when employee groups are friendly toward each other. Recommended research in this area would categorize the conflicts that arise between the various departments in commercial and educational stations.

How Are Rating Standards Used to Justify Discharge or Reassignment?

As Coulson mentions, rating standards are used quite often as guides for wage and other employee rewards. Researchers should determine the effects of the method of discharge on the employee-union management relationship and on the employee's morale. What alternative criteria are available if rating standards are not used? Field experimental work would seem justifiable for answering this question.

How Much Discrimination Exists in Employment?

With the Justice Department watching closely, the industry has been given warning by the Federal Communications Commission of the importance of minority group representation on station and network staffs. Meyer has condemned broadcasters for their lack of positive results in finding, hiring, and training minority groups. A 1968 study of educational radio and television stations by the National Association of Educational Broadcasters revealed that 7.72 percent of the responding licensee's personnel were from a minority group. The study, first of its kind, reported that 5.34 percent of 3,695 employees were Black.[24] Further empirical investigation of this question should be made to determine if there is justification for Meyer's charges. In addition to research into numbers of minorities currently employed at networks, stations, and related areas, research into methods of finding and training necessary personnel would be pertinent.

What is the Pattern and Result of Freelance Agreements?

Other questions related to contracts and the working environment may be profitably explored. Such things as: What are the problems for actors which are caused by pilot options? From Bakaly, this question: Does union jurisdiction affect the assignment of personnel? Finally, there are problems of dual loyalty which are hinted at in several chapters. Does the uniqueness of broadcasting make it difficult for the worker to be both a good union member and a good company employee? Several of these questions call for a relatively simple case history and questionnaire method employed for analysis of organizational life which might be profitably reported here, that of Blansfield.[25] The research methods employed are neither time consuming or especially expensive. The human relations or communication workshop methods which he used to produce change do, of course, require a high degree of skill on the part of a properly trained and experienced communication consultant. A summary of the Blansfield study might suggest for some broadcasting stations potentialities for change and assessment of change in the working environment.

The conditions for change were itemized and considered in relation to the goals of the organization. Managers subsequently participated in a five-day live-in communication workshop centered about the theory and methods of counseling with others — including extensive skill-practice sessions. Group analysis noted that the group consistently expressed grave concern over a number of matters not directly related to counseling but certainly affecting it. Matters of interpersonal tensions and hostilities, feelings of personal inadequacy, dissatisfaction with corporate policy and practices were often discussed with deep feeling. The training program allowed such communication problems which came up so importantly to be expressed and worked through in order that communication learning could occur. Results of the workshop as determined by questionnaire self-ratings of participants at the conclusion of the laboratory showed:

	More	About the Same	No Comment
Understanding the process of human behavior	78%	22%	
Awareness of reactions of others to self	82%	18%	
Ability to listen	80%	19%	1%
Consciousness of relations to others	84%	15%	1%
Flexibility	74%	25%	1%

If a broadcast station invests in an appropriate resource person or persons to conduct such a communication learning lab, this kind of study should be relatively economical to replicate.

What Are the Effects of Technological Change on Management Rights?

According to Coulson, technological change has resulted in new demands from the unions to protect their jobs and salaries. Each technological innovation generates a union-management confrontation that has to be resolved. Each technological advance has brought renewed pressures from the unions to protect themselves. What has this done to management rights? Is technological progress reducing management's power and increasing the power of the unions? This tends to become in part a question of social philosophy or ethics, perhaps, more than a single, researchable item.

What Are the Effects of the Profit Motive on Management's Decisions Regarding the Labor Unions?

Loper and McDermott emphasize the need to cultivate good relations with the commercial stations in the surrounding area, because commercial and noncommercial station managers face some of the same problems. The profit motive is obviously a factor that influences the eventual solution of the commercial manager's problems. It might be asked, What is the motivating force behind the non-commercial station manager? Comparisons between the solutions of ETV and commercial stations to similar problems would provide interesting insights into what moves the ETV manager. Such investigation would most likely benefit from the kind of understanding provided by the repertory grid or the use of something like Cattell's O-method.

What Are the Effects of the Availability of Recordings on Strike Length?

From Burkey and McCue we gain insight into how the broadcast employee is actually his own strike breaker because management can fall back on previously recorded tapes and film during periods of strikes. How long will the audience watch reruns during strikes before audience ratings drop drastically? Again, strike activity to analyze is almost a prerequisite for proper research into this area. Other questions of interest are, How are bluff, threat, and promise used in strike negotiation? How can moves and strategies during broadcast strikes be classified? The rating surveys themselves provide indices of actual viewing behavior, or at least of television *set* behavior, and what viewers *say* they watch. Rating data could be compared to broad classifications of repeated content. (See Budd, et al.) There are a variety of social indices for classifying interpersonal and group communication styles, such as the "interaction process analysis" method developed by Robert Bales,[26] and others being employed by the National Training Laboratories Institute for Applied Behavioral Science.

What Is the Best Method in Determining Lines of Delineation between the Job Jurisdiction of Contesting Unions?

Warnock's discussion of some of the jurisdictional problems faced in broadcasting and their outcome and McCue's description of the absence of interunion cooperation reveal the difficulties the unions face in putting forth a united front by reducing interunion disagreement over jurisdiction, issues, and contents. In published research related to this problem, Abrahamson reported the results of a study showing that orientation toward one another is necessary for accommodation, and that interpersonal interaction is not primarily a result of clearly defined roles and role expectations.[27] Deutsch, Epstein, Canavan, and Gumpert studied five behavioral strategies to find out which was best for gaining the cooperation of someone who was uncooperative initially or persistently. They found that the participants would exploit another subject who turned the other cheek, unless that behavior was a reform or change from some previous position.[28] But competition between unions is not all necessarily bad. For example, Fiedler found that competition among groups assisted employees in maintaining personal adjustment and eliminating the demoralizing effects of failure. Most likely, however, the competition will have a positive effect only when the groups have few members, which is probably true only in small and medium market stations. If used correctly, the competition increases morale and serves as a psychological boost.[29] Additional studies of this type, but broadcast oriented, could provide an understanding of duties, training, and employee expectations by job category, aiding the effort to find systematic solutions to the problems unique to unions. Experimental research which compares different methods of delineation and their effects on morale, productivity, job satisfaction, and absenteeism is needed, and should be fruitful. One way to identify the differences which exist between these variables would be with measures such as the Dartnell "self-administered employee opinion unit," The Jenkens "job attitudes survey," or the "work information inventory," or the like.[30] A comparison of one or more of these with measurement of work role and other variables, such as work quality and amount of work produced, could be made by employing principles of variance analysis.

What Is the Impact of Strikes upon the Audience?

Rating studies will only allow us to guess at audience attitudes toward management and the unions, and it is expected that possible shifts exist. Is the audience more aware of the issues in broadcast labor disputes and strikes than of those in other industries? Bakaly leads us to ask, How does management use the struck medium for propaganda purposes against the union during a strike? What opposing statements and methods of dissemination are used by the union to favorably dispose the public? What effects do these have on public attitudes? How does the public estimate the social and financial rewards of broadcast employees? Obviously many of these questions can only be investigated at times of strike activity. Both experimental and descriptive studies at the right moments in broadcast labor relations history would certainly provide results of worth. And generally there are warning signs of strikes before they actually occur, allowing sufficient time for set-up and pretesting where it is needed. Naturally some planning ahead is required if the researcher is to take advantage of the strike situation, making the most of what still is a rare event. Studies such as those conducted by the late Dr. Paul Deutschmann and others active in the diffusion of information studies allow us to understand such communicative processes. Studies of information diffusion could be profitably combined, as MacLean has done, with Q analysis of the same population. Such a combination of research designs allows the data to provide insight not only into information flow and personality styles but also into the relation between the two. Stephenson's Q-technique is also highly appropriate for studies of public images, and especially for assessing change of public meaning over time, as implied by some of the above questions.

What Are the Reasons for Increased Strike Activity?

McCue and others call attention to the rising trend to strikes in the industry and even predict that the no-strike clause will eventually be dropped from all broadcast union contracts. Research in other fields has shown that strikes only occur when the power balance is almost equalized. Some kinds of morale indicators mentioned earlier would provide indices which might predict predisposition to strike, and they are relatively economical. A more effective predictor would be the repertory grid,[31] if it is competently administered and analysis of the data conducted by a skilled researcher.

Conclusion

The questions presented in this chapter are only a sample of the wide range of labor relations problems facing broadcasting unions and management. The authors have directly and indirectly called attention to these areas of doubt where, at the moment, no easy and quick solutions exist. Whether dealing with the unions, the working environment, broadcast management, or contract negotiation and strikes, the questions reflect the uncertainty in an area too long ignored by researchers. No doubt they are answerable through systematic investigation, but in addition to attention by researchers, finding the answers would be aided by the active interest, encouragement, and cooperation of union leadership and network and station management. Without the cooperation of the two principals, the future for research in labor relations will not be bright. But with a strengthened dedication to labor relations research by the scholar and student and an increased awareness by unions and management of its importance to the industry, we can move forward toward hypothesizing, testing, analyzing, and encouraging application of sound, proven principles for solving the industry's labor relations problems.

NOTES

1. Warren Bennis, Kenneth D. Benne, and Robert Chin, eds., *The Planning of Change* (New York: Holt, Rinehart & Winston, 1961).
2. Edwin L. Miller, "Job Attitudes of National Union Officials: Perceptions of the Importance of Certain Personality Traits as a Function of Job Level and Union Organizational Structure," *Personnel Psychology* 19 (Winter, 1966), 395–410.
3. Charles E. Winick, "The Television Station Manager," *Advanced Management Journal* 26 (January, 1966), 53–60.
4. Barry E. Collins and Harold Guetzkow, *A Social Psychology of Group Processes for Decision Making* (New York: John Wiley and Sons, 1964).
5. See Robert R. Blake and Jane S. Mouton, *The Managerial Grid* (Houston, Texas: Gulf Publishing Co., 1964).
6. See William Stephenson, *The Study of Behavior* (Chicago: The University of Chicago Press, 1953), and George A. Kelly, *The Psychology of Personal Constructs*, 6 vols. (New York: W. W. Norton, 1955), 1, 2.
7. S. M. Klein and J. R. Maher, "Educational Level and Satisfaction with Pay," *Personnel Psychology* 19 (Summer, 1966), 195–208.
8. For an example of one union's decision-making process, see Allen E. Koenig, "American Federation of Television and Radio Artists Decision-making on the Transcription Code" (Ph.D. diss., Northwestern University, 1964).
9. See Charles E. Osgood, George J. Suci, and Percy H. Tannen-

baum, *The Measurement of Meaning* (Urbana: University of Illinois Press, 1957).

10. Morton Deutsch and Robert M. Kraus, "Studies of Interpersonal Bargaining," *Journal of Conflict Resolution* 6 (March, 1962), 52–76.
11. Robert L. Swirth, "The Establishment of the Trust Relationship," *Journal of Conflict Resolution* 11 (September, 1967), 335–44.
12. Ann Douglas, "The Peaceful Settlement of Industrial and Intergroup Disputes," *Journal of Conflict Resolution* 1 (March, 1957), 69–81.
13. Robert M. Kraus and Morton Deutsch, "Communication in Interpersonal Bargaining," *Journal of Personality and Social Psychology* 4 (1966), 572–77.
14. David W. Johnson, "Use of Role Reversal in Intergroup Competition," *Journal of Personality and Social Psychology* 7, no. 2 (1967), 135–41.
15. H. A. Hornstein and D. W. Johnson, "The Effects of Process Analysis and Ties to His Group Upon Negotiators' Attitudes Toward the Outcome of Negotiations," *Journal of Applied Behavioral Science* 2, no. 4 (1966), 449–63.
16. Raymond B. Cattell, ed., *Handbook of Multivariate Experimental Psychology* (Chicago: Rand McNally, 1966).
17. R. R. Blake and Jane S. Mouton, "Some Effects of Managerial Grid Seminar Training on Union and Management Attitudes Toward Supervision," *Journal of Applied Behavioral Science* 2, no. 4 (1966), 387–400.
18. Carl R. Rogers and Rosalind R. Dymond, *Psychotherapy and Personality Change* (Chicago: University of Chicago Press, 1954).
19. Richard W. Budd, Robert K. Thorp, and Lewis Donohew, *Content Analysis of Communications* (New York: The Macmillan Company, 1967).
20. See Robert K. Merton, Marjorie Fiske, and Patricia L. Kendall, *The Focused Interview* (Glencoe, Illinois: The Free Press, 1956).
21. Kenneth Harwood, "On Geographical Distribution of Payrolls of Broadcasting Organizations in the United States," *Journal of Broadcasting* 7 (Fall, 1963), 327–38.
22. Sherman P. Lawton, "Discharge of Broadcast Station Employees," *Journal of Broadcasting* 6 (Summer, 1962), 191–96.
23. Glenn Starlin, "Employee Attitudes Toward the Broadcasting Industry: A Report From the APBE-NAB Employment Study," *Journal of Broadcasting* 7 (Fall, 1963), 359–67; Glenn Starlin,

"The Broadcasting Employee: A Report From the APBE-NAB Employment Study," *Journal of Broadcasting* 7 (Summer, 1963), 233–45.

24. NAEB Office of Research and Development, "Minority Employment in Educational Broadcasting," *Educational Broadcasting Review* 3 (April, 1969), 15–18.

25. Michael G. Blansfield, "Depth Analysis of Organizational Life," *California Management Review* 5 (Winter, 1962), 29–42.

26. Robert R. Bales, *Interaction Process Analysis* (Cambridge, Mass.: Addison-Wesley, 1950).

27. Mark Abrahamson, *Interpersonal Accommodation* (Princeton, N.J.: D. Van Nostrand, 1966).

28. Morton Deutsch, Yakor Epstein, Donnah Canavan, and Peter Gumpert, "Strategies of Inducing Cooperation: An Experimental Study," *Journal of Conflict Resolution* 11 (September, 1967), 345–60.

29. Fred E. Fiedler, "The Effect of Inter-Group Competition on Group Member Adjustment," *Personnel Psychology* 20, no. 1 (1967), 33–44.

30. Oscar K. Buros, *The Sixth Mental Measurements Yearbook* (Highland Park, New Jersey: The Gryphon Press, 1965).

31. D. Bannister and J. M. Mair, *The Evaluation of Personal Constructs* (New York: Academic Press, 1968).

17 Summary
and a Look at the Future

by ALLEN E. KOENIG

This volume represents the first time a book or monograph has been devoted to the subject of labor and broadcasting. Although quite a bit of material has been written on the subject, there has been no attempt, until now, to look upon it as a specialized field in broadcasting. In the past the topic was treated on an *ad hoc* or news story basis. And as has been said, it was difficult to acquire this material, since labor and management seemingly desired to keep it confidential.*

At the outset Martin J. Maloney has set the scene by saying that the influence of the unions may provide documentation for McLuhan's view that the contents of a new communications medium is an old medium; that is, the roots of unionism entwined broadcasting before it had a chance to become an individual or unique medium. Maloney developed his theory on three hypotheses:

(1) Radio and television could be viewed as metaphors;

(2) These metaphors would determine what organizations (unions) should control the media;

For a list of periodical literature on the subject, see Allen E. Koenig, "Labor Relations in the Broadcasting Industry: Periodical Literature 1937–1964," *Journal of Broadcasting* 9 (Fall, 1965), 339–56.

(3) The pre-existing organizations would pass on their biases to the media and thus affect their content and developing styles.

Thus, according to Maloney, the unions' previous successes would eventually affect broadcasting, because unions would apply their successful techniques to inappropriate areas, an instance of "cultural lag."

His position is that "it is hard to imagine television developing a highly imaginative, idiosyncratic style where the workers who produced it were most likely to force it into a resemblance to the media with which they were most familiar."

Maloney's warning of a "cultural lag" is reinforced by Robert L. Coe's story of his years as a pioneer in broadcasting management and engineering, in St. Louis and New York City. In relating his story to Darrel W. Holt, Coe stated that "Over the years, needless to say, there has been a good deal of labor-management maneuvering to watch. From what I've seen — if we want to cast it into television terms — most of it has been a sophisticated remake of the same old plot. More." Later he amplified this statement: "In looking for other correlations, I've discovered that no matter how I've approached them verbally, the substance of each can be simply stated — cost. . . . If this cost notion is valid, then the wheel has come full circle, because cost is a function of the labor-management game called More."

Coe says that stations cannot afford to go dark because of the advertising revenue losses that are incurred. Because costs spiral, however, a unions' victory may not be economic, but rather psychological.

But what about these unions? In the spring of 1968, Professor James Lynch conducted the first graduate seminar on broadcasting unions offered at the Ohio State University. He and graduate student Gregory Schubert decided to pool the students' research in the seminar and present it here. They traced the history, structure, and impact of the eight major labor unions in broadcasting: the American Federation of Television and Radio Artists, the Screen Actors Guild, the Writers Guild of America, the Directors

Guild of America, the American Federation of Musicians, the International Brotherhood of Electrical Workers, the National Association of Broadcast Employees and Technicians, and the International Alliance of Theatrical Stage Employes.

From their study the authors concluded that "the unions and management have a long history of successful negotiation, because both sides were responsive to each situation and its implications." This view, however, may be overly optimistic in view of recent management-union confrontations in both the creative and technical fields.

Thus radio and television unionism relied on past union experience for answers to new problems encountered in radio and television. Economic gains were of prime concern to the workers, and they accomplished their goals through these eight major labor unions.

Another variable in the labor relations process is the "outside" decision, a factor which materializes whenever management and labor are unable together to solve a problem. It is manifested in either National Labor Relations Board decisions or binding arbitration awards. Warnock in his chapter traces the history of the Wagner, Taft-Hartley, and Landrum-Griffin Acts. The NLRB, operating under the authority of these acts, has dealt with broadcasting union problems in seven areas: NLRB jurisdiction, certification, scope of bargaining units, unfair labor practices by management, unfair labor practices by labor, union jurisdictional disputes, and grievances. It is Warnock's belief that most union objectives have been achieved insofar as wages and fringe benefits are concerned; and he reports the opinion of NLRB member Sam Zagoria that future labor-management negotiations will tend toward a consolidation of union forces which will be encouraged by management, and deal with increased problems caused by automation.

Robert Coulson, in the succeeding chapter, outlines another "outside" decision, binding arbitration. He points up the problem that although most labor contracts contain clauses for grievance solutions through arbitration, they do not provide for arbitration when a new contract cannot be reached. Coulson treats four types of cases that have been arbitrated: program competition; management decisions involving program production; jurisdictional disputes; and issues involving pay rates and job content. However, he believes that arbitration will dispose of the most difficult contract disputes, particularly those that depend upon an interpretation of contract provisions. By having experienced arbitrators, the industry can continue to resolve most of its labor problems without experiencing expensive work stoppages. He also predicts that labor and management will continue to have disputes because of technological and marketing changes that neither side will have anticipated.

Like Warnock and Coulson, Bakaly is dealing with the past decisions of the NLRB and arbitration awards, but with an emphasis on the problems of national networks and unions. He echoes Coulson's last prediction by remarking that he finds broadcasting labor problems interesting because of the constant change that automation and technology bring to the industry. This, he concludes, produces a unifying theme in the unions' concern for work preservation, which results from a rapidly developing technology, and this will continue to be the focal point in the future.

In addition to legal problems what other specific problems impinge upon labor and broadcasting? In treating the history of exporting and importing in broadcasting, and their effect upon labor and management, Cole and Goldstein point out that although a plateau may be reached in the distribution of American programming to foreign markets, there is still a large marketplace. The problems in the field have been those of residuals, the interchange of union personnel across national boundaries, "runaway productions," and union solidarity through international labor associations and agreements.

Because of the urgent problems of maintaining existing jobs and compensation at home, there will be "no startling change in union policies or union agreements covering the foreign market . . . in the very near future," according to Cole and Goldstein.

The creative artist not only faces the traditional economic problems but also creative ones, according to Evelyn F. Burkey. Performers, actors, announcers, writers, dancers, and musicians face the problems of:

(1) Exclusivity — how long will my contract run?
(2) Reruns — will I be in competition with myself?
(3) Credits — how will I be recognized?
(4) Creative control — will I make the creative decisions?
(5) "Runaway productions" — will I lose work because of foreign competition?
(6) Copyright — will new laws limit my current copyright protection?
(7) Satellite protection — will satellites eliminate my recordings?

The technical "artists" in broadcasting face problems of a different nature, probed by Lenihan and O'Sullivan. They emphasize that the role of the technical employee should be creative rather than routine, and they examine the major problems which he faces: automation job displacement, job alienation because of noncreative or boring tasks, and the encroachment of nontechnical employees into traditional engineering duties.

The authors also look at the current broadcasting setting in order to ascertain what variables affect the working conditions of the technician. Although they conclude that changes in society are inevitable, they end with this challenge: "The technician-engineer and his unions must stand ready to help make these changes, but make them in such a fashion that the public and the quality of broadcasting will benefit at the same time that the status and security of the technician-engineer is enhanced."

Loper and McDermott argue management's position on labor and ETV. They explain that the essential difference between commercial and educational broadcasting has been that the former receives support from advertising revenues while the latter must depend upon public support. Ergo, the ETV station is entitled to pay employees less than its commercial brethren. After developing this philosophy, the authors suggest ways for management to negotiate with broadcasting unions.

In my chapter on representation of TV teachers, I argue for labor's point of view. That is, the teacher should not accept less for his services simply because he is noncommercial. Furthermore, the new reality of collective bargaining in education is discussed, including its implications for television teachers. It is my belief that the rights of TV teachers can be best protected through collective bargaining, professional policy statements, and arbitration.

The broadcasting industry has recently turned to another problem, the black man. In Meyer's opinion, "during the decades prior to the Black Revolution of the 1960s, broadcasting did little or nothing to relate the civil rights struggle to the mainstream of American society. . . . Only black radio, beaming its message to black audiences, built its own images with a civil rights point of view." He questions why a black man would want to work in an industry that has portrayed him as an "Amos 'n Andy." He refers to the Plotkin Study delineating the underrepresentation of blacks in television, and leaves us with the question of whether "broadcasting, and especially television, [will] widen the racial gap, or is the medium proceeding with integration?"

Another sensitive problem in the broadcasting industry has been blacklisting, which Gumpert traces from its beginnings in the fear of a Communist threat, in the early 1950s and which, of course, affected much more than broadcasting. The author cites numerous broadcasting cases and actual blacklists which pointed up the critical nature of the problem. He feels that the subject is relevant today because "The climate and circumstances which stimulated it, and in which it proliferated, could occur again."

Special problem areas in labor and broadcasting have included the international labor market, problems of creative and technical personnel, negotiating lower wages for ETV personnel, representation for television teachers, employing blacks, and blackballing union members because of political ideologies.

Discussing the future of broadcasting labor relations from a frankly union viewpoint, McCue introduces one element that can be expected to be important: interunion cooperation. Broadcasting unions which have been tied to no-strike clauses by their contracts with management have been hindered in this cooperation, and McCue expects that they will take necessary action during future negotiations to abolish the clauses. He believes that it is "the height of folly for a single union to rely on its own bargaining strength," and he discusses the extension of interunion cooperation on all levels.

In another area of concern for the future, Hunter points up the low academic priority given to the study of broadcasting unionism. Although he advocates offering course work in this area for students majoring in broadcasting, he stresses that it is not the role of the university to train union or management personnel, and believes that the university can best serve the interests of both labor and management by:

(1) Offering courses in the history of unionism, labor and management law, and methods of negotiation;

(2) Having an interdisciplinary program of studies with other departments, thereby allowing radio and television majors to take these subjects;

(3) Encouraging graduate students to conduct research on broadcast unionism;

(4) Offering seminars or institutes on labor and broadcasting, and involving unions and management in these endeavors;

(5) Preparing audio-visual devices for formal teaching or professional use on labor and broadcasting.

Graduate student A. Edward Foote and Professor Robert R. Monaghan analyzed the chapters in this book before writing their chapter. Thereafter they stated a number of problems that researchers could investigate on labor and broadcasting. Also, they cited related literature or research findings that might pertain to this type of research. In some instances they gave brief strategies on how the studies could be conducted.

Too often it is dangerous and foolhardy to predict the future. In broadcasting and labor, however, there are several areas that can be prognosticated with some certainty because of current practice and philosophy.

Certainly the traditional pattern of negotiating and striking will continue, since both management and labor have not been innovative in their strategies. Research in the next ten years, however, may offer alternatives to these traditional patterns, if the unions and broadcasters are willing. For example, it is generally believed that a strike is economically wasteful for both sides. What would be their reaction to a controlled experiment to test whether an impasse could be solved more inexpensively and in a shorter period of time than a regular strike by diverting all the company's profits and employees' salaries to charity? Or, as another illustration of what might be done, what about a comparative study of whether arbitration is a more economical way of problem solving than either a lockout or a picket line?

It is to be hoped that education will play an increasingly important role in broadcasting labor relations. It can be expected that large corporations and unions will send some of their personnel back to school for a year or more of intensive graduate work leading to degrees in industrial-labor relations or related fields. At the same time the university will have to assume a position that is neither pro nor con unionism or management. It can serve as neutral ground on which both sides can explore the latest knowledge relating to labor relations. In this setting continuing education should play the role of keeping both labor and management up-to-date on the most effective techniques for negotiating and settling their problems. Certainly short courses on this subject should be offered on the university campus, or over educational television.

Although past issues have been largely economic (including fringe benefits), the future will be highlighted by the issue of job preservation. Already many radio stations and some television stations are fully automated for technical and even creative purposes. If creative problem-solving is not initiated in order to deal with this problem, prolonged and costly strikes can be expected. In order to fight automation unions will probably join together in exerting concentrated pressure on the employer. However, the answer to the problem is not to be found in fighting change, but in finding ways to adjust to it. Both management and labor should consider working together in creating new jobs for displaced workers, and giving them the necessary training to function in these positions.

Public or educational broadcasting employees, including teachers, will become increasingly unionized as federal money, through the Corporation for Public Broadcasting, and increasing foundation money is infused into the system. These employees will not be content with receiving less than their commercial counterparts when hundreds of millions of dollars are being spent yearly on public broadcasting! Also, as satellite and interplanetary television become more widely used, new union demands will in all probability be presented to management.

Unless there is drastic reevaluation on the part of broadcast management, the outstanding college graduates of the future will pursue careers in other fields that offer better starting salaries and more benefits. A questioning of young college graduates who majored in radio and television indicates that they believe that careers in education and advertising offer better beginning employment opportunities (see Craig R. Halverson and Allen E. Koenig, "The College Graduate's View of the Broadcasting Labor Market," *Journal of Broadcasting* 2 [Spring, 1968], 169–178). The broadcasting industry should emulate the advertising profession by actively recruiting on the campus and offering enough economic incentive to compete with the offers from business administration, science, law, and comparable fields. The quality of the future leaders of broadcasting will depend upon this effort.

Finally it seems to me that the tragedy of broadcasting labor and management lies in their ties to the establishment, to the status quo. Unless they are more innovative in their solutions "more of the same" can be expected, and the losers will be both sides. Thus far the labor relations process in broadcasting does not appear to be unique. Working men have been striving through collective bargaining for more of the "pie" in this country since 1648 when the Boston Coopers and Shoemakers Guilds were founded. Likewise management has been concerned with earning maximum profits since colonial days. What might make broadcasting labor relations different, however, is the way its leaders in the future identify and solve their problems.

REFERENCE MATTER

Report and Order of the FCC on Nondiscrimination in Broadcast Employment Practices

Adopted June 4, 1969, by the Federal Communications Commission, in the matter of Petition for Rulemaking to Require Broadcast Licensees To Show Nondiscrimination in Their Employment Practices.
By the Commission: Commissioner Bartley not participating; Robert E. Lee concurring in part and dissenting in part and issuing a statement.

1. On July 5, 1968, the Commission released a memorandum opinion and order and notice of proposed rulemaking, 33 F.R. 9960, 13 F.C.C. 2d 766, setting forth its view that discriminatory employment practices by a broadcast licensee are incompatible with operation in the public interest. We found that the Commission has a responsibility to implement the important national policy against discrimination on the basis of race, color, religion, or national origin, and we accordingly announced our intention to act upon substantial complaints of discrimination, either directly or by referral to an appropriate Federal, State, or local body. At the same time, we stated our doubt that embodying the policy in rule form and requiring periodic (e.g., at renewal time) showings of compliance with the policy would be useful. The tentative decision to proceed primarily upon a complaint basis [1] was substantially influenced by considerations related to our limited staff resources. However, we simultaneously instituted rulemaking to explore the questions of whether the basic nondiscrimination requirement should be embodied in a rule, whether a showing of compliance should be required, and whether notices of equal employment rights should mandatorily be posted in employment offices and placed on employment applications.

2. The comments and reply comments filed on these issues have been most helpful. The interested parties are essentially unanimous in support of the proposition that there ought not be discrimination

18 F.C.C. 2d

in employment practices of broadcast licensees. However, several parties have urged either that the Commission lacks authority to implement this policy, in light of the creation of a special Commission (the Equal Employment Opportunity Commission) to act across-the-board with respect to the problem of discrimination or, that, for the same reason, it would at least be better policy for the Federal Communications Commission not to attempt to duplicate the EEOC's processes with additional requirements in the broadcast field. For the reasons already stated in the July 5, 1968, memorandum opinion and order and notice of proposed rulemaking, we cannot agree with these latter contentions. Indeed, a substantial case has been made that because of the relationship of the Government of the United States to broadcast stations, the Commission has a constitutional duty to assure equal employment opportunity.[2] However, we need not decide this point. It is enough that the importance and urgency of the equal employment opportunity policy in the areas covered command its implementation on every appropriate front. Action by the Commission will complement, not conflict with, action by bodies specially created to enforce the policy, as the EEOC points out in its comments and as the Department of Justice has also advised us. It is also clear that we have an independent responsibility to effectuate such a strong national policy in broadcasting, and that we need not await a judgment of discrimination by some other forum or tribunal. *National Broadcasting Company* v. *United States*, 319 U.S. 190 (1943); *Southern Steamship Company* v. *Labor Board*, 316 U.S. 31 (1942).[3] As Assistant Attorney General Pollack urged:

> Because of the enormous impact which television and radio have upon American life, the employment practices of the broadcasting industry have an importance greater than that suggested by the number of its employees. The provision of equal opportunity in employment in that industry could therefore contribute significantly toward reducing and ending discrimination in other industries. For these reasons I consider adoption of the proposed rule, or one embodying the same principles, a positive step which your Commission appears to have ample authority to take.[4]

3. The fear has also been expressed, with respect to the complaint referral policy we announced in our July 1968 opinion, that inconsequential or spurious complaints of discrimination could be used to delay Commission consideration of applications. We agree that consideration of applications should not be held up because of inconsequential complaints. For that reason, our earlier opinion stated that we will refer to other agencies only ". . . complaint(s) raising a substantial issue of discrimination . . . against a station. . . ." In this

connection, we may also make our own preliminary investigation at our discretion in lieu of the complaint referral procedure. We will exercise care in the use of these procedures to the end that no licensee need fear undue delay arising out of the referral procedure. On the other hand, we do not believe that an application should be granted where a serious qualification question remains unresolved. The command of the Communications Act is to the contrary, whatever the nature of the particular unresolved public interest question. Therefore, while not every complaint of an isolated action, even if substantial, will warrant deferring a renewal or designating a renewal application for hearing,[5] renewal will not be appropriate where there is a pattern of substantial failure to accord equal employment opportunities.

4. The earlier opinion proposed almost sole reliance upon a complaint procedure and further stated our view that it was not necessary to adopt the policy on equal employment opportunity in rule form. A number of commenting parties have urged that a formal rule would be useful, not only to emphasize the policy and make it specific, but also to make available the remedy of forfeitures under section 503 of the Communications Act of 1934, as amended, 47 U.S.C. § 503, where there is noncompliance. They state, as we have recognized in other contexts, that denial of a license may sometimes be so severe a remedy that it becomes useless. We find these contentions to be meritorious, particularly since, as noted above, some complaints may be appropriately considered independently of consideration of renewal applications. It has also been urged by a substantial number of parties active in this field that the equal employment opportunity policy cannot be effectively implemented by relying solely upon individual complaints. They point out that consideration of complaints, particularly if referred to other agencies, is time consuming (a point also made by industry parties), and they state their experience that many people will not complain even though they suspect or know they have been treated unfairly in respect either to initial employment or management practices, that many people will not even seek employment where they believe discriminatory practices to exist, and that individuals have great difficulty in demonstrating the existence of discrimination where it does exist.

5. These parties urge that only a serious compliance program with the burden upon the licensee to demonstrate operation conforming to national policy will be effective. The U.S. Commission on Civil Rights thus has stated in its comments:

> It is not enough that no one comes forward to complain of its noncompliance, for that may leave discriminatory practices undisturbed, much as all other complaint-oriented procedures for enforcing State and Federal FEP requirements have had only a minor impact upon the widespread dis-

crimination the National Advisory Commission has found still exists. (Id. at 91.) The New Jersey Governor's Select Commission on Civil Disorder stated earlier this year: "If the enforcement of equal opportunity laws on the State level is predicated upon individual complaints, it is bound to be weak and ineffective." (Report for Action (1968) at 73.)

As appendix B to these comments indicates, there is substantial unanimity among FEP commissions and professional sources, including a number of persons who have specialized for a lifetime in problems of administrative law, that complaint-oriented procedures to enforce nondiscrimination requirements, for various reasons, do not work. They cannot, in light of two decades of experience, be expected to work.[6]

Moreover, reliance solely upon a complaint procedure to implement equal employment opportunity cannot cope with general patterns of discrimination developed out of indifference as much as out of outright bias. In this connection, the Committee on Government Contracts concluded in 1960 that:

Overt discrimination, in the sense that an employer actually refuses to hire solely because of race, religion, color or national origin is not as prevalent as is generally believed. To a greater degree, the indifference of employers to establishing a positive policy of nondiscrimination hinders qualified applicants and employees from being hired and promoted on the basis of equality.

The direct result of such indifference is that schools, training institutions, recruitment and referral sources follow the pattern set by industry. Employment sources do not normally supply job applicants regardless of race, color, religion or national origin unless asked to do so by employers.[7]

Despite the workload problems, these considerations impel us to adopt further requirements to assure equal employment opportunity, especially in view of the urgent national need cited in our earlier opinion. We believe it vital that such action be taken.

6. In order to accomplish the foregoing purposes, we are adopting rules modeled closely upon the equal opportunity program requirements which the Civil Service Commission has adopted for Government agencies, and which are the product of considerable experience.[8] We have decided upon the basis of the record before us that such rules should be adopted. They are set out in appendix A hereto.

7. We also believe, as stated in our earlier opinion, that statistical information should be obtained. Such information will give us a pro-

file of the broadcast industry, and may also be more useful in indicating noncompliance than we had previously thought. See *United States* v. *Wiman*, 304 F. 2d 53 (C.A. 5, 1962); *State of Alabama v. United States*, 304 F. 2d 583, 586 (C.A. 5, 1962). As the court stated in the latter case (304 F. 2d at 586): "In the problem of racial discrimination, statistics often tell much, and courts listen." We therefore propose to adopt an additional rule to obtain statistical data for the broadcast industry. We had considered as the vehicle for reporting statistical information the primary Employer Information Report EEO–1 developed by the EEOC, the Office of Federal Contract Compliance of the Department of Labor, and Plans for Progress. This form requires statistics on several general work categories[9] for employees who are Negro, oriental, American Indian, and Spanish surnamed American. It is already being prepared annually by many broadcasters, and its use by broadcasters already using it would have that advantage. However, we have devised a new form which we believe will be more useful for our purposes.[10] It utilizes the same job categories as the EEO–1 form,[11] but requires a station-by-station breakdown, which EEO–1 does not. We believe our proposed form has considerable additional advantages by way of simplicity and brevity. This form will still permit interindustry comparisons and should minimize industry burdens.[12] Preparation of the requested information should be of minimal difficulty. We seek the advice and suggestions of all interested persons concerning the proposed form. We proposed to include network personnel and so-called headquarters staffs for broadcast operations.

8. In accordance with the considerations set forth in paragraphs 4, 5, and 6, supra, we are also proposing to require the submission by licensees of more detailed equal opportunity programs as to significant minority groups (Negroes, orientals, American Indians, and Spanish surnamed Americans), which may be most in need of assistance in achieving equal employment. These written programs will enable licensees to focus, in terms of their individual situations, upon the best method of assuring effective equal employment practices. Supplemental to the adoption of such programs will be reports to be prepared with renewal applications whose purpose will be a review by the licensee of the effectiveness of his program. Since we have not hitherto proposed specific requirements in this area, we seek comment upon the particulars of the proposed provisions. See note 10, supra, for reference to the text of these provisions. We propose to require that each station with five or more full-time employees develop an equal employment opportunity program, taking due account of such factors as station size and location, and demographic makeup of the area.[13] The scope of the program would vary with the size of the station and the nature of the community and its racial makeup, but its essential purpose for

every station would be to assure equal opportunity in every aspect of station employment practice, including training, hiring, promotion, pay scales, and work assignments. While permitting flexibility, the programs would be expected to include specifics of the station's practices such as, but not limited to those listed in the additions to the application forms. See note 10, supra, for reference to the text of these additions. The proposed procedure would require that these programs be submitted by existing stations within an appropriate time, and by applicants for new and transferred facilities. They would be kept open for public inspection at the station and modified as required. In view of these requirements we see no need for a separate requirement on the posting of notices and statements on application forms discussed in the notice of proposed rulemaking. In addition, as mentioned above, we also believe that reports should be prepared at renewal time to enable the licensee to appraise the effectiveness and relevance to his own situation of his equal employment opportunity program. It should be most useful to know how the specific practices proposed in the station's equal employment opportunity program have been concretely applied and what effect they have had upon the flow of applications for employment, actual hiring, and the status of minority group members. This information would be submitted by each broadcaster in appropriate exhibits with the application for renewal of license.

9. It is important to emphasize in connection with the requirements of the general rule, and the equal opportunity programs proposed, that they do not cover certain areas of employment practice which we described as most appropriate for an appeal to conscience in our earlier opinion. The need for such further affirmative action along the lines suggested in the Kerner report is, however, strongly urged as a voluntary supplement to the requirements of the proposed rules. Thus, broadcasters might consider the adoption of special training programs for qualifiable minority group members, cooperative action with other organizations to improve employment opportunities and community conditions that affect employability, and other measures in addition to the employment practices suggested in the proposed rules. These voluntary measures may well be the chief hope of achieving equal employment opportunity at the earliest possible time, and the decision to take such action rests with the individual broadcaster.

10. *It is ordered,* pursuant to the authority contained in sections 4(i), 303, 307, 308, 309 and 310 of the Communications Act of 1934, as amended, 47 U.S.C. 154(i), 303, 307, 308, 309 and 310, that effective July 14, 1969, part 73 of the Commission's rules *Is amended* as set forth in Appendix A hereto.

FEDERAL COMMUNICATIONS COMMISSION,

BEN F. WAPLE, *Secretary.*

Appendix A

In part 73, §§ 73.125, 73.301, 73.599, 73.680, and 73.793, all to read identically, are added as follows:
§ 73.— Equal employment opportunities.

(*a*) *General policy.*—Equal opportunity in employment shall be afforded by all licensees or permittees of commercially or noncommercially operated standard, FM, television or international broadcast stations (as defined in this part) to all qualified persons, and no person shall be discriminated against in employment because of race, color, religion, or national origin.

(*b*) *Equal employment opportunity program.*—Each station shall establish, maintain, and carry out, a positive continuing program of specific practices designed to assure equal opportunity in every aspect of station employment policy and practice. Under the terms of its program, a station shall:

(1) Define the responsibility of each level of management to insure a positive application and vigorous enforcement of the policy of equal opportunity, and establish a procedure to review and control managerial and supervisory performance.

(2) Inform its employees and recognized employee organizations of the positive equal employment opportunity policy and program and enlist their cooperation.

(3) Communicate the station's equal employment opportunity policy and program and its employment needs to sources of qualified applicants without regard to race, color, religion or national origin, and solicit their recruitment assistance on a continuing basis.

(4) Conduct a continuing campaign to exclude every form of prejudice or discrimination based upon race, color, religion, or national origin from the station's personnel policies and practices and working conditions.

(5) Conduct continuing review of job structure and employment practices and adopt positive recruitment, training, job design, and other measures needed in order to insure genuine equality of opportunity to participate fully in all organizational units, occupations and levels of responsibility in the station.

NOTES

1. We did indicate our intention to acquire statistical racial employment data.
2. The contention is rested upon such decisions as *Burton* v. *Wilmington Parking Authority*, 365 U.S. 715 (1961).
3. The policy being so clear, our authority extends to its application to stations with fewer than 25 employees, although Congress chose to limit the particular remedies in the Civil Rights Act of 1964, entrusted to the EEOC, to those employers having at least 25 employees.
4. Letter of Assistant Attorney General Stephen J. Pollack, Department of Justice, Mar. 21, 1968, p. 4.

5. Adoption of a specific rule, which we are now proposing, will make forfeitures available where appropriate.
6. Comments of U.S. Commission on Civil Rights, Sept. 9, 1968, pp. 5–6.
7. "Pattern for Progress," final report to President Eisenhower from the Committee on Government Contracts, p. 14 (1960).
8. Equal Opportunity, agency program, 5 C.F.R. 713.203.
9. These categories are: Officials and managers, professionals, technicians, salesworkers, office and clerical, craftsmen (skilled), operatives (semiskilled), laborers (unskilled) and serviceworkers.
10. See the Commission's further notice of proposed rulemaking in docket No. 18244, "In the matter of petition for rulemaking to require broadcast licensees to show nondiscrimination in their employment practices." (F.C.C. 69–632), adopted June 4, 1969, for the text of the proposed rules, amendments to current FCC reporting forms and the proposed FCC form 325, annual employment report.
11. While the advantages of having the same job categories as those in the EEO–1 form prompted their use in the nw FCC form, we invite comment upon alternative categories which might be more directly related to the broadcast industry, and thus perhaps more useful.
12. We propose to obtain the requested information only for the broadcast operations of licensees also engaged in nonbroadcast activities, except for related subscription services, which we believe should be included.
13. We believe it reasonable to exclude stations with less than five full-time employees. While the rules now adopted apply to all employees and contain general requirements which can readily be adhered to even where minority group representation may be minimal, we also should make clear that a licensee need not prepare an equal employment opportunity program where the particular minority groups concerned are represented in the area in such insignificant numbers that a program would not be meaningful.

Statement of Commissioner Robert E. Lee Concurring in Part and Dissenting in Part

I concur in the report and order and dissent to the related further notice of proposed rulemaking. Since this report and order includes, in paragraphs 7 and 8, the reasons in support of the further notice of proposed rulemaking, both documents will be considered in this statement.

There is no disagreement as to the importance of equal employment opportunity in the broadcast industry, or as to the desirability of an FCC prohibition of employment discrimination by broadcast licensees. There is serious question about the effectiveness of the proposed reporting requirements as a basis for determining compliance, and consequent doubt as to the justification for the burdens they would impose on the industry and the Commission.

The proponents of periodic reporting treated it as a means by which stations would show compliance with the requirement that they afford equal employment opportunity, without discrimination because of race, color, religion or national origin. The concept is that annual reports showing compliance (or its lack) would provide a convenient and practicable way to enforce equal employment opportunity in the broadcast industry. But the allure of this idea fades on analysis. The proposed reporting requirements would not only be burdensome and impracticable; they could not possibly serve the intended purpose of reflecting — much less enforcing — compliance.

The proposed annual report is a profile of station payrolls, showing — for each of nine job categories — the total number of employees and those in each of four minority groups. The proposed form is based on form EEO–1 on which licensees with at least 100 employees already report annually to the Joint Reporting Committee at Washington. These reports provide a source of information concerning the major employers in the broadcast industry. The Equal Employment Opportunity Commission, which administers title VII of the Civil Rights Act of 1964, applicable to employers in interstate commerce with 25 or more employees, does not require the filing of form EEO–1 by employers with fewer than 100 employees. This indicates that profile reports are considered useful primarily as indicia of broad industry trends in minority employment, rather than as showings of compliance or noncompliance by individual employers.

There are several reasons why annual profile reports to the FCC could not provide a basis for determining whether a station is complying with the prohibition against discriminatory employment practices. The report simply reflects the numbers of Negroes, orientals, American Indians and Spanish surnamed Americans in the several job categories. It reflects nothing of the availability or nonavailability of persons in any of these minority groups who are qualified and locally available for work in the several job categories at the reporting broadcast station. Nor does it reflect comparative qualifications of persons in majority or minority groups, which are a proper and permissible basis for decisions by broadcast licensees concerning employment and promotion. It is pertinent to note that the Civil Rights Act expressly disclaims the intention that employers be expected to increase existing proportions of minorities on their payrolls by discrimination against applicants or employees who are not members of minority groups.

The clear goal is to increase employment opportunities for minorities. The method of achieving that goal is eliminating discrimination — in recruitment, employment, pay, privileges, opportunity for advancement, and employment terminations. However, it is almost self-evident that the proposed annual payroll profiles cannot serve the purpose of showing compliance with the requirement of nondiscrimination. There is no way by which staff could, by inspection of profile reports, rationally conclude, from the summary payroll data they would show.

whether the reporting station has or has not discriminated during the reporting period, in hiring new staff, reassigning work, promoting staff, setting rates of pay, providing training, dismissing staff, or in making any other decisions concerning staffing or working conditions at the station.

Furthermore, such reports would be burdensome, both to licensees and the Commission. In order to obtain consistently based, industry-wide statistics, either licensees with fewer than 100 employees would have to fill out and file the more detailed form EEO–1, which is designed for larger employers, or licensees who submit forms EEO–1 to the Joint Reporting Committee would have to prepare, in addition, the separate annual profile report which the general counsel proposes that all broadcast licensees with at least five employees be required to submit annually to the FCC. This, insofar as we have been able to ascertain, would be the first time employers with so few on their payrolls would be required to submit annual employment profile reports. It is difficult to understand the justification for the FCC to impose these additional reporting requirements either on the larger broadcasters (with 100 or more employees) or on the smaller ones.

As with profile reports, the proposed new section to the station application forms combines a desirable objective with a questionable method. The method is to have all applicants submit an extremely detailed statement (set out on pages 2 through 5 of the appendix attached to the further notice of proposed rule making), concerning the station's practices and policies for effectuating nondiscrimination.

The present staff of the Broadcast Bureau is not adequate in numbers, background, and training, to digest, evaluate, and arrive at sound judgments concerning additional reports of this magnitude and nature. Unless such reports could be subjected to searching analysis and well-founded judgment by staff expert in the difficult and sensitive field of employment discrimination, offending licensees would be in a position to paper-over discriminatory practice with artfully contrived, self-serving statements.

If, on the other hand, a meaningful analysis of the reports were to be carried out, the Commission would need a substantial staff and budget for the purpose. Should the Commission find it desirable to add the proposed new section to the application forms, the first needed step would be a thorough study of the staff and budgetary needs, which would include:

    (*a*) Qualified analysts and clerical staff to handle the resultant correspondence with reporting licensees and applicants.

    (*b*) Headquarters staff and field investigators to handle and inquire into the complaints which would probably arise upon local inspection by disappointed job seekers or job holders of the station's public file containing the detailed statements of employment practices and policies forming part of station applications.

(c) Added workload on the Hearing Division, hearing examiners, Review Board and the Office of Opinions and Review resulting from cases arising out of claims and disclosures made in the new section to the application forms.

Once careful estimates were made of staff and budgetary needs, the matter should be taken up with the Bureau of the Budget, and with interested committees of the Senate and House of Representatives. These bodies will have interest, not only in the costs involved, but also in related questions about the justification for separate employment reports to FCC by those licensees (with 100 or more employees) already required to file the EEO–1 report with another government agency.

Only when all these steps have been taken, and hurdles cleared, would it seem appropriate to arouse the expectations of those proposing reporting requirements by putting out specific rulemaking proposals on them.

Meanwhile, it would seem appropriate to announce in the report and order, in lieu of its present paragraphs 7 and 8, that the Commission is inquiring into the budgetary, staffing, and the other related questions posed, and that the docket will be held open for further announcements and possible action depending upon the findings reached and clearances obtained from (or withheld by) the Bureau of the Budget and on possibilities for obtaining sufficient appropriated funds to cover the added staffing needs.

Relatively few complaints — none so far adjudged substantial — have been received since the Commission last year announced the policy of receiving and referring to the EEOC or corresponding State and local agencies, complaints alleging discriminatory employment practices by broadcast licensees. The staff has managed to handle the small handful of such complaints without referral to other agencies. Whether it would be practicable to continue this after adoption of the proposal reporting requirements (appendix to the report and order) would depend on whether a substantial number of complaints would be generated by the availability to the public of the station's policy statements proposed to be included with applications.

Under these circumstances, I would:

(a) Delete paragraphs 7 and 8 of the report and order and not issue, at this time, the further notice of proposed rulemaking.

(b) Announce at this time that the Commission is still considering possible solutions to difficult problems raised by the reporting requirements advocated by a number of the parties, including budgetary and staffing needs for meaningful review of and — where necessary — action upon such reports.

(*c*) Clear these matters with the Bureau of the Budget and invite the attention of appropriate committees of Congress to such annual reporting requirements by licensees and such additional information as it may wish to require on station applications before inaugurating further rulemaking on these subjects.

Further Notice of Proposed Rulemaking on Nondiscrimination in Broadcast Employment Practices

Adopted June 4, 1969, by the Federal Communications Commission, in the matter of Petition for Rulemaking To Require Broadcast Licensees To Show Nondiscrimination in Their Employment Practices.
By the Commission: Commissioner Bartley not participating; Commissioner Robert E. Lee dissenting and issuing a statement.

1. Notice is hereby given of further proposed rulemaking in the above-entitled matter.

2. In its report and order in this docket, adopted June 4, 1969 (F.C.C. 69-631), the Commission adopted rules reflecting its basic policies in the area of licensee nondiscrimination in employment practices. The Commission also concluded that further rulemaking with respect to FCC reporting requirements would be appropriate (see F.C.C. 69-631, pars. 7-8). The proposed rules are set forth in the appendix hereto.

3. Authority for the proposed rules is set forth in sections 4(i), 303, 307, 308, 309, and 310 of the Communications Act of 1934, as amended, 47 U.S.C. 154(i), 303, 307, 308, 309, and 310.

4. Interested persons are requested to file comments on or before August 4, 1969, and reply comments on or before September 5, 1969, concerning the proposed rules and amendments to FCC reporting forms in the appendix hereto under applicable procedures set forth in section 1.415 of the Commission's rules and regulations. In accordance with the provisions of section 1.419 of the rules, an original and 14 copies of all comments, replies, briefs and other documents shall be furnished the Commission. All relevant and timely comments and reply comments will be considered before final action is taken in this proceeding. In reaching a final decision in this proceeding, other rele-

18 F.C.C. 2d

vant information, in addition to the specific comments invited by this notice, may be taken into account.

FEDERAL COMMUNICATIONS COMMISSION,

BEN F. WAPLE, *Secretary.*

Appendix

A. Parts 0 and 1 of the Commission's rules are amended to read as follows:

1. In § 0.455(b), subparagraph (3) is added to read as follows:

§ 0.455   Other locations at which records may be inspected.

✿   ✿   ✿   ✿   ✿   ✿   ✿

(*b*) *Broadcast Bureau.* ✿ ✿ ✿

(3) Annual employment report filed by licensees and permittees of broadcast stations pursuant to § 1.612 of this chapter.

✿   ✿   ✿   ✿   ✿   ✿   ✿

2. In § 1.526, the introductory text of paragraphs (a) and (e) is amended and a new subparagraph (a) (5) is added to read as follows:

§ 1.526   Records to be maintained locally for public inspection by applicants, permittees, and licensees.

(*a*) *Records to be maintained.*—Every applicant for a construction permit for a new station in the broadcast services shall maintain for public inspection a file for such station containing the material in subparagraph (1) of this paragraph, and every permittee or licensee of a station in the broadcast services shall maintain for public inspection a file for such station containing the material in subparagraphs (1), (2), (3), (4), and (5) of this paragraph: *Provided, however,* That the foregoing requirements shall not apply to applicants for or permittees or licensees of television broadcast translator stations. The material to be contained in the file is as follows:

✿   ✿   ✿   ✿   ✿   ✿   ✿

(5) A copy of every annual employment report filed by the licensee or permittee for such station pursuant to the provisions of this part; and copies of all exhibits, letters and other documents filed as part thereof, all amendments thereto, all correspondence between the permittee or licensee and the Commission pertaining to the reports after they have been filed and all documents incorporated therein by reference and which according to the provisions of §§ 0.451–0.461 of this chapter are open for public inspection at the offices of the Commission.

✿   ✿   ✿   ✿   ✿   ✿   ✿

(*e*) *Period of Retention.*—The records specified in paragraph (a) (4) of this section shall be retained for the periods specified in §§ 73.120(d) 73.290(d), 73.590(d), and 73.657(d) of this chapter (2 years). The records specified in paragraphs (a) (1), (2), (3), and (5) of this section shall be retained as follows:

✿   ✿   ✿   ✿   ✿   ✿   ✿

3. Section 1.612 is added to read as follows:

§ 1.612   Annual Employment Report.—Each licensee or permittee of a commercially or noncommercially operated standard, FM, television, or international broadcast station (as defined in part 73 of this chapter) with five or more full-time employees shall file with the Commission on or before April 1 of each year, on FCC form 325, an annual employment report.

B. *Proposed additional section to be added to FCC forms 301, 303, 309, 311, 314, 315, 340, and 342.*

A new section VI in FCC forms 301, 303, 309, 311, 314, 315, 340, and 342 would be adopted as follows: (Applicants for construction permit, assignees, transferees and applicants for renewal would file equal employment opportunity programs or amendments to those programs in the following exhibit.)

I. Submit as exhibit No. —— the applicant's equal employment opportunity program, indicating specific practices to be followed in order to assure equal employment opportunity for Negroes, Orientals, American Indians, and Spanish surnamed Americans in each of the following aspects of employment practice: recruitment, selection, training, placement, promotion, pay, working conditions, demotion, layoff, and termination. The program should reasonably address itself to such specific practices as the following, to the extent they are appropriate in terms of station size, locations etc. A program need not be filed if the station has less than five full-time employees or if it is in an area where the relevant minorities are represented in such insignificant numbers that a program would not be meaningful. In the latter situation a statement of explanation should be filed.

1. To assure nondiscrimination in recruiting:

(a) Posting notices in station employment offices informing applicants of their equal employment rights and their right to notify the Federal Communications Commission or other appropriate agency if they believe they have been the victim of discrimination.

(b) Placing a notice in bold type on the employment application informing prospective employees that discrimination because of race, color, religion, or national origin is prohibited and that they may notify the Federal Communications Commission or other appropriate agency if they believe they have been discriminated against.

(c) Placing employment advertisements in media which have significant circulation among minority-group people in the recruiting area.

(d) Recruiting through schools and colleges with significant minority-group enrollments.

(e) Maintaining systematic contacts with minority and human relations organizations, leaders, and spokesmen to encourage referral of qualified minority applicants.

(f) Encouraging present employees to refer minority applicants.

(g) Making known to all recruitment sources that qualified minority members are being sought for consideration whenever the station hires.

2. To assure nondiscrimination in selection and hiring:

(a) Instructing personally those of your staff who make hiring decisions that minority applicants for all jobs are to be considered without discrimination.

(b) Where union agreements exist:

(1) Cooperating with your unions in the development of programs to assure qualified minority persons of equal opportunity for employment;

(2) Including an effective nondiscrimination clause in new or renegotiated union agreements.

(*c*) Avoiding use of selection techniques or tests which have the effect of discriminating against minority groups.

3. To assure nondiscriminatory placement and promotion:

(*a*) Instructing personally those of the station staff who make decisions on placement and promotion that minority employees are to be considered without discrimination, and that job areas in which there is little or no minority representation should be reviewed to determine whether this results from discrimination.

(*b*) Giving minority group employees equal opportunity for positions which lead to higher positions. Inquiring as to the interest and skills of all lower-paid employees with respect to any of the higher-paid positions, followed by assistance, counseling, and effective measures to enable employees with interest and potential to qualify themselves for such positions.

(*c*) Reviewing seniority practices and seniority clauses in union contracts to insure that such practices or clauses are nondiscriminatory and do not have a discriminatory effect.

4. To assure nondiscrimination in other areas of employment practices:

(*a*) Examining rates of pay and fringe benefits for present employees with equivalent duties, and adjusting any inequities found.

(*b*) Advising all qualified employees whenever there is an opportunity to perform overtime work.

II. (Assignors, transferors, and renewal applicants would file the following exhibit): Submit a report as exhibit——indicating the manner in which the specific practices undertaken pursuant to the station's equal employment opportunity program have been applied and the effect of these practices upon the applications for employment, hiring, and promotions of minority group members.

III. (Assignors, transferors, and applicants for renewal, would file the following exhibit): Submit as exhibit —— whether any complaint has been filed before any body having competent jurisdiction under Federal, State, territorial, or local law, alleging unlawful discrimination in the employment practices of the applicant, including the persons involved, the date of filing, the court or agency before which the matter is or has been, the file number (if any), and the disposition or current status of the matter.

FCC Form 325

ANNUAL EMPLOYMENT REPORT
(Please see instructions)

1. Check one, to indicate type of reporting unit(s) covered in this report:
   [□] Station   [□] Headquarters   [□] Consolidated
2. Identity of reporting unit(s) covered in this report. (Answer A, B, or C.)
   A. If a station report:
      (1) Check one: [□] AM   [□] FM   [□] AM–FM combination
                       [□] TV   [□] International
      (2) Give station call letters and location: _____

      (3) Check if station is noncommercial. [□]

   B. If a headquarters report:
      List here (or in an appendix, if this space is insufficient) the headquarters office or offices covered in this report.

Name of headquarters office(s)	Location(s) of headquarters office(s)	Stations supervised by listed headquarters offices

C. If a consolidated report:
List here (or in an appendix, if this space is insufficient) the headquarters and stations covered in this consolidated report.

Headquarters offices names and locations	Stations call letters and location

3. Employment data:

Job categories	All employees [1] total	Minority group employees [2]			
		Negro	Oriental	American Indian	Spanish surnamed American
Officials and managers					
Professionals					
Technicians					
Sales workers					
Office and clerical					
Craftsmen (skilled)					
Operatives (semiskilled)					
Laborers (unskilled)					
Service workers					
Total					
Total employment from previous report (if any)					

(The data below shall also be included in the figures for the appropriate occupational categories above)

On-the-job trainees [3]
White collar
Production

1. Insert here the total of all employees at the places covered in this report (permanent, temporary, and part-time), not merely those in minority groups.
2. See instructions for identification of minority groups.
3. Report only employees enrolled in formal on-the-job training programs.

CERTIFICATION
(This report must be certified: by licensee or permittee, if an individual; by partner of licensee or permittee, if a partnership; by an officer of licensee or permittee, if a corporation or association; or by attorney of licensee or permittee in case of physical disability of licensee or permittee or his absence from the Continental United States.)

I certify that to the best of my knowledge, information, and belief, all statements contained in this report are true and correct.*

Signed _____ Title _____

Date _____ 19____ Name of company _____

Instructions for Annual Employment Report (FCC form 325)
1. Who must file.

All licensees and permittees of commercial and noncommercial AM, FM, television and international broadcast stations with five or more full-time employees must file the annual employment report on FCC form 325.

2. When and where to file.

A single copy of each annual employment report required under these instructions must be filed with the Federal Communications Commission, 1919 M Street NW., Washington, D.C. 20554, no later than April 1 each year.

3. Reporting period.

The employment data filed on FCC form 325 must reflect the facts as of the preceding December 31. Such data may be taken from the payrolls for the period in which December 31 falls.

4. Reporting units.

A separate annual employment report (FCC form 325) must be filed:

(a) For each AM, FM, TV, and international broadcast station, whether commercial or noncommercial; except that a combined report may be filed for an AM and an FM station, both of which are:

      (1) under common ownership, and

      (2) assigned to the same principal city or to different cities within the same standard metropolitan statistical area.

(b) For each headquarters office of a multiple station owner at which the employees perform duties related to the operation of more than one broadcast station (a separate form 325 need not be filed to cover headquarters employees whose duties relate to the operation of an AM and an FM station covered in a combined AM–FM report under instruction 4(a), if all such employees are included in such combined AM–FM report).

(c) As a consolidated report, covering all station and headquarters employees covered in the separate reports which a multiple station owner must file under instructions 4 (a) and (b).

5. Job categories.

Persons performing functions in more than one category should be classified according to their major function.

6. All employees.

Include in this column all employees in the reporting unit covered in the individual FCC form 325, not just the total employees falling within the four categories of "Minority group employees."

7. Minority group identification.

(*a*) Minority group information necessary for this section may be obtained either by visual surveys of the work force, or from post-employment records as to the identity of employees. An employee may be included in the minority group to which he or she appears to belong, or is regarded in the community as belonging.

(*b*) Since visual surveys are permitted, the fact that minority group identifications are not present on company records is not an excuse for failure to provide the data called for.

(*c*) Conducting a visual survey and keeping post-employment records of the race or ethnic origin of employees is legal in all jurisdictions and under all Federal and State laws. State laws prohibiting inquiries and recordkeeping as to race, etc., relate only to applicants for jobs, not to employees.

(*d*) FCC form 325 provides for reporting Negroes, American Indians, Orientals, and Spanish surnamed Americans, wherever such persons are employed. For purposes of this report, the term Spanish surnamed Americans is deemed to include all persons of Mexican, Puerto Rican, Cuban, or Spanish origin. Identification may be made by inspection of records bearing the employees' names, by visual survey, by employees' use of the Spanish language, or other indications that they belong to this group. The following States are among those having large concentrations of Spanish surnamed Americans: Arizona, California, Colorado, Florida, New Jersey, New Mexico, New York, and Texas. Large concentrations of Spanish surnamed Americans are found in particular localities in other States. The term "American Indian" does not include Eskimos and Aleuts.

8. Separate instructions applicable to broadcast networks will be furnished from the Federal Communications Commission.

Dissent of Commissioner Robert E. Lee

For the reasons stated in the statement attached to the report and order released this same date in this proceeding, I dissent.

Index

AAUP. *See* American Association of University Professors

ABC. *See* American Broadcasting Company

Actors Equity Association: organized, 14; influence on AFRA, 16; member of Television Authority, 43

Advertising: on radio and television, 176

AFL. *See* American Federation of Labor

AFM. *See* American Federation of Musicians

AFRA. *See* American Federation of Radio Artists

AFT. *See* American Federation of Teachers

AFTRA. *See* American Federation of Television and Radio Artists

Altieri, James: arbitrator, 94

American Arbitration Association, 86, 87

American Association for Higher Education, 200

American Association of University Professors, 194, 195, 198, 200

American Broadcasting Company: early TV station, 37; formation, 56; case before NLRB, 77; NABET strike, 78; unfair labor practices case, 102; arbitration case, 106–7; nondiscrimination policy, 216; defendant in blacklisting complaint, 241–42; blacklisting incident, 251; split from NBC, 262

American Business Consultants: formation, 233; use by clearance officers, 241

American Civil Liberties Union: warning on blacklisting, 234–35; blacklisting complaint to FCC, 241–42; position on loyalty oaths, 249–51

American Communications Local 16: NLRB case involving Greater New York Broadcasting Company, 76

American Council on Education, 194

American Federation of Labor: organized, 6; established American Federation of Musicians, 54; and IATSE, 60, 61; investigation, 62; internal disputes procedure, 91–92; runaway production, 142

American Federation of Musicians: first union demand on radio operators, 10–11; founded, 15; move into broadcasting, 28; in St. Louis, 28–29; history and structure, 53–56; representation election, 102; foreign residuals, 125–27, 132; runaway music scoring, 143; respect for AFTRA pickets, 269; mentioned, 41

American Federation of Radio Artists: formed, 14; influence of Actors Equity, 16; negotiation with KMOX, 42; founding and development, 42–45; certification election, 72–73; foreign residuals, 125, 129, 132, 133; isolationist position, 264